HELPING RELATIONSHIPS

Basic Concepts for the Helping Professions

SECOND EDITION

Arthur W. Combs
University of Northern Colorado

Donald L. Avila
University of Florida

William W. Purkey
University of North Carolina at Greensboro

Allyn and Bacon, Inc.
Boston, London, Sydney, Toronto

10 9 8 7 6   85 84 83 82

Library of Congress Cataloging in Publication Data

Combs, Arthur Wright.
  Helping relationships.

  Bibliography: p.
  Includes indexes.
  1. Counseling. 2. Helping behavior. I. Avila,
Donald L., joint author. II. Purkey, William Watson,
joint author. III. Title.
BF637.C6C48 1978   361'.06   77-20972
ISBN 0-205-0595-7

CONTENTS

Preface   *vii*

Section I   Psychological Bases for Helping   1

CHAPTER 1   What Is a Professional Helper?   3

The "Why" of the Helping Professions • What Makes an Effective Helper? • The Self As Instrument Concept • Importance of Belief • Becoming a Helper

CHAPTER 2   Perception and the Self   15

Perceptual Psychology • What Is the Self-Concept? • Self-Concept Determines Behavior • How the Self-Concept Is Learned • Self-Concept and Self-Report • Self-Concept and the Helping Professions

CHAPTER 3   A Humanistic View of Motive   34

Two Views of Motivation • Older Concepts of the Nature of People • A Perceptual View of Motive • Need for Self-Actualization • Determining Effect of Need on Behavior • Maladjustment—A Problem of Deprivation • Freedom and the Rights of Others • Some Implications for the Helping Professions

CHAPTER 4   Learning and Helping as Change in Personal Meaning   51

Facts, Meaning and Reality • Some Dynamics of Meaning • Learning as Discovery of Meaning • Effects of Threat and Challenge on Perception and Learning • Relation of Meaning to Memory, Emotion, and Feeling • Some Implications for Helpers

CHAPTER 5   The Range of Human Potential   69

Capacity and the Physical Model • Intelligence as Functional Capacity • What Intelligence Tests Measure • Determinants of Intelligence • Some Implications for the Helping Professions

CHAPTER 6   Dimensions of Self-Fulfillment   84

What Is Self-Actualization? • Positive View of Self • Openness to Experience • Freedom and Identification • Freedom and Self-Actualization

CHAPTER 7   Two Frames of Reference for Working with People   101

Closed and Open Systems of Thought • The Psychology of Closed and Open Systems • Selecting Tools for Helping

Section II   Helping Processes   113

CHAPTER 8   Goals and Responsibilities of Helping   115

Changing Goals of the Helping Professions • The Basic Dynamics of Helping • How Helpers Are Alike • Some Ethical Considerations • Professional Accountability

CHAPTER 9   Empathy: Essential Skill of Helping   130

Developing Sensitivity • The Use of Self in Empathy

CHAPTER 10   The Helping-Learning Atmosphere   143

The Special Nature of the Helping Atmosphere • Two General Approaches to the Helping Atmosphere • The Helper's Impact on the Atmosphere for Helping •

Helping Begins with Acceptance • Challenge and Threat in the Atmosphere for Change • Removing Barriers to Involvement • Limits in Helping Relationships

CHAPTER 11   Providing Experience and Information   159

Communication: A Function of Common Meanings • Communication Must Be Related to Need • Information Must Be Related to Existing Meanings • Openness and Communication

CHAPTER 12   Modes of Helping   177

Some Possible Modes of Working • Some Management Aspects of Helping • Some Management Techniques of Limited Value for Helping

CHAPTER 13   Being and Becoming Helpers   199

Becoming Helpers • The Helper's Own Self-Actualization • The Helper as Person and Citizen • Helping Professions: A Two-Way Street

Bibliography   217

Reference Guide to Relevant Research and Writing   249

Index   257

PREFACE

People need people and the more complex the society, the more pressing is the need for the help of others. For most of human history, the only helping relationships available were hit-or-miss affairs provided by well-meaning neighbors and friends or local wise men whose primary source of skill was age or association with religion. The story today is quite different. In less than one hundred years, social sciences like anthropology, sociology, political science, psychiatry and psychology have developed expressly to study the nature of human beings and their interrelationships. From the knowledge gained in these studies a whole new group of helping professions has come into being. Among these are counseling, school psychology, clinical psychology, social work, nursing, play therapy, remedial and rehabilitative services of many kinds and, most recently, professions helping people through basic encounter, sensitivity training, and T-groups. These professions join the very old helping professions of teaching, medicine, and the clergy.

Out of all this ferment and experience we now have far better principles and understanding about the nature of human beings and the processes of helping than ever before. Step by step, the social sciences have achieved increased understanding of helping relationships and have formulated better and better guidelines for their construction. The best of these new understandings, we think, may be found in modern humanistic psychology. Accordingly, we have tried, in this book, to set down principles of behavior widely accepted among humanistically oriented psychologists and to examine what such concepts mean for people who work in the varied helping professions. Especially, we have tried to answer two questions: (1) What ideas about human behavior have special value for understanding the helping relationship? and (2) What do these ideas imply for effective practice in the helping professions?

Humanistic psychology currently includes a wide variety of persons, practices, and beliefs. Among these, the authors have found the position described as *perceptual psychology* to be most pertinent for the helping professions. In our experience it speaks with special relevance to helpers and provides a framework for understanding students, clients, or patients that is immediately applicable to the practical problems helpers confront. In fact, at times, perceptual psychology has been called "the practitioner's psychology." Many of the concepts discussed in this book are based upon the systematic outlines for perceptual psychology first proposed by Snygg and Combs in 1949 and most recently updated by Combs, Richards and Richards in *Perceptual Psychology: A Humanistic Approach to the Study of Persons* (New York: Harper & Row, Publishers, 1976).

Each of the authors of this book began his professional training in orthodox, behavioristic psychology, but over the years increasingly learned to appreciate the special values of a humanistic frame of reference for the problems of the helping professions. Among those professions we have practiced are teaching, counseling, supervision, clinical psychology, administration, and school psychology. We have also been responsible for psychological aspects of the training of nurses, teachers, social workers, administrators, and pastoral counselors. In the course of continuous dialogue with helpers in many fields, we have had opportunities to explore and refine psychological theory on one hand, and to test its applicability in professional practice on the other. We sought to share this experience in the first edition of *Helping Relationships* which was published in 1971. Response to that volume was so encouraging, we are emboldened to offer this second edition incorporating many suggestions from readers of the first. These changes include:

1. A greatly condensed text
2. An updated bibliography
3. New sections on: professional responsibility, open and closed systems, behavioral contributions to helping, and being and becoming helpers

For ease of reading we have limited the designation of helpees to *student, client,* and *patient.* However, readers should understand that these terms are interchangeable, and the application of general principles is intended to apply to all helpees regardless of what they may be called in the respective helping professions.

The literature available for helping relationships is now so great that, in the interests of easier reading, we have arranged documentation in a special Reference Guide to Relevant Research and Writing. This removes extensive footnoting and interjection of authors, dates, etc. from the running text and, at the same time, provides interested readers with easy reference to additional research and writing. The topics under discussion are listed in the Reference Guide by page and paragraph of the text. Additional alphabetical listing of references by authors may be found in the Bibliography.

A book devoted to basic principles and their meaning for the helping professions cannot hope to deal with all topics in detail. Serious students will want to become acquainted with original sources or pursue topics in greater depth. To meet these needs, Selected Readings relevant to the topics in the chapter have been listed at the end of each chapter. To make pertinent and original articles more readily available, many of the shorter Selected Readings have also been included in a companion volume, *The Helping Relationship Sourcebook,* by Donald L. Avila, Arthur W. Combs, and William W. Purkey (Boston: Allyn and Bacon, 1977).

The authors would like to express their deep appreciation to the many persons who have assisted in the production of this book, especially:

To the authors and publishers who have so generously permitted quotation from their sources.

To Susan Kannel, Ruth Kannel and Bonny Clute for preparation and critical reading of the manuscript.

To the thousands of students, clients, and patients with whom the authors have worked and from whom they have learned so much. Out of the dialogue of those interactions, thinking was stimulated and hypotheses were formulated which were subjected to critical examination and tested in the encounters of real life helping relationships.

The years spent in the helping professions have been a rare privilege for the authors. Few occupations are so greatly needed in current society or so deeply rewarding for its practitioners. That, in itself, is a highly fulfilling experience. If this book can serve, in turn, to assist new members of the helping professions toward better understanding of themselves, their clients, and the processes of helping, the authors will rest content. What more could professional helpers ask than to write a helpful book?

A.W.C.
D.L.A.
W.W.P.

I
PSYCHOLOGICAL BASES FOR HELPING

Whatever helpers do in their interactions with others will be determined by their beliefs about what people are like and why they behave as they do. To assure effective, responsible practice, beliefs must be based on the clearest, most accurate conceptions possible, so helpers must be keenly aware of the best psychology can offer about the nature of human personality and the dynamics of behavior. The first half of this book is, therefore, designed to explore several basic psychological concepts of special relevance for the helping professions.

Chapter 1 begins with a short statement about the "why" of the helping professions and examines what research and theory have to say about the nature and characteristics of good and poor helpers. The chapter concludes with suggestions for becoming a helper.

Chapters 2 through 6 present basic concepts from perceptual psychology of special relevance for the development of helping relationships. These include: the nature and functions of perception, the self-concept, motivation, learning, human potential, and some characteristics of fully functioning persons, the goal of helping professions.

Section I ends with an examination of two ways of looking at human problems and their accompanying psychological schools of thought.

1

1
What Is a Professional Helper?

What are professional helpers and how can psychology help them to carry out their professional tasks successfully? The formal study of human beings is now nearly a hundred years old, and the information psychologists have accumulated is overwhelming. To select from this mass those understandings most likely to be useful for helping persons, we must first ask two questions: What are the helping professions? What are effective helpers like?

THE "WHY" OF THE HELPING PROFESSIONS

Each new person born into our society must, in comparatively few years, work his or her way through the public schools, develop some form of satisfying relationships with other people, and make a living from one or more of the thousands of occupations required to keep our economy running. One way or another, people must find ways to fulfill both their own needs, and society's expectations. For a few people, life will be a marvelous experience, satisfying for themselves as well as the society in which they live. Others will never achieve such high peaks of realization but will manage to work out a tolerable balance between their own and society's needs. Still others will succeed in meeting the demands of society well enough, but will fall far short of realizing the levels of personal fulfillment they hope for. And some deeply deprived persons will be unable to satisfy *either* society's needs or their own. Such desperate persons are not only disappointing to themselves; they are dangerous for the rest of us.

It is a tragedy for everyone concerned when people are unable to realize the potentialities that lie within them. When societies were less complex and interdependent, the failure of individuals to achieve satisfactory growth and development could often be overlooked. In today's world, human unhappiness affects far more than the individual; it reaches out to touch the lives of everyone. One angry driver on a freeway can endanger the lives of hundreds of innocent persons. A Lee Harvey Oswald, armed with a rifle, can turn our political world upside down.

Even if practical reasons for being concerned about the fulfillment of human potential were not enough, we should still be concerned about helping people on purely humanitarian grounds. Frustration and unhappiness are not just matters of economics. They are tragic human conditions, and are in themselves reasons enough to warrant concern. As a nation, the "pursuit of happiness" is a major tenet for our society. But if we "never made a nickel" from achieving that goal, it would still be worth striving for, both for ourselves and for our fellow citizens, simply because life is better that way.

The concept of democracy implies a belief in the basic dignity and integrity of persons. We believe that when people are free and informed they can find their own best ways. Our forefathers dared to adopt this dream as a basic value of their way of life, and little by little, over the years, we have come closer and closer to making it a reality. The fulfillment of the democratic ideal, however, depends upon how successfully we can produce persons who act with intelligence, independence, and responsibility.

To aid in the achievement of these ends, we have invented the helping professions. Some of these professions are rehabilitative; they help the sick and discouraged, the casualties of the system. Some are preventive, seeking to forestall illness. Some are fulfillment oriented, helping people scale the highest levels of human possibilities. The people who work in these professions are called by many names. Among them are teachers, doctors, psychologists, social workers, nurses, supervisors, counselors, human relations experts, psychiatrists, visiting teachers, personnel workers, guidance counselors, child care specialists, encounter group leaders, and group therapists. Each profession has its unique aspects, but all are concerned with the "people problem," helping people achieve more effective relationships between themselves and others or with the world in which they live.

What is a profession? A profession is generally defined as a vocation requiring some special knowledge and skill. The crucial quality of a profession, which distinguishes it from other occupations, however, is its dependence upon the professional worker as a thinking, creative being. Professional workers are problem solvers. They begin their training from some field of intellectual content. Beyond this, professions call for high degrees of self-discipline, skill in judgment, and adherence to an appropriate code of ethics. The helping professions, more specifically, are concerned with service to people. Their special responsibility is human welfare, a ministry to human beings.

WHAT MAKES AN EFFECTIVE HELPER?

Knowledge and the Helping Professions

It seems obvious that effective professional helpers must know their subject. Almost everyone, however, has had experience with people who knew their subject but were ineffective in putting it to work. We have seen intelligent medical students who failed as doctors, gifted scholars who couldn't teach, brilliant ministers unable to hold a parish, and clever psychiatrists with obvious problems of their own. Clearly, knowledge alone is no guarantee of successful professional work.

The helping professions are applied professions and require *doing* something with knowledge. In all the helping professions there exist the knowers and the doers, the scholars and the practitioners. In medicine, for example, there are specialists in anatomy or biochemistry and the physician who puts this information to work at the bedside of his patient. In education, there are scholars researching some aspect of knowledge and teachers helping students to understand it. Psychology has experimental psychologists investigating principles of human behavior and counselors putting this information to work with clients. There are sociologists examining the conflicting forces of the social scene and social workers helping clients adjust to them.

While knower and practitioner may, of course, exist in the same skin, it does not follow that knowledge alone is enough to make an effective helper. This fact has been clearly demonstrated in many research studies attempting to distinguish between good practitioners and poor ones in a number of the helping professions.

Methods in the Helping Professions

Becoming an effective helper is also not just a matter of using the right methods. One cannot clearly distinguish between good and poor practitioners on the basis of the methods they use. For example, a review of all the research available on good and poor teaching, sponsored by the National Education Association in 1961, was unable to discover any method of teaching clearly associated with either good or poor teaching. This review covered hundreds of studies, and the conclusion seems unquestionably definitive. Apparently there is no such thing as a "good" or a "right" method of teaching. Research in helping professions other than teaching corroborates this point.

People seem to be helped by the most unexpected things. We are frequently surprised by sudden waves of public enthusiasm over some weird new technique supposedly helpful to people in trouble. Doctors are well aware that nostrums with no demonstrable chemical value frequently help patients to get well if the patient believes the nostrum will help. The effects of stimuli on human behavior are determined by the perception of the stimulus in the person who receives it. The value of a dollar, for example, varies greatly in the eyes of a poor or wealthy person. The incentive effect of food is quite different when people are stuffed than when they are starving.

The methods helpers use to carry out their tasks depend on a wide variety of factors, which shift and change from moment to moment, so attempts to isolate specific methods as "good" or "necessary" for helping processes prove generally sterile. The *meaning* of the methods as perceived by the persons on whom they are employed, rather than the methods themselves, determine their effect. These meanings are so personal and unique that they make the search for methods invariably related to effective or ineffective helping an exercise in futility.

THE SELF AS INSTRUMENT CONCEPT

In examining the activities of the helping professions, it becomes apparent that their common characteristic is instantaneous response. All of the helping professions seem to differ from more mechanical vocations in the immediacy of reaction required of the helper. For example, when a child says something to a teacher, the teacher must respond. The interchange between teacher and pupil will be different every moment, and the teacher must be prepared to react to each child in terms of the unique question, idea, problem, and concern being expressed at that particular instant. Similarly, the patient asking the nurse, "Am I going to get well?" must be answered. A delay in the nurse's answer while stopping to think what should be said is already an answer. This immediate nature of helping relationships is characteristic, too, of the relationship between social worker and client, pastor and parishioner, or counselor and client. All depend upon instant response.

Professional helpers must be thinking, problem-solving people; the primary tool with which they work is themselves. This understanding has been called the *self as instrument* concept. In the helping professions, effective operation is a question of the use of the helper's self, the peculiar ways in which helpers are able to combine knowledge and understanding with their own unique ways of putting them into operation.

The self as instrument concept helps to explain why the attempt to distinguish between effective and ineffective helping professionals on the basis of knowledge or method falters. If effective operation in the helping professions is a personal matter of the use of the helper's self, then the search for a common knowledge or a common method is doomed before it begins. Since each individual is unique, the search for a common uniqueness is, by definition, hopeless!

At this point we are confronted with a difficult problem. If effective helping calls for an instantaneous response appropriate to the peculiar needs of the person to be helped, and if it depends upon the effective operation of the unique self of the helper, how can we be sure that the instantaneous use of the self will be good for the client? Helping, after all, must be a predictable process, one in which we can be sure of positive results. In answering this question, it is helpful to draw an analogy with a giant computer. The modern computer is a magnificent machine capable of receiving great quantities of outside data and combining it with information stored in its "memory bank" to give an almost instantaneous "best answer" to the questions asked of it. Like a human being, it provides appropriate responses to mountains of data. The kind of answers the computer provides out of the data available is dependent upon the formula (the program) entered in the machine. Similarly, the peculiar responses that occur as people interact with the world they live in is the product of the program in the person. But the formula in human beings is not a mathematical equation. It consists of the individual's perceptions, especially those we call values, beliefs, and purposes.

IMPORTANCE OF BELIEF

In an article on the nature of the helping relationship, Carl Rogers once observed that it didn't seem to make much difference how the helper behaved so long as his "intent" (purpose) was to be helpful. From personal experience we know that our own behavior is an expression of our beliefs. Indeed, this intimate effect of belief on behavior is so strong that it betrays us even when we consciously try to hide it. As the old Indian said, "What you do speaks so loudly I cannot hear what you say." Beliefs have a controlling, directing effect. This is especially true with respect to what we believe is important.

A young woman teaching first grade in one large city had a magnificent head of blonde hair, which she often wore in a ponytail down her back. For the first three days of the new school year, she wore her hair this way. Then, on Thursday morning of that first week she decided to put it up in a bun on top of her head. As often happens when a person changes hairstyles, she looked quite different, and one of the little boys in her class didn't recognize his teacher. Thinking he was in the wrong room, he turned away in confusion. Soon the bell rang for the start of the day, and he found himself standing in the hall not knowing where to go or what to do. He was still there crying when a supervisor came along a bit later. Questioning the child, she could not discover what his teacher's name was. He didn't know. Nor did he know what room he belonged in. He'd looked in there and it was clearly not the right place! She said to him, "Come along. Let's go together and see if we can find your teacher," and they set out hand in hand, to see if they could find his classroom. They opened the doors of several rooms without any luck. Finally, they came to the right one. As the door opened, the teacher turned, saw the little boy and said, "Why Joey! It's so good to see you! We wondered where you were. We're glad to have you back! We missed you so!" The little boy let go of the supervisor's hand and threw himself into his teacher's arms. She gave him a hug, patted him softly, and he trotted off to his seat. She believed that little boys are important.

Let's suppose she had not acted in this manner. She might very well have thought other things were important, in which case she would have behaved quite differently. For example, she might have thought that supervisors were important and in that case probably would have said, "Why, good morning, Miss Jones. Do come in. We've been hoping you'd come to see us. Haven't we, boys and girls?" The little boy would have been ignored. Or, she might have felt that discipline was important, in which case she could have punished him for being late. But she didn't. She believed the little boy was important and so behaved in terms of his feelings. So it is with each of us.

The Crucial Effects of Beliefs

What we believe to be important inevitably determines the techniques we employ when dealing with other people. There are a vast number of methods one could conceivably use in establishing helping relationships. There are so many, in fact, that without some kind of philosophy or frame of reference for making choices, the helper is likely to remain forever ineffectual rather than becoming a potent force for human welfare. A clear understanding of purposes and goals provides guidelines for the selection of methods, and helps to establish a frame of reference to use in choosing from the great welter of possibilities. Without this, helpers may find themselves behaving in such confused fashion as to confuse the very people they seek to help.

There is a widespread belief that eclecticism—that is, the use of whatever seems best from whatever source—is most likely to produce an effective teacher or counselor. Unfortunately, this seemingly logical and practical way of selecting methods of operation often misfires. It produces what William Snyder once called "the Smorgasbord Approach in which a little of everything is tried." Some years ago at an American Psycho-

Psychological Bases for Helping

logical Association convention, a well-known psychologist reported upon a difficult counseling case. He described how, over the years, the staff had used a large number of methods selected from a dozen different schools of thought. At the conclusion of this description of methods used and results obtained, the psychologist concluded: "Well, now I've told you what we did with this client and what happened, but do not ask me why. The best I can say about this case is that the patient got better in the presence of the therapist!" There can be no doubt that eclecticism sometimes works. But then it is true that almost anything works with some people, sometimes, in some places. The competent professional worker cannot be content with so hit-or-miss an approach to his job. There is a place, even a need, for helpers to employ a wide variety of methods. How and when such methods are used, however, cannot be fortuitous. Effective helpers must possess internal systems of beliefs certain to produce behavior likely to be good for those they seek to help.

The dynamics of a helping relationship cannot be understood solely by what may be observed by an outside observer. What goes on can only be understood in terms of what the helper is trying to do and what the student-client-patient thinks happened. The authors are acquainted with a very fine teacher, a former marine, who runs his fourth-grade class in a bluff and hearty manner. He is deeply beloved by all the children in his class. On one occasion, the writer heard him say to a little boy, "Eddie, that was a pretty stupid thing to do!" Now, everything in this psychologist's thinking must ordinarily recoil from such a "put down" of a child. But not in this case! The child's reaction was to look up at his teacher adoringly and reply, "Yeah wasn't it?" No matter what this event may have seemed like to an outside observer, the teacher's behavior was determined by a whole system of understandings and beliefs, which the teacher himself would have difficulty in fully expressing. But this much is certain, putting the child down was no part of his purpose. For the child it was no "put down" either. The message conveyed was one of love and camaraderie, which the child enjoyed as a kind of "game we play together."

What makes helpers effective is the nature of the beliefs they hold. In the important events of life we are governed by our beliefs, our values, our understandings, and the goals we think are important. An effective helper is one who has acquired an extensive, accurate, internally consistent personal set of perceptions or beliefs, which serve as guides for the helper's moment to moment behaviors with students, clients, and patients.

Beliefs of Professional Workers

A series of studies on the perceptual organization of workers in the helping professions carried on by Combs, his colleagues, and students at the

University of Florida sheds light on the kinds of beliefs specifically related to effective professional work.[1] These studies examined the belief systems of teachers, counselors, professors, nurses, politicians, and Episcopal priests. They show a high degree of similarity in the perceptual organizations of "good" and "poor" workers in all of these fields. The Florida investigators have suggested six major categories into which the perceptions of effective helpers may be divided:

1. Content or subject matter
2. Frame of reference
3. What people are like
4. The helper's self-concept
5. Purposes—society's, the helper's own, and those related to the helping task
6. Helping methods or techniques

1. *Content or Subject Matter*

We have already seen that a profession is a vocation requiring some specialized knowledge. Effective professional workers must be well-informed about their subjects. We have also observed that mere knowledge is not enough. For effective professional work, knowledge about the subject must be so personally meaningful to the helper as to have the quality of belief. The practitioner, without commitment to his knowledge, cannot be counted upon to use this knowledge when it is called for. Even an Einstein must believe in his theory to put it into practice. The teacher who knows that the children in her class differ widely from one another but does not believe this fact important cannot be expected to teach as though the information existed at all. It is precisely because the discovery of the meaning of information is so essential for professional workers that so much of their training is devoted to discussion, observation, experimentation, internship, and various forms of clinical experience. Here they discover the personal meaning of knowledge and convert it to belief.

2. *The Helper's Frame of Reference*

The perceptions people have are always determined by the frame of reference from which they make their observations. If administrators,

1. See A. W. Combs et al., *Florida Studies in the Helping Professions* (Gainesville, Florida: University of Florida Press, 1969). The interested reader will find in this monograph an expanded discussion of the theory and development of this approach to the helping professions and a more detailed description of the research designed to test it. Additional research completed since 1961 may be found in this book's bibliography in dissertations by R. G. Brown, C. Choy, C. V. Dedrick, D. A. Dellow, E. J. Doyle, G. D. Jennings, R. G. Koffman, A. O'Roark, J. Parker, P. W. Pendergrass, J. L. Swanson, R. H. Usher, and H. G. Vonk.

whose primary concern is production, see workers as part of the machinery, they are likely to treat workers so. When administrators see themselves as facilitators and workers as important persons in the processes of production, they will behave quite differently toward workers, because they are looking at quite different problems. Generally speaking, there are two major frames of reference available to helpers: (a) an objective, external approach, primarily concerned with facts, things, organization, management, systems and machinery or (b) an internal, subjective one, focusing on people, feelings, attitudes, beliefs, and the facilitation of human processes. Good helpers in all of the Florida studies mentioned above could be clearly distinguished from poor ones on the basis of these broad frames of reference.

3. What Are People Like?

Among the most important beliefs determining what we do as members of the helping professions are the perceptions we hold about what people are like and why they behave as they do. If I believe a child is hungry, I will feed him. If I believe he is lonely, I will befriend him. If I think he needs to know, I will teach him. How we behave as helpers will depend upon our particular concepts about people and the ways in which they behave. No matter if the ideas we hold about other people are accurate or false; if we believe them, they affect our behavior. The goals we set for our professions, the methods we use, the rules we make, even the buildings we design will be dependent upon our understanding of human nature. It is of vital importance, therefore, that professional helpers carefully examine their beliefs about human beings.

4. The Helper's Self-Concept

Effective helpers must have the ability to share self and, at the same time, possess the capacity for extraordinary self-discipline. The tasks of professional workers can be accomplished only by entering into some kind of relationship with others. Since one cannot have a relationship with a nonentity, effective helpers must have a clear sense of self. The giving of self called for in the helping professions is probably possible only to the degree that helpers themselves feel basically fulfilled. A deeply deprived self cannot afford to give itself away. A self must possess a satisfactory degree of adequacy before it can encounter and commit itself to others. This same feeling of personal adequacy is also necessary for self-discipline. Only when persons feel fundamentally adequate can they transcend their own needs and give attention to the needs of others. People who feel inadequate cannot afford the time and effort required to assist others.

Because beliefs about themselves are so very important, training programs for professional workers increasingly deal with the self of the helper. Thus, social workers and counselors are encouraged and often required to enter into personal counseling relationships as a part of their professional training. Training programs for teachers, supervisors, school psychologists, and nurses likewise concern themselves more and more with the personal qualities of the people entering these professions.

5. The Helper's Purposes

Human behavior always has purpose. Professional helpers will perform their tasks according to what they believe are the purposes of those with whom they must work, the purpose of their particular kind of helping profession, and their own personal and professional purposes at any moment. Some of these purposes in the helping professions are highly specific and related to the particular kind of helping function workers are involved in. Others are much more general and seem to be held in common by a number of the helping professions.

6. Appropriate Methods or Techniques

Earlier in this chapter we reported that investigators were unable to discover any method of helping clearly associated with either good or poor helpers. There is, however, at least one essential general characteristic about methods—the authenticity of the method employed.[2] Helping techniques must fit the helper, the client, the purposes of helping, and the peculiar settings in which they are employed. To achieve these ends, training programs provide opportunities for prospective helpers to examine a wide variety of techniques to discover those most appropriate for a particular helper. The helper's search for an individual "idiom" is never ending. Effective helpers become more unique, more genuinely themselves, the longer they live.

BECOMING A HELPER

Good helpers are not born, nor are they made in the sense of being taught. The development of a professional helper is a process of becoming, of learning how to effectively use one's self to carry out one's

2. To the best of our knowledge this characteristic has not yet been formally researched. It is, however, very strongly suggested by such categories in the Florida Studies as: self-revealing–self-concealing purposes, openness-closedness frame of reference, and perceptions of self like trustworthy-untrustworthy, identified-apart, and able-unable.

own and society's purposes. In the legal profession we do not say of the trainee, "He is learning how to law." We say, "He is becoming a lawyer." In the medical profession we do not say the trainee is "learning how to doctor." Rather, we say, "She is becoming a doctor." Similarly, the making of professional helpers is not a question of learning *how to;* it is a matter of *becoming* a teacher, counselor, or social worker.

The helper's personal frame of reference begins with some new experience, concept, or idea and is thereafter modified as a consequence of the individual's personal discovery of meaning. By confronting practical problems and conceptual ones, by trial and error, by consideration and evaluation—by experience—helpers steadily build their perceptual organizations, developing deeper and more consistent personal meanings.

To facilitate this process, training programs can provide helpers with the stimulation of ideas from people and events. They can provide opportunities to learn about processes and dynamics through reading programs or through interaction with significant scholars and practitioners. Programs can also provide student helpers with the opportunity to confront problems and situations that require an examination of self and personal beliefs for their resolution. But no matter how excellent the opportunities provided by a training program, in the final analysis no one but helpers themselves can make the personal explorations required to develop internally consistent perceptual frames of reference. Effective growth calls for trying methods that are both new enough to be challenging and close enough to the helper's current capacity to be likely of success.

Becoming a helper is a time-consuming process. It is not simply a matter of learning methods or of acquiring gadgets and gimmicks. It is a deeply personal process of exploration and discovery, the growth of unique individuals learning over a period of time how to use themselves effectively for helping other people. There can be no "quickie" programs for producing such persons. Becoming a teacher, nurse, counselor, social worker, or pastor is not learned in a two-week course. Neither is it accomplished by the presentation of a degree or a license. Becoming a helper is a life-long process, composed of many small steps that lead both to broader and deeper conceptions of the nature of persons and the processes by which they grow and develop and to the growth of helpers, themselves, into more effective, self-actualizing persons committed to the welfare of their fellow human beings. The process never ends, but neither does its potential for fulfillment of self and others.

Some of the beliefs that enter into the making of a helper are so very personal that information from outside sources will be of little value. Others may be obtained from interaction with the world of ideas, and it is here that exploration of psychological thought can be of assistance. In the pages to follow the authors have examined some of the most significant concepts from humanistic thought, which provide bases for thinking about helping relationships. From concepts like these, which have stood the test of research, expert opinion, time, or experience, helpers may find some of the building blocks they need to construct their own systems of beliefs about what people are like and why they behave as they do. Such beliefs, in turn, will inevitably affect the ways they go about constructing helping relationships for others.

Selected Readings

Starred entries indicate appearance in whole or in part in Donald L. Avila, Arthur W. Combs, and William W. Purkey, *The Helping Relationship Sourcebook,* Boston: Allyn and Bacon, 1977.

Arkoff, A. "Some Workers in Improvement." In *Adjustment and Mental Health,* pp. 284–307. New York: McGraw-Hill Book Co., 1968.

Brammer, L. *Helping Relationships: Process and Skills.* Englewood Cliffs, New Jersey: Prentice-Hall, 1973.

Carkhuff, R. R., and Berenson, B. G. *Beyond Counseling and Therapy.* New York: Holt, Rinehart and Winston, 1967.

Combs, A. W.; Blume, R. A.; Newman, A. J.; and Wass, H. L. *The Professional Education of Teachers: A Humanistic Approach to Teacher Preparation.* Boston: Allyn and Bacon, 1974.

*Combs, A. W.; Soper, D. W.; Gooding, C. T.; Benton, J. A.; Dickman, J. F.; and Usher, R. H. *Florida Studies in the Helping Professions.* University of Florida Social Science Monograph no. 37. Gainesville, Florida: University of Florida Press, 1969.

*Purkey, W. W. "The Task of the Teacher." In *Self-Concept and School Achievement,* pp. 43–65. Englewood Cliffs, New Jersey: Prentice-Hall, 1970.

*Rogers, C. R. "The Characteristic of a Helping Relationship." *Personnel and Guidance Journal,* 1958, pp. 6–16.

Wass, H.; Blume, R. A.; Combs, A. W.; and Hedges, W. D. *Humanistic Teacher Education: An Experiment in Systematic Curriculum Innovation.* Ft. Collins, Colorado: Shields Publishing Co., 1974.

2

Perception and the Self

Human behavior is always a product of how people see themselves and the situations they are involved in. Although this fact seems obvious, the failure of people everywhere to comprehend it is responsible for much of human misunderstanding, maladjustment, conflict, and loneliness. Our perceptions of ourselves and the world are so real to us that we seldom pause to doubt them. Since persons behave in terms of their personal perceptions, effective helping must start with the helper's understanding of the nature and dynamics of perceiving.

PERCEPTUAL PSYCHOLOGY

The concepts of perceptual psychology help us to understand persons through studying the processes of perception—how things seem to the person at the moment of action. It is a psychology that looks at persons through the "eye of the beholder"; from the perspective of the person's own experience.[1] This point of view is especially useful for the helping professions.

Perceptual psychologists take the position that all behavior is a function of the perceptions that exist for an individual at the moment of behaving, especially those perceptions about self and world. The term *perception,* as these psychologists use it, refers not only to "seeing" but also to "meaning"—the personal significance of an event for the person

1. For a more extensive, systematic view of psychology from a perceptual orientation, the interested reader is referred to A. W. Combs, A. C. Richards, and F. Richards. *Perceptual Psychology: A Humanistic Approach to the Study of Persons* (New York: Harper & Row, Publishers, 1976).

experiencing it. Such meanings extend far beyond sensory experience to include such perceptions as beliefs, values, feelings, hopes, desires, and the personal ways in which persons regard themselves and other people. Behavior is understood in terms of the ways people see themselves and their world now, in the present, at this instant. For persons in the helping professions, this concept is of enormous significance.

Immediate Guidelines to Action

It is interesting that most modern schools of psychotherapy are predicated upon the understanding that effective changes can be accomplished through helping clients directly in the present. The long, agonizing delving into the client's past, which formerly was considered absolutely essential for effective treatment is no longer so regarded. One can see many instances of this in daily life. Nurses, for example, may help patients feel less depressed without knowing the facts of their lives outside the hospital. Businessmen can help employees to feel better about themselves and their jobs and still be unaware of the lives of their employees off duty. One of the authors has often noted, in his experience as a psychotherapist on a college campus, that clients who spend long hours exploring their past are, almost without exception, graduate students in psychology! From their studies they know that behavior is a function of their pasts. When they come for therapy, then, they set about exploring it in detail. Clients who have not learned so thoroughly that behavior is a function of the past spend very little time digging into it. They begin at once to explore their present feelings and perceptions. Often they get well despite the fact that at the end of therapy the counselor may still not know how they became unhappy in the first place!

Because an immediate frame of reference does not impose on the helper the necessity to search, probe, diagnose, and analyze, it also facilitates the development of rapport and cooperative relationships. Working with a person's immediate perceptions, means working on the person's own ground in a subject matter he knows and understands. As a consequence, he is likely to feel much closer to the professional helper, more readily understood, and willing to communicate with him.

It should not be supposed from this discussion that we are denying the truth of the genetic principle that behavior is a product of the individual's past experience. Generally speaking, the more data we have about any problem, the more likely we are to be able to arrive at correct solutions. Not all data, however, is of equal value in all situations. Relevant data is determined by the helper's goals and his method of reaching them.

From the perceptual frame of reference, an individual's behavior is understood to be the direct consequence of the total field of personal meanings existing at that instant (the perceptual field). At any moment a person's perceptual field contains some perceptions clearly differentiated from the rest and toward which behavior is directed. At the same time, the person's field contains many other perceptions. These vary in degrees of awareness, from those in very clear figure at the center of attention to those perceptions so vague and undifferentiated that the person would not be able to report them if we were to ask about them. This sounds very much like the Freudian concept of conscious and unconscious awareness. In a sense it is; but perceptual psychologists prefer not to speak of "conscious" and "unconscious," because they give the impression of two distinct conditions rather than varying levels of awareness with different degrees of clarity.

At the core of each person's perceptual field are the perceptions about self. While situations may change from moment to moment or place to place, the beliefs people have about themselves are always present factors in determining behavior. The self is the star of every performance, the central figure in every act. Because this is so, persons working in the helping professions need clear understandings of the nature, origins, and functions of the self-concept.

WHAT IS THE SELF-CONCEPT?

The self-concept includes all those aspects of the perceptual field to which we refer when we say "I" or "me." It is the organization of perceptions about self that seems to the individual to be who he or she is. It is composed of thousands of perceptions varying in clarity, precision, and importance in the person's peculiar economy. Taken altogether, this organization is called the self-concept.

Each of us has literally thousands of ideas or concepts about self: who we are, what we stand for, where we live, what we do or do not do, and the like. A particular person might see herself as Sally Blanton—wife, mother, part-time social worker, American, white, young, resident of Tampa, Florida, measurements 34-25-34, good swimmer, poor tennis player. These and many other perceptions or beliefs about herself make up the personal and unique self-concept of Sally Blanton. Not all concepts about herself are equally important to her. Concepts like her age or occupation may be recognized as transitory. Others, like her concept of herself as a woman, mother, or wife are probably extremely important and difficult to change.

Descriptive perceptions like those of Mrs. Blanton serve to distinguish her as unique from other selves. Self-description does not stop there, however, since we are seldom content with description alone. Even more important are the values a person places upon the various qualities of self. People do not regard themselves only as fathers or mothers, but as "good" or "bad" fathers and mothers. They see themselves, not simply as persons, but as attractive or ugly, pleasant or unpleasant, fat or thin, happy or sad, adequate or inadequate. These perceptions, too, are part of the person's self-concept.

The self-concept, it should be understood, is not a thing but an organization of ideas. It is an abstraction, a gestalt, a peculiar pattern of perceptions of self. The different parts may seem only like ideas to outsiders, but for the owner they have the feeling of reality. In fact, the self-concept is even more important to its owner than the body in which it exists. The body, according to Earl Kelley, is but "the meat house we live in," the vehicle in which the self rides. We recognize the distinction between body and self when we complain that "the spirit is willing but the flesh is weak," or "I would have come to the meeting, Joe, but my old body let me down, and I had to stay in bed with the flu."

This distinction between the self-concept and the physical self may be observed in other ways. For example, the self-concept may be defined in such a way as to include matters quite outside the skin. This often happens with respect to one's most cherished possessions. A man may regard his desk as so much a part of him that he treats interference with it as a personal violation. Consequently, his reaction to a secretary who has intruded upon his territory by disturbing things in or on the desk may be so angry and forceful as to bewilder her. She exclaims to the other people in the office, "You'd think I'd wounded him, or something!" Of course, she had. What seems to be only a piece of furniture to the secretary is an extension of self to the owner of the desk.

The extension of self is even more common with respect to persons. Psychologists refer to this experience as "identification." They mean the feeling of oneness we have with those persons or groups who have come to have special value for us. The feeling of oneness with those we love may sometimes be so strong that awareness of physical separation may be temporarily lost. A young mother describes this feeling with respect to her newborn child:

> When they brought my baby to me I unwrapped her and lay for a while in awe examining the marvelous way she was made. Then, after a while, I placed her on my stomach with her head between my breasts and lay there with a curious feeling of triumph and exquisite peace. Now and then I would raise the covers a little and peek down at her. As she lay there I honestly couldn't tell where she began and I left off. I remember I wept a little because I was so happy. I'll never forget the moment as long as I live.

The expansion of self-concept also extends to feelings about groups. One reason groups come together in the first place is to have the expe-

18   **Psychological Bases for Helping**

rience of oneness. In becoming a member of a group, the self-concept is expanded to include the other members. Thereafter the individual begins to behave as though the members are an extension of self. He speaks of "my gang," "my school," "my friend," "my church," "my neighborhood," or "my country." Depending upon the strength of the identification, he also behaves with respect to them as though they were part of self.

The Self: Personal Center of the Universe

For each person, the self-concept is the frame of reference from which observations are made. It is our personal reality, the vantage point from which all else is observed and comprehended. We speak of things as "right" or "left," "near" or "far," and, of course, we mean from ourselves. The self is also used as a yardstick for making judgments. Others are regarded as taller, shorter, smarter, more unscrupulous, older, or younger than ourselves. As the self changes, the yardstick changes, and what we believe to be true changes with it. What is considered "old" is likely to be quite differently defined at ages six, sixteen, thirty-six, or sixty.

Generally speaking, we feel quite at home with "what is me." Toward what is "not me," we are likely to be indifferent, even repelled. Allport pointed out, for example, that when a person cuts a finger he may put it in his mouth and so, drinks his own blood without the slightest concern. Once the finger has been bandaged, however, a suggestion to lick blood from the bandage would likely be regarded with revulsion. Similarly, an individual is continuously engaged in swallowing the saliva that collects in his mouth. This same saliva, collected in a glass and offered to the person to drink, is a very different matter!

Experiences consistent with the existing self-concept are readily accepted. They are treated as though they belong even when accepting them may be painful. A failing grade for a student who already believes he is a failure may not concern him at all, because it only represents further corroboration of what he already believes. On the other hand, incongruous experiences may produce feelings of great discomfort. For example, one of the authors once counseled a young lady who complained with tears and near hysteria that she was flunking out of college. Taking what she said at face value, he began dealing with the problem as one would with a student who was failing. A great deal of time and effort was wasted before the author discovered that the student's perception of failing was based on the fact that, in three years of college, she had just gotten her first grade of C. All the others were A's!

Doctors and nurses often find it difficult to get patients newly diagnosed as diabetic to care for themselves properly. Such patients often find it difficult to accept this new concept of self and the accompanying use of insulin and special dietary requirements. It takes time to assimilate new definitions of self. The disturbing effect of inconsistent experiences will occur even if the new thought is something the person would like to believe. This can be observed in the embarrassment people feel when, after long periods of failure, they are told they have done something very well.

SELF-CONCEPT DETERMINES BEHAVIOR

The importance of the self-concept in the economy of the individual goes far beyond providing the basis of reality. Its very existence determines what else the person may perceive. The self-concept has a selective effect on perceptions. People tend to perceive what is congruent with their already existing concepts of self. Men perceive what is appropriate for men to perceive, while women see what is appropriate for women to perceive. So it happens that on the way home from a party, Mrs. Adams may say to her husband, "John, did you notice what Helen was wearing?" John is quite likely to reply, "No, I didn't notice that." But, being a man, there were other things he noticed which almost certainly, his wife will not think to ask him about and probably would not want to hear about if she did!

Once established, the self-concept begins to mediate subsequent experience. For example, if a potential self-perception appears to the perceiving individual as congruent with those already present in the self-system, the perception is easily assimilated. If a potential idea about self is dissonant with ideas already incorporated, then it will likely be rejected. So the self-concept becomes a kind of personal gyrocompass providing stability and direction for the interaction of self with the world. It provides a screen through which everything else is seen, heard, evaluated, and understood.

Psychological literature is overflowing with articles and research studies dealing with the effect of the self-concept on a variety of behaviors including failure in school, levels of aspiration, athletic prowess, mental health, intelligence, delinquency, industrial productivity, and the behaviors of ethnic groups and the socially disadvantaged. The self-concept exerts its influence on every aspect of human endeavor. When we know how people see themselves, much of their behavior becomes clear to us, and often we can predict with great accuracy what they are likely to do next.

Circular Effect of the Self-Concept

The selective effect of the self-concept has another important consequence. It corroborates and supports already existing beliefs about self and so tends to maintain and reinforce its own existence. This circular characteristic of the self-concept may often be observed in the problems of children learning arithmetic, spelling, public speaking, physical education, history, music, or any other school subject. Take the case of reading, for example. Rarely these days does the child coming to the reading clinic have anything wrong with his or her eyes. With modern methods of testing children's health, sight deficiencies are usually discovered routinely. Instead, youngsters who come to the reading clinic are much more likely to be handicapped because they *believe* they cannot read. Take the case of Jimmy Brown. Having developed the idea that he is unable to read, thereafter, Jimmy is caught in a vicious circle. Because he believes he cannot read, he avoids it, thus avoiding the very activity that would help. Because he avoids reading, he doesn't get any practice and continues to read badly. When his teacher asks him to read, he reads very poorly, and the teacher says, "My goodness, Jimmy, you don't read very well!" This, of course, is what he already believed in the first place! To make matters worse, a report card is often sent home telling parents how badly the child reads and they, too, join in the act, confirming the child's belief that he is, indeed, a very poor reader. In this way a poor reader is frequently surrounded by a veritable conspiracy in which all experience corroborates the deficiency. This conspiracy, moreover, is produced for the most part by persons whose intentions were excellent. They *wanted* the child to be a good reader, even though the net effect of their pressures was to prove the child was not.

You may be one of the thousands of people who believe they cannot do mathematics, make a speech, or spell. With such a belief, you may avoid those occasions where it is necessary to use the particular skill. Many research studies show the effects of student beliefs upon achievement in a wide variety of school subjects. Evidence even suggests that the self-concept may be a better predictor of a child's success in school than time-honored IQ scores.

The self-perpetuating effect of the self-concept is by no means limited to success or failure in academic subjects. The same dynamics may be seen at work in all walks of life. Dr. Walter Reckless and his colleagues at Ohio State University carried out a series of studies on the self-concepts of delinquent and nondelinquent boys. Among their findings are the following: The twelve-year-old "good" boy in a slum area perceives of himself and his friends as staying out of trouble, of himself as finishing school, and of his family as good. The mothers of the "good" boys also had favorable perceptions and prognostications of their sons. On the other hand, the so-called "bad" boy, spotted by his sixth-grade teacher as a drop-out and trouble-maker, has the opposite perception of himself. He perceives himself as headed for trouble, of his friends as delinquents, and of his family as a "bum" family. The "bad" boy's mother echoed his perceptions. In a follow-up study at the end of four years, these investigations found that the "good" boys were practically delinquency free, while forty percent of the "bad" boys were in the juvenile court one to seven times.

As this example shows, the circular effect of the self-concept operates in both positive and negative directions. Persons with positive self-concepts are quite likely to behave with confidence causing others to react in corroborative fashion. People who believe they *can,* are more likely to succeed. The very existence of such feelings about self creates conditions likely to make them so. The nurse who feels sure of herself behaves with dignity and certainty, expecting positive responses from other people. These expectations in turn call forth responses from her coworkers and patients that tend to confirm the beliefs she already holds. So, the circular effect of the self-concept creates a kind of spiral in which "the rich get richer and the poor get poorer." This self-corroborating characteristic gives the self-concept a high degree of stability and makes it difficult to change once it has become firmly established.

Self-Concept and Social Problems

The self-perpetuating characteristic of the self-concept makes it of special concern in dealing with some of the great social problems of our time. Millions of citizens are caught in a vicious circle in which their experience seems always to confirm their unhappy or disastrous concepts of self. Having defined themselves in ways that preclude much hope of success, they remain forever victims of their own self-perceptions. Believing they are only X much, that is all the much they do. Other people seeing them behave so, label and treat them as "X much people" which, of course, only confirms what the person felt in the first place! How to help these desperate victims of their own perceptions off the treadmill of self-corroboration is one of the great problems faced by society.

The self-concept also plays its part in the social and philosophical problems posed by our great international dilemmas. People who see themselves as Americans behave like Americans, while people who see themselves as Russians, Chinese, Japanese, Germans, British, or Ghanians behave in ways appropriate to their conceptions of themselves. Sometimes diverse ways of seeing even create differences and misunderstandings where none would really exist, were it possible to penetrate to the basic issues beneath the surface. U Thant, once Secretary-General of the United Nations, expressed this in a description of his own growth and philosophy, which had brought him to a point where he could see himself as a "person in the world" rather than as a representative of Burma, his native country. Feeling so, he said that he could watch a wrestling match between a man from his own and a different country and rejoice for whomever won. For most of us, such a "citizen of the world" self-concept is still beyond our experience.

HOW THE SELF-CONCEPT IS LEARNED

The self-concept, we have said, is an organization of beliefs about the self. We acquire these concepts in the same way we acquire all other perceptions—as a consequence of experience. Before a child is born it has already begun to differentiate between self and the world. After birth, the infant spends a very large part of its waking hours in continuous exploration. Everything is smelled, felt, tasted, listened to, and looked at. Very early he or she begins to distinguish between what is "me" and "not me." With continued exploration, these perceptions become increasingly differentiated into more and more explicit definitions. As language use develops, it soon becomes possible to give "me" a name, and the whole process of differentiation and concept formation accelerates. Before long the child possesses many perceptions about self and the world, and a sense of identity emerges. The child becomes aware of himself or herself as a unique person of many qualities and values, which all together contribute towards a feeling of personness. A new self-concept has come into being. Once established, this self-concept will exert its influence on every behavior for the rest of its owner's life.

Some of the things people learn about self are discovered by interacting with the physical world. From these experiences they learn how big or how little they are, how fast they can walk or swim, or where they are located in the space they live in. They also learn what they can lift or not lift, what they can control, what dangers they must avoid or protect themselves from, what things are good or enhancing, and thousands of other perceptions used for getting along in the physical world.

Role of Significant Others

Of much more importance to the growth of the self, however, are the concepts acquired from interaction with other human beings. Persons are primarily social animals, and they derive their most crucial self-concepts from experiences with other people. People learn who they are and what they are from the treatment they receive from the important people in their lives—sometimes called *significant others*. From these interactions people learn that they are liked or unliked, acceptable or unacceptable, successful or failures, respectable or of no account. We learn very little from unimportant people even if they are teachers, parents, social workers, counselors, priests, or rabbis. Only the persons the individual considers significant have much effect on the self-concept.

Although the self-concept is primarily learned from experience with significant others, this is not simply a matter of what one is *told* by the important people in one's life. What people say to each other may, of course, have considerable importance, but not always. The effect of words does not lie in what is said, but in how it is interpreted by the hearer. Understanding this fact is especially important for persons in the helping professions, because so much of their work is dependent upon verbal interaction in one form or another. Believing that words are terribly important or that any problem can be solved by talk can result in making the helper ineffective. Talking is one of the most valuable tools we have for influencing the behavior of others, but it is easy to exaggerate its contribution. It is not enough to be told one is loved; one must *feel loved,* and by someone who matters. Speech is by no means infallible and is often vastly overrated. One need only remind himself how seldom he takes "good advice" from others.

A great deal of what we learn about ourselves comes about through nonverbal communication. Everyone expresses feelings, attitudes, and beliefs through "body language": the ways we sit or stand, the gestures we use, facial expressions, and a thousand other more or less subtle signs that convey our personal meanings. We become very skillful in reading such signals so that we know what others think of us with never a word being spoken. Indeed, the fact that something was not said that should have been, may, itself, be the most significant idea expressed between two people. Children learn about themselves, for example, from the atmosphere of the classroom, from the moods of teachers, and from the overt or covert indications of success or failure implied by approval or disapproval of teachers and classmates. This unplanned learning is likely to be much more significant and permanent than what the teacher "taught." The child in fifth grade who is reading at second-grade level has a daily diet of failure imposed by the rigidity of a system that insists on teaching all children at a given level as though they were alike. In the face of this daily experience, calling the child "a good girl or boy" is like a drop of water in a dry lake bed.

What is learned about self is a matter of the individual's own experience, not what seems to some outsider to be happening. A parent who scolds a child for not doing well in school may do so with the best of intentions, hoping to motivate the child to greater effort. To the child the meaning of this event may only be that he is stupid, unacceptable, or not much good. This kind of "incidental learning" is often more important in determining behavior than what the counselor or teacher or social worker expected to convey. A grasp of the crucial effects of significant others on self-concept is not only important to helpers for understanding the persons they seek to help. It is also necessary for the guidance of helpers themselves as they strive to serve as significant others in the lives of their students, clients, and patients. In a later chapter, we will examine some ways in which prospective helpers can learn to perceive the self-concepts of others.

Place of Trauma in the Growth of Self

Many believe the self-concept is primarily a product of the dramatic events that happened to the child while growing up. The development of this idea is based upon concepts introduced by Sigmund Freud and his students. As he listened to his patients retrace their development during psychoanalysis, Freud found them concentrating on shocking events from their pasts. Naturally he assumed that these events had had powerful influences on the formation of personality and the creation of the problems his patients carried into adult years. This impression was further confirmed by the patients themselves, who frequently spoke of traumatic events as critical. Yet we know that two people can experience the same kind of tragedy and react quite differently. One person may lose an entire family in an auto accident and be totally destroyed psychologically, while another person may quickly recover from such an experience. One woman may suffer total mental collapse on being raped; another may survive the experience and eventually become a stronger person than before.

We now understand that most important changes in the self-concept probably occur only as a consequence of many experiences repeated over long periods of time. The little day-to-day events repeatedly chipping away at an individual's feelings produce the most pervasive effects on the self. A child learns that he is acceptable or unacceptable—not so much from dramatic events as from the thousands of little everyday nuances of attitude and feeling picked up from those about him. These are often so subtle and indistinct at the time they occur that the grownup will find it quite impossible to distinguish the particular childhood event that produced a current feeling. Looking backward down the years of our growth, dramatic events provide the hooks on which we can hang *accumulated* meanings. As a consequence, an adult may recall how shy he was as a child and how devastated he was the day in third grade "when all the children laughed at me." What makes the difference in human personality is not the trauma itself, but the complex of other experiences that hammered and molded a person's meanings to a state later triggered into explicit expression by some traumatic event.

Stability of the Self-Concept

We have described the self-concept as an organization of concepts varying in importance to the individual. We have also observed that, once established, the core of self-concept has a high degree of stability. Peripheral aspects of the self can often be acquired or changed fairly quickly. For example, a person can be taught to play tennis and come to think of himself as a "tennis-player." By taking a person for a ride in an airplane, we may produce a change in her self-concept to "one who has been in a plane." These kinds of changes are comparatively simple to bring about, but they are seldom significant enough to produce important changes in personality. Important changes in self-concept, like those related to values, attitudes, or basic beliefs, occur much more slowly and sometimes only after very long periods of time. While this is often frustrating to those who would like to help people quickly or easily, we need to remind ourselves that this same resistance to change is also our best guarantee against control by a demagogue. It is a good thing people do not change easily.

Generally speaking, the more important the aspect of self is in the economy of the individual, the more experience will be required to establish it and the more difficult it will be to change. Fritz Redl once illustrated this slow development of individual feelings about self in the course of a lecture on juvenile delinquency. Delinquents, he pointed out, are not made by any one thing:

> It takes fourteen years to make a good delinquent. Before that you can't really be sure you have one. To make a good delinquent everything has to go wrong, not once, but over and over again. The home has to go wrong, the school has to go wrong, the church has to go wrong, the community has to go wrong, his friends have to let him down, not once, but over and over again. They have to make a habit of it! Then, after fourteen years of that you may have a good delinquent.[2]

After fourteen years of such experience it is also understandable why it takes time to change such a child's beliefs about self and the world.

SELF-CONCEPT AND SELF-REPORT

If the self-concept plays so important a role in the determination of behavior as modern psychologists believe, then members of the helping professions must be sensitive to the self-concepts of their students, clients, or patients, and skillful in helping them change concepts of self. At first glance, understanding someone's self-concept seems like an easy proposition, if you would like to know how someone sees himself, why not just ask him? Unfortunately, it is not that simple. A person's self-perceptions are very private, and what the person is able to tell you about self will

---

2. From notes taken by A. W. Combs at Dr. Redl's lecture. Since Dr. Redl was speaking *ex tempore*, the accuracy of the quotation cannot be checked.

depend upon his or her willingness to reveal self to you. Even if the person is willing, there is still a question as to whether he or she can accurately describe self to you on demand. Members of the helping professions should develop a clear understanding of the differences between a person's self-report and self-concept.[3]

The self-concept is what a person perceives himself to be; it is what he *believes* about self. The self-report, on the other hand, is what a person is willing or able to divulge, or what he or she can be induced into *saying* about self. The self-report is a behavior; the self-concept is a system of beliefs. These categories are not the same.

What people say about themselves may be accepted as interesting and informative data, but not, without question, as a direct indication of the self-concept. The self-concept can, however, be understood indirectly through a process of inference from some form of observed behavior. The rationale is as follows: If it is true that behavior is a product of the individual's perceptual field, then it should be possible, by a process of reading behavior backward, to infer from observed behavior the nature of the perceptions that produced it. This is, in fact, what all of us do with people who are important to us. We deduce what they are thinking and feeling from the behavior we observe. The psychologist in research and the helper in the professional role do exactly the same thing, although with greater control and precision than the general public.

The question may legitimately be raised as to why inferences about the self-concept, made from observed behavior, are more acceptable indicators of the self-concept than a person's own self-report. First, the inferred self-concept is more accurate on theoretical grounds; it approaches the self-concept as an organization of *perceptions* that *produce* behavior rather than accepting the person's behavior as synonymous with self-perception. Second, it recognizes the existence of distorting factors in the self-report and attempts to eliminate as many of these as practicable. Making inferences about the self-concept, for example, can eliminate or reduce errors introduced by social expectancy, lack of cooperation of the subject, lack of adequate language, or the subject's feelings of threat. One may argue that inference procedures introduce other errors in the perceptions of the observer, but that is a problem in every human observation that scientists must deal with, no matter what the nature of the observations.

3. This is a matter currently in great confusion in the psychological literature. Most of the studies presented through 1975 as researches on the self-concept, turn out, on closer examination, to be studies of self-report. Purporting to be researches on the self-concept, they used measures of the self-report as though these concepts were identical. Treating these terms as though they were synonymous has greatly complicated the literature, and serious students need to be aware of this in interpreting research findings.

A person's *real* self, of course, is measured neither by the inferred self-concept nor the self-report. The question is: Which of these provides the closest approximation for the purposes we have in mind? Despite criticism of the self-report as a measure of self-concept, the self-report has value in its own right. What a person has to say about self is observable behavior. Because of its symbolic character and the uses the behaver makes of it for self-expression, it has more than ordinary value for helping us understand another person. Employed as behavioral data, a self-report can provide valuable clues to the nature of the self-concept when subjected to processes of inference. Despite its distortions, the self-report may also provide sufficient data for the citizen operating in daily life. The scientist, student of behavior, or practitioner in the helping professions, however, will generally need descriptions of self more carefully and rigorously obtained.

SELF-CONCEPT AND THE HELPING PROFESSIONS

Any aspect of human personality that affects behavior so fundamentally as the self-concept must be of vital concern to workers in the helping professions. It is, in fact, their primary subject matter in whatever arena they practice their art. Counselors, teachers, social workers, and priests are in the business of helping students, clients, and parishioners to explore and discover better, more effective relationships between themselves and the world they live in. Whether or not they are successful practitioners depends upon the effects they have on the self-concepts of those who seek their help. Major principles of human personality structure cannot be set aside because they are inconvenient. If the self-concept has the central importance suggested by modern psychology, then those whose responsibilities require that they work with people can ignore it only at the risk of making themselves ineffective.

In a fascinating experiment in New South Wales, J. W. Staines found marked differences in the sensitivities of teachers to the self-concepts of children. This sensitivity was accompanied by greater evidence of growth in the children they worked with. What is more, Staines found that the self-concepts of children were affected whether the teacher was consciously attending to their self-concepts or not. In the conclusion of his experiment he says:

> The educational significance of the self is re-affirmed when it is realized that changes in the self picture are an inevitable part of both outcomes and conditions of learning in every classroom, whether or not the teacher is aware of them or aiming for them. They occur, as in A's class where the teacher deliberately included them in his teaching goals and adopted

them in his methods accordingly, and they occur in B's class where the teacher aimed at orthodox goals and was ignorant of these correlative factors. Since both classes were reasonably typical and both teachers recognized by their headmasters as competent teachers, it is reasonable to generalize and expect such factors to operate in all classrooms.[4]

The self-concept is important to helpers for another reason. Students, clients, and patients judge the value of their experience with helpers from the frame of reference of the self-concept. If the helper continually misses the subject's self, sooner or later the student-client concludes that the relationship is a waste of time and, one way or another, physically or mentally departs the scene. People do not listen long to those who have no significant message. They also evaluate helpers in terms of this significance and report their findings to anyone else who may ask their opinion. People bring their self-concepts with them everywhere they go. To ignore the self-concept and its impact upon behavior seriously handicaps the helper's effectiveness. His position is as ridiculous as the man who says, "I know my car needs a carburetor, but I think I'll run mine without one!"

Changing the Self-Concept

Because the self-concept is learned, it can be taught. This fact provides the theoretical basis upon which the helping professions depend. The purpose of these occupations is to assist other people in exploring and discovering more effective relationships between themselves and the world. To accomplish this objective, helpers need to understand the nature of the self-concept and how it changes. Generally speaking, the self of another person may be modified in two ways: (1) through confrontation with some experience calling for a different view of self, or (2) through evaluation of already existing experience.

The first of these routes to change is familiar to everyone. This is the way each of us learned our identities from the beginning, as a consequence of the ways we were treated by those who surrounded us while we were growing up. Helpers affect the self-concepts of students, clients, and patients by arranging appropriate experiences. So teachers help children feel able by providing success experience, and counselors help clients feel able by treating them as though they were.

Helpers engage in a subtle process of teaching whether they are aware of it or not. They cannot be nonentities. The helping relationship is an active one, and a completely passive helper is unlikely to teach his client anything but his or her own futility. The personality of the helper must play a vital part in any helping relationship.

4. J. W. Staines, "The Self-Picture as a Factor in the Classroom," *British Journal of Educational Psychology* 28 (1958).

The second way in which the self changes comes about as a consequence of new ways of seeing old experience. This kind of learning, often called "insight," occurs when the elements of perceptual organization are put together in a new pattern or gestalt. So a person talking about concerns with a teacher or counselor, may conclude his original way of perceiving the matter was not accurate or appropriate and change his point of view about the event and about himself.

Changing Self Takes Time

Changing important aspects of self is rarely accomplished quickly. A proper perspective of the limitations of these changes can forestall the helper from setting impractical goals and contribute to the helper's own mental health and probabilities of successful practice. Generally speaking, the more fundamental or important the aspect of self we hope to change, the longer it is likely to take. Persons who have been deeply deprived, for example, have a great void within that requires filling. Helping them is something like trying to help a person who has fallen deeply in debt. For a very long time all the money he makes must go just to keep himself solvent from day to day. All efforts are spent in just trying to balance the budget. Until that is done, little can be used to get ahead. The matter is made more difficult by interest charges or withdrawals to meet new emergencies. It may take a long time to help such a person recover to the point where he can take some positive action on his own. Helpers often have to believe their efforts are worthwhile despite the lack of tangible evidence for a considerable period of time. For deeply deprived persons, a single experience is rarely enough to make much difference.

The impatient helper may begin the task intending to help and end by making the client worse. The following scenario with a tough delinquent is all too common:

Here he is—surly, angry, against the world, feeling as a result of his long experience, "Nobody likes me. Nobody wants me. Nobody cares about me. Well, I don't care about nobody neither!" Now the well-meaning social worker, with the best of intentions, says to him, "Eddie, I like you." Much to her dismay, her friendly words are met with a stream of profanity. The inexperienced social worker may be deeply hurt by this rejection and outraged by the violence of the child's reply. Why should the child behave in this way? He does so, because from his point of view, "you can't trust people who talk like that." All his past experience has taught him so. The social worker's words are a mockery to the child. They sound like outright lies, or worse still, like someone is making fun of him. Small wonder that he lashes out at his attacker and lets her have "what she deserves." Unless the social worker knows what she is about and possesses a great deal of patience, she may succumb to the "natural" thing and slap him across the mouth. This, of course, only proves what the youngster felt in the first place—"you can't trust people who talk like that!" What started out as an attempt to help becomes shipwrecked by the helper's own lack of perspective about the self-concept, and confirms the child's beliefs more deeply than ever before. Worse still, the experience may increase the child's distrust of persons in the helping professions generally.

Helping Is Never in Vain

Despite the high degree of stability characteristic of its central aspects, the self-concept is always capable of change. Indeed, throughout life it is continually changing. Good examples are the changes in feeling about self which occur from childhood to adolescence, to maturity and finally to old age. Even very old people sometimes make considerable changes in self-concept, albeit not so easily as they did in their youth. Change, to be sure, is more rapid in the peripheral and less important aspects of self; but learning goes on continuously and even the central aspects of the self-concept may change as a consequence of experience over the years.

Life is not reversible; every experience a person has is forever. One cannot unexperience what has happened! Every experience of significant interaction has its impact upon those who were involved in it. Meaningful experiences provided by a helper may not be sufficient to produce the changes hoped for; but they are always important. The importance of the helper in the life of a client is never without meaning unless the helper makes it so.

Professional helpers often complain that there is little they can do because they do not have control over the outside lives of clients, students, or patients. They complain that their work is spoiled by the unhappy experiences visited upon their clients by bosses, parents, or society in general. As a matter of fact, even a holding operation may make a very important contribution. When everything in a child's life outside of school is teaching him that he is unliked, unwanted, and unable, a loving teacher, who provides experience of success, may make a world of difference. A teacher may not be able to turn the tide completely, but if he or she does no more than help such a child keep his head above water the effort is surely not wasted. Teachers rarely get credit for this kind of help, but it probably occurs with far more frequency than any of us realize. Similarly, the social worker who helps a young delinquent stay only "as bad as he is" when everything else in his world is pushing him downhill can make a contribution of tremendous importance—even if the social worker does not succeed in making him over into a more socially acceptable image.

Helpers must not fall into the trap of thinking their efforts are futile. To do so may only contribute further to the inadequacies of their clients and students. After all, because a child is rejected at home is no good reason to reject him in school as well. What happens to an individual outside the helper's sphere of influence may operate in directions opposite to those sought by the helper. This does not mean that what the helper does is of no avail. Take the case of the teacher who exclaims, "What can you do with a child from a home like that?" It seems to her that all her hard won gains are negated by what happens to the child in his family. Such an attitude is most unfortunate. It overlooks the fact that a family is a dynamic unit in which each person interacts with all the others. What happens to any one member must affect everyone else. Let us take the hypothetical case of George Anderson, who is driving his mother to distraction by his hostile behavior. Let us also suppose this child is fortunate enough to have a teacher who provides some warmth, friendship, and experience of success. When George goes home from school these days he feels better than he did when school was a more unhappy place. As a consequence he doesn't upset his mother quite so much. Mr. Anderson, coming home tired from work, discovers his wife is easier to live with, and his home is a more restful place. When Judith Anderson, George's little sister, claims her father's attention while he is trying to read the paper, instead of pushing her gruffly away, as he often does, he makes room for her to climb in his lap, and Judith gains from her father a greater measure of the love and care she needs. Because she feels better, she feels less need to nag her brother George, as she usually does, and we have come full circle! Every good thing a helper does is forever. It may not be enough, but it is never futile. There is always the further possibility that someone else may contribute something elsewhere, and such cumulative experiences may in time be sufficient to bring about the changes hoped for.

The self-concept, we have said in this chapter, lies at the very heart of the helping process. A proper knowledge of the self-concept and its dynamics can add immeasurably to understanding people in need of help. It can also provide the guidelines by which persons in the helping professions may focus their practice more effectively and efficiently, and so contribute with greater certainty to the health and growth of clients.

Selected Readings

Starred entries indicate appearance in whole or in part in Donald L. Avila, Arthur W. Combs, and William W. Purkey, *The Helping Relationship Sourcebook*, Boston: Allyn and Bacon, 1977.

Bettelheim, B. "Where Self Begins." *Child and Family* 7, 1968, pp. 5–12.

Canfield, J., and Wells, H. C. *100 Ways to Enhance Self-Concept in the Classroom: A Handbook for Parents and Teachers.* Englewood Cliffs, New Jersey: Prentice-Hall, 1976.

Combs, A. W.; Richards, A. C.; and Richards, F. *Perceptual Psychology: A Humanistic Approach to the Study of Persons.* New York: Harper & Row, Publishers, 1976.

Giorgi, A. *Psychology as a Human Science: A Phenomenologically-Based Approach.* New York: Harper & Row, Publishers, 1970.

Hamachek, D. E. *Encounters with the Self.* New York: Holt, Rinehart and Winston, 1971.

*Kelley, Earl C. "What May We Now Believe." In D. L. Avila, A. W. Combs, and W. W. Purkey. *Helping Relationships Sourcebook.* Boston: Allyn and Bacon, 1977.

La Benne, W. D., and Greene, B. I. *Educational Implications of Self-Concept Theory.* Pacific Palisades, California: Goodyear, 1969.

*Patterson, C. H. "The Self in Recent Rogerian Theory." *Journal of Individual Psychology* 17, 1961, pp. 5–11.

Piaget, J. *The Mechanisms of Perception.* Translated by G. N. Seagrim. New York: Basic Books, 1969.

Purkey, W. W. *Self-Concept and School Achievement.* Englewood Cliffs, New Jersey: Prentice-Hall, 1970.

3
A Humanistic View of Motive

Next to our beliefs about ourselves, perhaps no others are more important than those we hold about what people are like and why they behave as they do. These provide the bases for every human interaction. Whatever we do in dealing with other people is always predicated on some conception of what they are like and what we believe they are trying to do. It makes a great difference in my behavior, for example, if I believe a man running toward me wants to walk along with me, ask for directions, deliver a message, or rob me. For helpers, a clear understanding of human motivation is essential for successful practice.

TWO VIEWS OF MOTIVATION

Two ways of examining motivation are commonly used. One looks at motivation externally—from the point of view of an outsider seeking to influence another person's behavior. The other is an internal approach to motivation concerned with what people want, need or are trying to do.

Underlying the external approach to motivation are several assumptions about the fundamental characteristics of the human organism. The more scientific of these conceptions sees human beings as objects, products at the end of a long chain of molding influences originating at conception. Other, less scientific, views regard the human organism as essentially untrustworthy, likely to revert to its perverse original nature if something isn't done to assure its proper behavior. In either case, the external approach views motivation in terms of what one person does to another to cause the behavior that the motivator has in mind. This is essentially a matter of management, involving the application of stimuli to control behavior, generally through some form of reward or punishment. Control may be exerted by various forms of manipulation like directing, ordering, making, convincing, telling, exhorting, threatening, or coercing. Coercion can be subtle, with a velvet glove masquerading as "guidance." Control may also be exerted by "carrot on a stick" techniques of reward with concrete rewards like cash, food, and presents, or by various kinds of seduction like, "Please," or, "If you do this, I will love you," or, "He-men shave with ——." In an external view of motivation, the person is treated as an object to be molded or manipulated toward preconceived ends.

Seen from the internal view, motivation involves human needs, goals and aspirations. These are internal matters arising from an understanding of human behavior as a consequence of a person's perceptions of self and the world. Helpers may sometimes find it useful to operate in terms of external approaches to motivation, but more often their efforts at helping will be directed toward facilitating change in the perceptual worlds of those they seek to help.

OLDER CONCEPTS OF THE NATURE OF PEOPLE

The Basically Evil Person

Throughout history, people have been intrigued by the problem of the "nature of man." and many explanations have been proposed. Each of these ideas has had its effects upon the generations that believed them, and many still influence modern thought. One of these concepts is the doctrine of original sin. This doctrine maintained that children entered the world innately evil. The purpose of life was to correct this evil and strive toward goodness. Since adults used their own behavior as the criteria for judging others, the child who did not conform to adult standards was considered "naughty" or "bad." And, since most children who behaved in approved ways managed to develop into satisfactory adults, it seemed evident that people grew better as they grew older. Assuming that tendencies toward good and evil were innate, parents did not regard themselves responsible for the outcomes of their offspring. People felt sorry for parents with "bad" children and regarded them as unlucky or as having to bear such a cross because it was God's will.

For many centuries this concept was part of certain religious dogmas and so was given the additional authority of the Church. More recently it had the apparent endorsement of science. Darwin's concept of evolution, for example, seemed to give credence to the basic animal quality of human nature. Freudian psychology also seemed to support this view in its concept of the *id*, defined as primeval impulses representing a person's roots in the uncivilized animal world. The concept of persons as basically evil is very old. Even today the principles of this essentially pessimistic view of human beings are accepted by people in all walks of life, including some members of the helping professions.

The Person at War with Himself

The concept of the person at war with himself is even more common than original sin. Those who hold this view see the person as a battleground on which both good and evil forces are constantly striving for supremacy. It is supported by the observations we make about the behavior of people around us. People do, indeed, behave well and badly. Conflict, competition, and struggle seem to be going on everywhere. Reflecting on one's own behavior, we can recall our struggles against temptation, grief or shame over harmful actions, or feelings of self-approval from fighting against an evil impulse. The personality-in-conflict view seems to explain a great many of our experiences.

The concept of the person divided can also be found deeply imbedded in tradition, not only in our culture but in most others. It exists in the folklore, myths, fables, and traditions in primitive tribes and highly civilized cultures. In the Western world, it has long been a classic concept of Judeo-Christian philosophy. In psychology, the concept of conflict is illustrated by need systems like: Succorance-nurturance, dependence-abasement, and aggression-deference. It is also advanced by psychoanalysts who describe maladjustment as the outcome of a person's struggles between the primitive impulses of the id and the civilized functions of the "super ego."

Some Implications of Older Concepts

Human nature seen from these older points of view poses difficult problems for the helping professions. The original sin and the person-in-conflict views require working with an organism that can never be trusted. If human nature is inherently evil, one is always confronted with the possibility of a reversion to bestiality the moment a person is permitted to operate freely. Helpers proceeding from this frame of reference constantly struggle against great odds and their task is doomed to eventual defeat. The person in need of help must be regarded with suspicion. The helper must always be on guard for signs of reversion to type and ready to head off such tendencies as they appear. With this view and its characteristic lack of trust, helper and helpee are cast in the roles of antagonists.

The methods required to deal with such perverse tendencies must be powerful ones. Saving people in spite of themselves calls for vigorous measures. Persons growing up in such traditions often come to believe that there is something innately good about work and that discipline for its own sake is a wonderful thing. They operate on the philosophy, "if it's hard it's good for them." Helpers with this orientation believe they are battling for the very salvation of the individual and the maintenance of civilization. This is a task that can brook no nonsense.

Such a philosophy calls for methods of helping people that rely upon various forms of control and direction—for example, rewarding the taking of right paths and punishing the taking of wrong ones. This results in a way of dealing with people sometimes called "the fencing in" approach, in which persons are guided toward chosen goals through the imposition or removal of barriers, much like a rat in a maze or controlling traffic on a modern freeway. Controls may be physical (walls, traffic lights, or electric shocks) or verbal (prohibitions or threats). Motivation is provided by outside manipulation, usually through some form of punishment or reward.

A PERCEPTUAL VIEW OF MOTIVE

In more recent years, humanistically oriented psychologists have arrived at a different view of the basic nature of human beings. They agree that persons do, indeed, sometimes behave well and sometimes badly. They point out, however, that because people *behave* so, it cannot be assumed that they *are* so. Who has not hurt or embarrassed a friend while intending to be especially nice? Perceptual psychologists have developed a conception that provides a different understanding of motivation and establishes a different set of guidelines for the helping professions.

From biology we learn that a basic characteristic of protoplasm is its "irritability," that is, its capacity to respond. Awareness is thus a quality of life itself. The ability of organisms to respond, furthermore, is not haphazard; it is response with direction. Haphazard or fortuitous response would quickly result in elimination of the organism in the course of evolution. The response of an organism is not accidental; it is goal-directed toward fulfillment. Even the lowly amoeba moves toward food and away from danger, at least as far as it is capable of doing so. Mushrooms turn away from light, whereas sunflowers grow toward it. Wounded flesh heals. Animals mate and care for their young. Each life in its own peculiar way continuously seeks fulfillment. The search for fulfillment is characteristic of life itself.

Human beings, like all other organisms, are continuously in search of fulfillment. The dynamic, striving character of persons has its origins in the nature of protoplasm itself. People begin their lives with a built-in motivation towards self-fulfillment, and thereafter make of it what they can within the limits of their capacities.

The expression of our basic striving translated into behavior may seem good or evil to an outside observer. But movement towards fulfillment is, of itself, neither good nor bad. That is a value judgment about behavior made by persons observing it from the frame of reference of a particular culture. We cannot say that the organism itself is basically good or evil. However, since striving for fulfillment seems to be a constructive force in human existence, there is some justification for considering this basic drive to be more positive than negative.

The Growth Principle

The basic striving of organisms for fulfillment has been called the *growth principle,* because the effect is to move them continuously toward health and growth for as long as possible. This is true whether we are talking of a single cell like a paramecium or of the great organization of cells that make up a complicated mammal like a human being. Growth is characteristic of the very essence of life and finds expression in all of life's ramifications.

The growth principle is so important to the physiological well-being of people that the practice of medicine is predicated upon it. The physician knows that it is not she who cures her patients; rather it is the patient who cures himself. When the body is invaded by germs, many forces swing into action to defend the organism by destroying or immobilizing the offending invaders. The doctor's task is to minister to this process. She assists the body in its normal striving toward a healthy condition. To this end, she may try to impede or destroy invading germs with medication or resort to surgery to remove or repair a disabled organ. By prescribing rest, nourishing food, or proper innoculations, the physician may further assist the body's attempts to return to a state of health by building up its resources. Whatever the doctor does to help the process along, in the final analysis the body gets well of itself.

The growth principle operates in behavioral as well as physiological terms. The entire organism strives toward growth. People do not just seek to be physically adequate; more important, they strive for personal fulfillment. To achieve psychological satisfaction they will even risk their physical beings. To feel important or worthwhile, they may even court death. Examples in everyday life are the professional football player, racing driver, test pilot, or astronaut to name but a few. Throughout history, heroes have gone to certain death for their fellows. In doing so the hero sacrifices his physical self to enhance another self more important to him: his self-concept.

NEED FOR SELF-ACTUALIZATION

We have seen in the previous chapter how the self-concept transcends the physical body. The fulfillment of self that human beings seek is actualization of the *concept of self,* not simply its container. As a consequence, people may strive very hard for self-enhancement, not only in the present but for the future as well. Many people spend large portions of their lives and fortunes seeking to perpetuate a favorable image of self in the minds of others. In certain cultures, even suicide may be seen as a form of self-enhancement. To achieve as adequate and effective a self as possible, a man may kill himself today rather than suffer the humiliation he knows is coming tomorrow. For the Japanese nobleman, committing hari-kari guaranteed prestigious immortality.

The growth principle at work has also been called by biologists "homeostasis," "the wisdom of the body," and "the drive to health." Among psychologists, it has been described by Maslow as a need for self-actualization, by Allport as a process of becoming, by Lecky as self-consistency, by Festinger as dissonance reduction, by Frankl as a search for meaning, and by Rogers as a search for self-fulfillment. In their earliest work, Combs and Snygg described it as a need for the maintenance and enhancement of the self; in a later work it was described as a need for personal adequacy. By whatever name it is called, the principle refers to the striving of human beings constantly searching for personal adequacy or fulfillment.

Maslow's Hierarchy of Needs

People do not seek enhancement in the same ways or through the same goals. They have learned many different ways of seeking fulfillment and operate on varied levels of enhancement. Abraham Maslow called these goals *needs* and arranged them in a kind of hierarchy from basic physiologic ones to high level self-actualization as follows:

1. Physiological needs (for example, food, water, oxygen).
2. Safety needs—security, stability, freedom from fear (for example, needs for structure, limits).
3. Belongingness and love needs—affectionate relationships with people and the feeling that one belongs in some social context.
4. Esteem needs—achievement, adequacy, mastery (for example, needs for reputation, recognition, importance).
5. Self-actualization needs—self-fulfillment, to actualize one's potential, "to become more and more what one idiosyncratically is, to become everything that one is capable of becoming."[1]

Maslow suggests that such hierarchies of need represent a demand system in which the more basic needs must be satisfied before higher ones can be achieved. This observation is demonstrated by the lower end of

1. A. H. Maslow, *Motivation and Personality,* 2nd ed. (New York: Harper & Row, Publishers, 1970): 35–58.

need hierarchies. A man dying of thirst is in no condition to appreciate a symphony, and people with empty bellies respond very badly to demands that they consider the fine points of democratic government.

While the idea of a hierarchy of needs has merit as a way of thinking about human striving, the practitioner should not regard it as universal. The fundamental need of the organism is for self-fulfillment. The ways people seek to achieve that need, in the terms of perceptual psychology, are goals through which the search is expressed. These may shift and change as time and circumstances determine, but the reach for fulfillment of self goes on unceasingly.

Is Human Nature Selfish?

Perhaps it will appear distressing to some readers that the basic nature of human beings as we have described it here is a striving for self-fulfillment. They may ask, "Is human nature really so fundamentally selfish?" The answer is yes and no. There is no doubt that the basic drive for self-fulfillment is a concern for self. We have also seen how the self-concept is the individual's basic frame of reference. In this sense, human beings appear to be selfish. The picture, however, is not nearly so egocentric as it seems.

In the previous chapter we saw that the self-concept is capable of expansion. If a child, born with a basic drive for self-fulfillment, has good experiences with the people about him, then little by little he comes to expand his self to include those significant others. He comes to feel "one with" his parents, his siblings, playmates, and friends. As he grows older, the circle of those he includes within his self may expand to include wider and wider groups of people. In time, he may come to identify with "my country" and "my school." In the case of saintly persons, the feeling of identification may eventually extend to all humanity. In that state, the problem of selfishness has completely disappeared; when the self is identified with all mankind then what one does for self, one does for everyone, and what one does for everyone, one does for self. Selfishness is determined by the boundaries of the self. A restricted self is a selfish one; an expanded self is a saintly one. Basic nature is selfish only in the extent to which the self has failed to grow by identification with others.

DETERMINING EFFECT OF NEED
ON BEHAVIOR

How people behave at every moment of their lives is determined by the basic need of the organism for self-fulfillment. No one is ever free of the operation of the growth principle. It is a function of life itself and has its effect upon every act. It also determines what we are able to see, to hear, and even to think and believe. Persons participating in food deprivation experiments, for instance, report that it is extremely difficult to think of anything but food as hunger and the need for food increases. Under these circumstances off-hours are spent drawing up menus for Thanksgiving dinners, and the slightest stimulus in the environment is likely to start such thinking although the stimulus may have no relation to food whatever. Similar effects of need upon perception have been demonstrated in a wide variety of human activities. Aside from research demonstrations, all of us have had experiences indicating how perceptions are affected by felt need. When a man feels in need of a new suit, he is much more aware of advertisements for men's clothing. In the course of our insatiable attempts to satisfy need, certain goals and values become differentiated as leading to satisfaction. Others, which seem to us to lead to the frustration of need, become differentiated as negative goals, to be avoided at all costs.

Because of the selective effect of need upon perception, the behavior of people becomes predictable if we know the peculiar nature the striving for growth and fulfillment takes in them. From their own points of view, people try to fulfill themselves as best they can in the conditions they confront. How they do this may not always seem intelligent, desirable, or appropriate to those who judge them, but from the individual's frame of reference the striving is positive and predictable. The juvenile delinquent who finds it impossible to gain status and prestige in a broken home, in school, or in a church that rejects him may discover that he can find at least partial fulfillment in a gang. There is a certain kind of prestige and status to be gained from stealing cars, flaunting with police, or getting involved in street-fights. What contributes to the delinquent's self-actualization is not what society thinks desirable, but what the delinquent thinks will lead to that end. Seen from his point of view, his behavior makes sense. It is even predictable.

An understanding of need can often cause the most puzzling behavior to make sense. For example, some coeds on a certain college campus expressed extreme reluctance to using oral contraceptives despite their expectations to become involved in sexual relationships. On questioning by the physician, their reasoning went like this: If they took the pills they would obviously be planning on sexual activity. This was considered improper outside of marriage and unacceptable to their concepts of self as "good" girls. If they did have sexual relations and weren't taking the pills, it would then be because they were "swept off their feet in a moment of passion." This was regarded as enhancing, even excusable, since it could happen to anyone!

A Humanistic View of Motive 41

A Trustworthy, Predictable Organism

The need for fulfillment is a single need with a single direction. This makes the behavior of human beings predictable and the organism trustworthy, providing we know the peculiar expression of need in a given person.[2] From the person's own point of view, far from being at war with himself, he is an organized totality with direction and purpose. "But," one may argue, "that does not seem to fit my personal experience. I remember when I had to make this or that difficult choice and it wasn't easy at all. Isn't this an indication that I was at war with myself?" Not at all.

Whenever we examine our own behavior, we must remember we are looking at it after the fact. That is, we observe it like any other outsider. From this position there may appear to be simultaneously existing desires, but this seems so only because the matter is being observed externally. At the moment of behaving, the individual does what seems *at that instant* most likely to lead to fulfillment and actualization. To be sure, it may have been perceived quite differently before or after the act. The illusion of conflict occurs because one is looking at two different events separated in time. The reader may test this against his or her own experience. Recall some instance where you may recently have "misbehaved." Now, looking back on this act from your present position, it may seen as though the act was stupid, undesirable, or even morally wrong. Even before the act occurred, if you had contemplated its consequences, the action may have seemed unsatisfying or immoral. At the moment it happened, however, it seemed like a good thing to do. The act appeared desirable and need-fulfilling, perhaps even necessary, to accomplish your purpose at that instant.

While there may be occasional confusion about ways of achieving fulfillment, there is no conflict of motives. Fulfillment is the motive no matter how it is accomplished. This basic drive for fulfillment is also characteristic of the societies people create to achieve their purposes. All kinds of groups—schools, clubs, communities, nations—are formed to provide fulfillment for their members. They thrive so long as they achieve it and are destroyed or disintegrate when they can no longer provide it.

---

2. This does not mean that every person is trustworthy in a moral sense. The authors, too, have been robbed, lied to, and deceived in their lifetimes. The point here is that there is nothing *innately* untrustworthy about people. The human organism can be counted on to behave in predictable fashion. If it appears untrustworthy, this judgment lies in the "eye of the beholder" who may not have enough data to make accurate predictions possible. Had the authors known enough about their deceivers, they could have predicted the times they were robbed and lied to.

MALADJUSTMENT—A PROBLEM OF DEPRIVATION

The striving of human beings for self-actualization goes on as long as it is possible to do so. The need is insatiable. As soon as a person has achieved one goal there is always another just beyond so that no one is ever completely fulfilled and the drive for self-actualization continues as long as one lives. For some people, unhappily, the force of this drive may be more or less permanently blunted or its direction diverted to unfortunate channels because of some form of deprivation.

The achievement of a satisfactory degree of fulfillment constitutes psychological health. Persons who are successful in attaining a measure of self-actualization are likely to be happy and contented with themselves and effective in their relationships with the world. People who are unsuccessful or frustrated in their attempts to achieve fulfillment become sick and maladjusted. Just as the body's failure to achieve proper growth and fulfillment results in physiologic disease, so, too, failure of the individual to achieve satisfactory fulfillment of self brings psychological ill health.

Maladjusted persons are unfulfilled, and the seriousness of their condition is almost directly a function of the degree of deprivation they have suffered or think they have suffered. Most of us can tolerate mild degrees of failure to achieve fulfillment. When failures become chronic or strike people in important aspects of self-structure, people soon become unhappy. If deprivations are serious or persist for long periods, persons become increasingly neurotic. Depending upon the degree of frustration, people become discouraged, dispirited, angry, or hostile. Severe deprivation can lead to depravity. Almost certainly, deprived people will frustrate other people. If deprivation is too great or too long continued, people finally may feel defeated and without hope. When this happens, they become burdens or dangerous to the rest of us. Such unfortunates are the people who fill our mental hospitals and our penitentiaries.

People are not "naturally" sick. We now understand that sickness and maladjustment are products of human deprivation, failure, and frustration. In earlier times we regarded criminality as willful immorality. Treatments devised for this condition were appropriate to that belief and were often unbelievably harsh and brutal. Today we have a more enlightened view and regard such persons as psychologically sick rather than inherently evil. Slowly we are learning to extend this understanding to the problems of the less dramatically ill, the poor, and to the victims of prejudice. At one time we could regard the problem of the sick and the deprived as inevitable expressions of the will of God. We no longer regard them as inevitable, and if they continue to exist they do so, not as the will of God, but as the lack of will of human beings.

Seen in this light, maladjustment is not a willful seeking of destructive or negative behavior. The observed behavior of persons suffering deprivation and low self-esteem must be understood as efforts to protect the self or achieve some measure of personal fulfillment. Maslow[3] once described the behaviors of the maladjusted as "the screams of the tortured at the crushing of their psychological bones."

Failure to understand the defensive character of such behavior often results in the complaint, "They like it that way." This statement is usually made in a tone of shock, frustration, disappointment, or condemnation, depending upon whether the speaker is surprised, thwarted, blaming, or rejecting. It is often used to explain the failure of social reforms when, for example, we provide new housing for ghetto areas and the residents destroy the property. We apply it also to our friends and neighbors whose behavior we do not comprehend. The assumption is that what people do is what they want to do. If that is so, it follows, they deserve what happens to them.

"They like it that way" is not only a judgment about other people, it is also a beautiful excuse for inaction. If "they like it that way," we really ought not interfere. What happens to other people can thus be ignored without feeling guilty for not having helped. For some, belief in this myth is more than an excuse for inaction. It provides an outlet for hostility and a satisfying feeling of superiority over the stupidity of other people. There are even persons for whom the myth may be a source of enjoyment when watching other people "get what's coming to them."

If the view of human nature that we have been discussing is accurate, vastly different attitudes toward human frailty and error are called for. So many of us are quick to blame our fellows for their foibles and misbehaviors. We get angry at parents for what they do to children. We scorn patients for the stupidities that made them ill, and blame teachers for their inabilities to cope with the children they sent to the counselor. We overlook the fact that the behaver always acts in ways that seem reasonable, even necessary, under the circumstances. We forget that others have problems and that their behavior is a consequence of those conditions. If the basic character of human beings is striving for fulfillment, if every person is forever engaged in a search for self-actualization, if each human being is searching to become the best he can, who then, can we blame for what?

FREEDOM AND THE RIGHTS OF OTHERS

To this point we have spoken of the need of the individual to achieve personal fulfillment. But what of fulfilling the needs of society? The

3. From unpublished comment at the First Annual Conference on Personality Theory and Counseling Practice, University of Florida, Gainesville, Florida, 1961.

answer to that question is that if a person is truly free to seek self-fulfillment and is achieving it to a reasonably satisfactory degree, the person will behave in ways that satisfy the needs of society as well. Why should this be so?

First, it is necessary to remind ourselves that each of us lives deeply imbedded in a social structure. We have created a world so cooperative and interdependent that few of us could last but a few hours without the aid and assistance of other people. The self-concept is learned from the behavior of others toward us, and most of our satisfactions are results of human relationships in one form or another. Human maladjustment is a product of the breakdown of this vital condition. Dialogue between the person and society is absolutely necessary for effective living. This means that successful fulfillment can only be achieved through some form of successful interaction with others.

We have already seen that selfishness disappears as people become fulfilled. As the self expands, increasing numbers of other people are brought into its organization and treated as extensions of self. In the degree to which fulfillment occurs then, persons become increasingly responsible. In fact, the dynamics we are describing are an essential precondition for truly responsible behavior. Irresponsible behavior is a consequence of the breakdown of dialogue, a feeling of alienation or lack of commitment to others. Since the self is learned from the feedback of others, its enhancement is dependent upon successful interaction. *Providing they are free to do so,* it follows that people can, will, *must* move in directions that are good, not only for themselves but for others as well.

This relationship between the person and society was described by Ruth Benedict as *high-synergy culture* and defined as one "in which the individual by the same act and at the same time serves his own advantage and that of the group."[4] Fred and Anne Richards have further described a high-synergy society as "the healthy or helping society in which the individual process of self-actualization and the cultural process of socialization, rather than mutually antagonistic, are complementary or reciprocal. The fulfillment of one's potential for growth and well-being and the realization of society's provides the maximum climate for the full development of the potentiality of the greatest number of its members . . . The individual, by participating in the social order, participates in and affirms his own personal growth."[5]

Persons confronted with this idea for the first time will no doubt find that it strains their credulity. It may even seem to be hopelessly naïve. However, if the basic motive of the organism is a drive toward health,

4. As quoted by A. H. Maslow, in "Synergy in the Society and in the Individual," *Journal of Individual Psychology* (November 1964): 153–164.
5. F. Richards, and A. C. Richards. *Homonovus: The New Man* (Boulder, Colorado: Shields, 1973).

and if it is free to move, it must progress in healthy directions. The essential condition in the statement lies in the phrase, "if it is free to move." The drive toward fulfillment is innate, but the conditions for freedom are not; they exist in the perceptions of the individual and in the world he must cope with. If creation of those conditions is in fact feasible, the democratic concept that "when people are free they can find their own best ways" becomes a clearly defensible principle. What is more, if persons are interacting openly and meaningfully with other people, the ways they find for achieving self-fulfillment will contribute to the fulfillment of all.

The growth principle can be counted upon to provide the motive power for the helping professions. The problem for helpers is to create the conditions for freedom in which the principle can operate. Just as the physician attempts to free the physical organism to move toward recovery and growth, the task of counselors, teachers, parents, psychologists, social workers, and all others engaged in the helping professions is to minister to human beings in such fashion that this basic drive may be set free. If we are successful in creating these conditions, the person's own basic drive for actualization and fulfillment can be counted upon to move him in positive directions.

SOME IMPLICATIONS FOR THE
HELPING PROFESSIONS
People Are on Our Side

If it is true that human beings are relentlessly driven toward health and adequacy, it follows that the helping professions always have a powerful ally—the person himself. The discovery that the human organism is trustworthy means that the people helpers seek to assist are not enemies perversely, stubbornly, or maliciously resisting the efforts of professional workers. Rather, they are deeply and fundamentally motivated by the need to be the very best they can as they see it. So, persons engaged in the helping professions are not dealing with unpredictable, fortuitous matters. They can formulate ways of working with their clients, students, and patients with real hope that these may result in certain and predictable outcomes. Helper and helpee seek the same goal—fulfillment of the client. This makes the relationship a kind of partnership. Such a partnership, to be sure, might occasionally be uneasy or filled with difficulties. A partnership, however, no matter how uneasy, is far more likely to produce positive results than open battle between enemies.

People Are Always Motivated

Most people regard the problem of motivation as a matter of management or manipulation to get others to do the things they would like them to. Motivation is accomplished by rewards or punishments designed to get other people to do "what is good for them," or to keep them from behaving in some fashion considered harmful or against the best interests of the motivator. In light of the growth principle we have been discussing, a different view of motivation is called for.

If people are always seeking self-fulfillment then they are forever motivated. They are never unmotivated until they die. To be sure, they may not be motivated to do what some outsider believes they ought or should. The little boy in school who pokes the pretty little girl in front of him during the arithmetic lesson is not very motivated at that moment to do arithmetic, but he is surely not unmotivated! In the light of our discussion of the growth principle, motivation is not a problem of external manipulations; it has to do with what goes on inside people. It is always there, a characteristic of the life force itself.

Looked at externally, motivating people is a problem of getting them to do the right things. From the internal point of view, the task of the helper becomes one of helping the person to discover new ways of becoming more effective as a human being. To do this, teachers, for example, seek to help each person fulfill the needs he already has, and then help him discover additional needs he never knew he had. As Frymier and Thompson describe it: "Motivation to learn in school is something which students *have* or *are* rather than that which teachers *do* to help them learn. It is a function of one's personality structure, his goals and values, his conception of self and others, and his attitude toward change. These aspects of human behavior are learned and they are subject to modification. Nevertheless, teachers concerned about their youngster's motivations have to do much more than use a carrot on a stick or a paddle on the behind if they hope for significant changes in any way."[6]

Understanding human motives in the terms we have described will have salutary effects upon the helper's relationships with clients, patients, or students. Rapport is likely to be much better, because helpers will more likely be seen as compassionate, concerned, and sympathetic. Operating under the assumption that human nature is fundamentally perverse is apt to make the helper suspicious of helpees. When behavior is not understood in relation to the individual's fundamental need for fulfillment, it is likely to seem puzzling, stupid, and depraved to the outside observer. Such an attitude will not endear the helper to those he seeks to help.

The irate father who viciously beats his child may be a figure of loathing and contempt until we understand that his attacks on Jimmy are motivated by a desire to "make him a good boy!" His problem lies not

6. J. R. Frymier, and J. H. Thompson, "Motivation: The Learner's Mainspring," *Educational Leadership* 22 (1965): 567–570.

in his motives, but in his ways of solving the problem. One can like a father who wants his son to be a good boy, but a father who seems viciously intent on destroying his son is in danger of being hated. It is a hard task to build an effective relationship with people who seem antagonistic and condemnatory. People in the helping professions who find it necessary to begin by blaming those they wish to help may turn out to be their own worst enemies.

In the view of motivation based on the concepts of perceptual psychology, the goal of the helping professions becomes one of ministering to a trustworthy, striving organism rather than controlling a perverse, unpredictable one. It calls for methods of helping designed to encourage and facilitate growth, and provides assurance that if helpers are successful in creating the conditions for freedom, then persons will move toward whatever degree of fulfillment is possible for them. This understanding of human nature is also basic to democracy. The basic tenets of democracy are not just "nice ideas" but have roots in the fundamental character of life itself. Helpers need not be split personalities. The beliefs they hold for working with their students, clients, and patients can be consistent with those they employ for guiding their own behavior and that of the societies in which they operate.

A Process Orientation for the Helping Professions

The purpose of helping relationships is the stimulation and encouragement of growth. This growth is internal and calls for encouragement and stimulation rather than threat and coercion. To grow a healthy plant we use the best possible seed we can find and plant it in the best possible soil available. We provide it with optimum conditions of light, moisture, temperature, and the nutrients it needs in order to grow. After that, we get out of its way and let it grow. In similar fashion, applied to persons, helpers actively involve themselves in the process of searching, perceiving themselves as facilitators in a cooperative process of exploration and discovery. The work of helpers is congruent with the fundamental striving of persons toward health. They seek to "get with it," by entering an encounter with clients or students that is designed to help explore and discover more effective relationships between self and the world.

Expertise rests not so much in knowing answers as in providing processes by which they may be discovered. This removes a tremendous weight from the shoulders of helpers. They do not have to play God or know in advance exactly how clients or students will emerge from the experience. Helpers can devote full attention to the creation of conditions for freedom, and rest assured that the end results will be positive if they are successful in doing so.

48   **Psychological Bases for Helping**

Unless helpers believe people are trustworthy, they do not dare trust them! Unless the helper is satisfied in his own mind as to the positive nature of human striving, he cannot afford to risk permitting helpees to make decisions. Indeed, if teachers, social workers, and clergymen do not believe their clientele can make good decisions, it would be downright unethical to permit them to do so. It takes a very certain belief about the basic nature of persons to be able to sit by and watch a helpee make a decision different from one's own. The kind of assurance demanded for the truly effective helping relationship calls for helpers able to follow this line of reasoning to its ultimate conclusion, to a position that says, "If I truly created the conditions for freedom for my client, student, patient, worker, or parishioner, and he has arrived at a solution different from my own, then I must be prepared to examine my own position with care. I could be wrong!"

The process orientation to the helping professions we have been discussing is characteristic of modern approaches to helping others in a wide variety of areas. In open-ended approaches to social work the social worker will not let her client become dependent upon her, and devotes her energies instead toward helping the client find his own solutions to problems. Experts in pastoral care advocate a similar approach for the clergy. In education it is represented by student-centered concepts of teaching designed to encourage and facilitate the student's own search for meaning. In counseling existential and client-centered approaches to treatment help clients to discover their own answers to problems in a relationship with counselors especially trained to facilitate this kind of exploration. In supervision and administration, it finds expression in emergent concepts of leadership that stress the facilitating aspects of administration rather than control and direction. Each of these modern developments in the helping professions is predicated upon the assumption that the human organism is predictable and, provided it has the proper conditions for freedom, can be counted on to move toward desirable ends.

Selected Readings

Starred entries indicate appearance in Donald L. Avila, Arthur W. Combs, and William W. Purkey, *The Helping Relationship Sourcebook,* Boston: Allyn and Bacon, 1977.

Brennecke, J., and Amick, R. *The Struggle for Significance.* Beverly Hills, California: Glencoe Press, 1971.

*Buhler, C. B. "Human Life Goals in the Humanistic Perspective." *Journal of Humanistic Psychology* 7, 1967, pp. 36–52.

Cantril, H. "Sentio. Ergo Sum: Motivation Reconsidered." *The Journal of Psychology* 65, 1967, pp. 91–107.

Combs, A. W.; Richards, A. C.; and Richards, F. *Perceptual Psychology: A Humanistic Approach to the Study of Persons.* New York: Harper & Row, Publishers, 1976.

Frankl, V. E. *Man's Search for Meaning: An Introduction to Logotherapy.* New York: Washington Square Press, 1963.

Fromm, E. *Art of Loving: An Inquiry into the Nature of Love.* New York: Harper & Row, Publishers, 1956.

*Kelley, E. C. The Meaning of Wholeness. In S. I. Hayakawa, ed., *ETC: A Review of General Semantics* 26, 1969, pp. 7–15.

National Education Association. *Learning and Mental Health in the School,* 1966 Yearbook. Washington, D.C.: Association for Supervision and Curriculum Development, 1966.

Redl, F., and Wineman, D. *Children Who Hate: Disorganization and Breakdown of Behavior Controls.* New York: Collier, 1962.

*Snygg, D. The Psychological Basis of Human Values. In D. Ward, ed., *Goals of Economic Life,* pp. 335–364. New York: Harper & Brothers, 1953.

4

Learning and Helping as Change in Personal Meaning

How people behave at any moment is a function of how things seem to them. Helping people achieve more satisfying ways of living and being is, therefore, a matter of facilitating change in what people think and believe about themselves and the world. To do this well, effective helpers need to understand the nature of personal meaning and how the perceptual field is modified and enriched.

FACTS, MEANING, AND REALITY

No matter how strongly it may be bombarded from without, a person's perceptual field of feelings, attitudes, ideas, and convictions remains forever the sovereign possession of the person himself. Meanings are the facts of life. In behavioral terms, a fact for any person is what that person *believes is so*. If Joe Green believes his boss is unfair, he behaves as though he were. Whether other people think Joe's boss is unfair has little or nothing to do with the matter. Joe can only behave in terms of what seems to him to be the fact of the matter. So far as Joe's behavior is concerned, the "real" facts as they appear to an outsider are irrelevant and immaterial. Indeed, if we try to convince Joe that he is wrong, we run the risk of having him conclude we don't understand him either!

The simplest, most obvious facts about the world around us are only true for members of a common culture. So long as we stay in the same culture, a given fact may never be seriously questioned. When we step outside our own culture we quickly discover that many facts we consider to be reality have no validity in the new setting. Even something so commonplace as a "table" may be called a different name in another culture or may not even be regarded as a table at all. Instead, it may be seen as a platform for dancing, a seat for the village chief, a bed to lie on, a roof for shelter from the rains, or a useless object to be used for firewood.

The personal quality of meanings and the importance they have in the private worlds of individuals is of tremendous significance to workers in the helping professions. The moment we understand other persons in terms of personal meaning, a great deal that was formerly puzzling or inexplicable becomes meaningful and reasonable. A student in one of our psychology classes raised the following question: "I just got a paper from home. I read where a man was arrested for shoplifting. He had a whole sack of things he had taken. When they searched him, he had a hundred pounds on him! How do you account for his stealing?" The student was obviously puzzled. The instructor, too, was puzzled. Here was a statement of fact. There is nothing puzzling about a man being caught with a hundred pounds of shoplifted loot. Why should this student be so puzzled about that? Then, suddenly, the teacher remembered that the student was from Jamaica, a former British colony. "Pounds" in the eyes of the student did not refer to weight, but to money! At once the problem was clear. Why, indeed, should a man shoplift when he has several hundred dollars in his pocket? The puzzle was clear when the instructor was able to perceive the problem through the eyes of his student.

Because of the individual character of meaning, people often fail to understand one another. This is particularly true of persons raised in different cultures, but it is also true of persons with different experiences raised in the same culture. Witness the difficulties in communication for men and women; adults and teenagers; or persons of differing occupations, religion, and locality. Without an understanding of the unique meanings existing for the individual, the problems of helping are almost insurmountable.

SOME DYNAMICS OF MEANING

Stability of Meaning

Development of meaning is a creative act occurring as a consequence of people interacting with the world they live in. People invest events with meaning. The perceptual field is a gestalt, an organization, in which some meanings develop an importance or centrality around which other meanings are organized. The most important of these fundamental meanings is the self-concept about which we have already spoken. Other organizations, called *anchorages,* provide additional orientation and direction by providing a kind of reference point to which other meanings can be referred. Some anchorages are aspects of the physical world like the horizon, which orients us with respect to distance and location.

Others are the relative positions of earth and sky, the discovery that far objects are smaller than near ones, and that bright things are generally closer than far ones. For most of us these seem so natural we take them for granted. But we were not born with them. We learned them, and having discovered their stability came to rely upon them.

Anchorages also exist in respect to personal, social, and political relations. Children, for example, may regard one or more parents as infallible referents for what is or is not so. For many a young child, "My daddy told me!" is the absolute clincher—the quintessence of truth in an argument. Later, "my teacher told me" may become the ultimate weapon at the dinner table. Adults develop similar highly stable feelings about husbands and wives, religious beliefs, and even philosophies or governments.

Anchorages have great value in providing expectancies or handy frames of reference against which new experience can be quickly tested and judged. They can also cause great distress when eliminated from experience. In experiments on sensory deprivation, for example, psychologists sometimes suspend subjects in water at body temperature with ears plugged and eyes blindfolded. Cut off from the usual anchors to reality, most subjects under these conditions have difficulty concentrating and often experience wild delusions. Similar anxiety and distress, usually on a less intense scale, may be experienced by almost anyone when his anchors to reality are destroyed. The first reaction to the assassination of a beloved president or to the loss of a husband or wife may be to deny the fact entirely. Little children may cling to the idea of Santa Claus long after they have begun to suspect he does not really exist, and may become extremely upset at the efforts of others to deny his existence.

Values, generalized attitudes toward events or persons, are organizations of meanings much like anchorages. Like all other meanings, they are learned from experience, but because of their generalized character, tend to add to the stability of the person's perceptual field. They also provide a frame of reference for experience—a kind of shorthand determination of the meaning of events for the behaver. This often makes a person's behavior so predictable that other people, observing its stability, develop an expectancy and sometimes can be heard to say, "Well, of course! What do you expect of Jane? You know how she is!" So important is the stabilizing effect of values upon behavior that in time it can be said in truth of an individual that he becomes his beliefs.

Selective Effect of Existing Meaning

We have seen how perceptions are affected by need and by the self-concept. We now add a third factor—namely, the effect of the existing field of meanings on new experience. Meanings, once discovered, tend to be relied upon and are seldom questioned unless the person is forced to do so because new experience does not fit his expectations. In part this is because some perceptions cannot be made until others have preceded them. The best examples of this are to be seen in learning school subjects with a highly sequential character—for instance, mathematics. Here, concepts are built in step-by-step fashion. Before one can grasp more complex concepts, simpler ones must first be perceived. In this fashion the existing field of meaning exerts a degree of control upon what further meanings can be readily acquired. Piaget spent a large part of his career studying concept formation in children, and was able to accurately map the step-by-step progressions by which the children he studied moved from simple to more and more complex concepts. While the children often moved through these phases at varying speeds, the sequences of development were highly stable.

The individual's need for adequacy also exerts a selective effect upon perceptions. To achieve fulfillment the organism requires a stable perceptual field. New experience that fits the existing organization is quickly and easily incorporated. It corroborates and reinforces what is already differentiated. When, however, new experience does not fit existing meanings, the behaver is confronted with a problem of disparate perceptions (called cognitive dissonance by some psychologists) and some adjustment must be made. Generally speaking, this may occur in one of three ways:

1. New experience may be denied or ignored while the person clings to old meanings. Facts that do not fit existing patterns may simply be bypassed. Letters about overdue payments may remain unread. Warning signs may not be seen. Unacceptable evidence is treated as though it did not exist.

2. A second way of handling meanings that do not fit is to distort them so they will. In this way the experience is given a meaning that does not require reorganization of the field. This can often be observed in the common practice of rationalization wherein a good reason for behavior is substituted for the real one. "I bought it because my old car was beginning to use oil." "I really need to eat to keep my strength up." "She probably had a date already." "The speed limit on this stretch of road is absolutely ridiculous."

3. A third way of dealing with divergent meanings is to confront the new experience and make whatever changes in currently existing meanings are appropriate. This could result in acceptance or rejection of the new concept. Such actions, however, are taken on the basis of willingness to confront the matter at hand and subject the existing field of meanings to the new data. This way of dealing with new experience is probably healthiest in the long run.

The above ways of dealing with new meanings are seldom found in isolation. More often than not, the person will use all three ways when confronted with a new problem. Depending on what seems to satisfy need most effectively some meanings will be ignored, some distorted, and some changes will be made in the individual's personal field of meaning.

The Circular Effect of Meaning

The process of discovering meaning from the world on the one hand and imposing on it on the other produces a circular effect. Having acquired a particular field of meanings, people behave in ways that tend to call forth from others reactions that corroborate existing meanings. For example, the child who is afraid of the water may be so terrified in early attempts to swim that he behaves out of panic and splashes water in his face, which frightens him more, and so proves what he already believed at the start. Similarly, what teachers or counselors believe about children or clients is likely to cause them to behave in ways that confirm existing beliefs. The "incorrigible" boy is likely to be more carefully watched and restricted, thus producing a feeling that he is "being picked on"—a feeling almost certain to result in aggressive behavior and further defiance of authority.

In a very real sense, each person is the architect of his own personality. Every experience a person has that produces a change in meanings must have its effects upon behavior, and so, changes the person himself. Each choice we make in life both opens up new possibilities and closes others. The decision to become a priest makes it unlikely that a person will become an engineer. At the same time, such a decision opens whole new areas of meaning that are unlikely to exist in similar degrees for the person who makes the decision to become an engineer. As Tillich has pointed out: "Man is his choices." People are also increasingly unique, for they acquire fields of meaning from their own individual experiences. So, people become more unlike each other and more individual the longer they live.

LEARNING AS DISCOVERY OF MEANING

Learning—A Human Problem

Effective learning always involves two aspects: the acquisition of new information or experience; and the individual's personal discovery of the meaning of the experience. The provision of information can be controlled by an outsider with or without the cooperation of the learner. It can even be done, when necessary, by mechanical means that do not require a person at all. The discovery of meaning, however, can only occur with the involvement of persons.

It is a naïve assumption that the acquisition of facts alone will make a difference in human behavior. All we need do is examine ourselves to be quickly aware of how false this assumption may be. Most of us know what we ought to eat, but we don't eat those foods. We know how we ought to drive, but we don't drive that way. We know we ought not to be prejudiced, but we are. Few of us misbehave because we do not know any better. Most of us have far more information than we ever can possibly use. A school dropout is not a dropout because he did not receive the same information as everyone else. He received it, but unhappily he never discovered what it meant.

A great deal of what passes for learning is no more than the production of temporary awareness. As a consequence, students do not behave in the terms they set down on the test, nor do clients and patients do what they know they should. The capacity to report back acquired information is but the first faint glimmering of meaning. Unfortunately, it can seldom be relied upon to produce a change in behavior the moment the necessity for reproducing it is past. Real learning—learning that produces a change in behavior—calls for a deeper, more extensive discovery of meaning. It calls, especially, for the discovery of the relationship of events to the self, for truly effective learning is a deeply personal matter.

Learning and the Self

Whether or not any meaning is sufficiently important to exert an effect on behavior is a function of its relationship to the person's self. Combs and Snygg have stated the basic principle of learning as follows: "*Any information will affect a person's behavior only in the degree to which he has discovered its personal meaning for him.*"[1]

Let us use an example to see how this works.

At breakfast you read the morning paper's statistics on pulmonic stenosis. There have been thirty-five cases in your state during the last year. Will this have any effect on your behavior? Probably not. For most readers this bit of information is probably little more than a foreign language. It has little personal meaning and so affects behavior very little. Later in the day you hear pulmonic stenosis mentioned, and because you have nothing better to do and a dictionary is handy, you look it up. You learn that this is a disorder of the heart having to do with a narrowing or closing up of the pulmonary artery. You continue to read and discover that this is a disorder with which some children are born. The information now has a little more meaning, and you may feel vaguely uncomfortable. Now, let us suppose you are a teacher and hear

1. A. W. Combs, and D. Snygg, *Individual Behavior: A Perceptual Approach to Behavior* (New York: Harper & Row, Publishers, 1959). The principle is more recently found in A. W. Combs, A. C. Richards, and F. Richards, *Perceptual Psychology: A Humanistic Approach to the Study of Persons* (New York: Harper & Row, Publishers, 1976).

that a child in a school across town is afflicted with this disorder. The matter is closer now to your personal concerns. As a consequence it has more effect on your behavior. Perhaps you pay more attention, listen more intently, think about the matter.

Suppose we now give this topic even more personal meaning. Let us say that you are a teacher who has received a letter from the mother of a child in your class. She writes that her child has this disorder and will need to be operated on in the near future. She asks that you consider the child's problem in assigning her school tasks. This item of information now has a much more personal bearing and produces a number of effects in your behavior. Perhaps you write a note to the mother. You certainly discuss the matter with other teachers and are especially nice to this child. This is no longer mere "information." It is something that is happening to one of *your* children. Because the information has more personal meaning, moreover, your behavior is more sharply focused and more precisely oriented.

Let us go one step further now and assume that you have just been told by a doctor that your son or daughter has this disorder. Now, indeed your behavior is deeply affected.

To conceive of this matter visually, we might think of a person's field of experience as shown in Figure 4.1. Let us assume that all information can be spread out on a continuum from that closely related to self at point A on this diagram to that having no relationship to self at point E. The closer events are perceived to the self, the greater will be the effects such perceptions have in producing behavior. The farther they exist toward the periphery of the perceptual field, the less influence they will exert. Plotting our discussion about the concept of pulmonic stenosis from the paragraphs above, we might illustrate the relationships to self on the line A–E and represent them as shown in Figure 4.1. Helping people learn is a matter of helping them discover closer, more meaningful relationships of information to self.

A Source of Learning Failures

Students who do not see the personal meanings of events are likely to be unaffected by learning experiences. For a long time a great deal of educa-

Figure 4.1. Diagram for Learning and the Self.

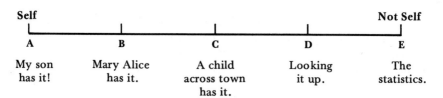

tional theory has been operating from an inadequate concept of learning, generally derived from some form of stimulus-response psychology. Seeing the problem of learning in this way leads logically to a preoccupation with manipulation of events outside the learner. The distressing thing about this is not that it is wrong, but that it's partly right. People do, indeed, need new information or experience. Preoccupation with this phase of learning, however, can have disastrous results by encouraging the belief that the problems of learning will be solved if we continue what we have been doing with more precision, more frequently, or with greater intensity. So we are led to polish and repolish our techniques of providing information in the fond belief that if a little is good, a lot must be much better.

Failure to deal with the second aspect of the learning equation explains why so much of what is learned in school is forgotten. At one time, most of us learned the capital of North Dakota, the number of miles to the moon, the date of the Battle of Waterloo, and a million other such facts. But where are they now? A great deal of educational activity often seems expressly designed to discourage the search for personal meaning while concentrating almost exclusively on the ingestion of information. Preoccupation with the information half of the learning equation is also responsible for many of the problems of dehumanization, depersonalization, and alienation we have created for young people.

Knowing and Behaving

There is a vast difference between knowing and behaving. Knowing comes from getting new information. Change in behavior comes from the discovery of meaning. Some of our most important learnings actually have nothing to do with new information but everything to do with the deeper and richer discovery of the meanings we already have. The majority of Americans know there is a strong possibility that smoking will significantly shorten their lives. They have had access to innumerable "facts" about the matter. Yet, the behavior of many clearly demonstrates that they do not really believe it. The act of smoking continues to be for them more self-enhancing than the possibility of developing lung cancer. They manage to hold the facts at arm's length, and keep from perceiving the relevance to self.

Most people in the helping professions know how to give information very well. Exposure to new information can often be greatly speeded up. The process of changing meaning is a slower, more difficult task, which cannot be done by an outsider. It must be done by the learner himself. People need information, of course. The danger comes when we lose our perspective and expect that "telling" or giving advice will result in permanent changes. The things we have learned but have not yet seen in relationship to self are quickly discarded when school is out or the pastor is not around. Good examples of reversion to what is personally significant can be found in the training of persons for the helping professions. It is fairly simple to teach beginners a new concept or technique. A counselor, for example, learns several "proper" approaches to working with clients. He knows them, can pass a test about them, can even talk about them convincingly. Then he goes to work with a client and may behave as though he had never heard of them. Confronted with real problems, he does not have time to think about what to do. Instead, he does what comes naturally to him, the things most closely related to self and his past experience.

EFFECTS OF THREAT AND CHALLENGE ON PERCEPTION AND LEARNING

Effect of Threat Upon Perception

In Chapter 3 we saw how the fundamental need of the organism for fulfillment has a selective effect upon the person's perceptual experience. This focus of attention is especially pronounced when people feel threatened, and the effects upon perception under such circumstances have extraordinary importance for persons in the helping professions.

Tunnel Vision

Psychologists are aware of two effects of the experience of threat. The first has been called *tunnel vision*. When a person feels threatened, the perceptual field narrows and focuses on the object of threat. Almost everyone has experienced this phenomenon under frightening circumstances. What can be perceived is narrowed to the point where it is difficult to see anything but the threatening object—like looking through a tunnel. One of the authors recalls asking his daughter at the dinner table what she had learned in school that day. "Oh, nothing," she replied. "But was our teacher mad!" Under the threat of an angry teacher, little or nothing else made very much impression.

If the threat is very great, attention becomes sharply focused on the threatening event, to the exclusion of all else. The child in school, for example, who feels threatened by his mother's being sent to the hospital is obviously in no condition to perceive the nuances of a Shakespearean line, the importance of the raw products of Arizona, or the implications of constitutional law. Sometimes the narrowing effect of threat may even result in apparently stupid actions in an emergency. Once, in the midst of a party given by one of the authors at his home, a grass mat in front of the fireplace caught fire. Seeing this, the author picked up the burning rug, ran across the crowded room to the front door, and threw the rug outside into the snow. When the excitement had quieted down, someone asked, "Why didn't you just kick it into the fireplace?" Why not, indeed? At the moment of the emergency, the only thing he could think of was to get the burning rug out of the house, and the simple solution of kicking it into the fireplace never occurred to him. His perceptions were focused on getting the fire out, not in!

The tunnel vision effect is equally operative when the feeling of threat is only very mild. Combs and Taylor, for example, asked subjects to translate short sentences into a simple code. Some of these sentences were mildly threatening or unflattering. They found that, even under conditions of very mild degrees of threat, performance in translating was significantly disturbed. Nearly every subject made more errors and took longer to complete the code under conditions of very mild threat.

This restricting effect of threat on perception is antithetical to effective learning and helping whether it takes place in the classroom, during a group activity, or in the counseling office. We do not want our clientele's perceptions narrowed. What we seek is the broadest, richest experience possible.

Defense of Self

A second effect of threat upon perception makes it even more important a consideration in helping relationships. When a person feels threatened, he is forced to defend the perceptions he already has. This effect of threat upon perception is well-known to most people, but it is truly amazing how little attention it has been given as a principle that affects learning. One need only look about to see examples of the principle in operation. People in the midst of an argument do not seem to hear what others are saying. Children dig in their heels and refuse to cooperate. Grown men and women become unreasonably stubborn. People resist perfectly clear demonstrations of how wrong they were. Almost everyone is aware that when one feels threatened, the first reaction is to defend the self in any way possible. What is more, the greater the degree of threat to which one is exposed the more tenaciously a person holds to the perceptions, ideas, or practices he already has.

The fundamental need of the organism to maintain and enhance the self will not ignore threats to self. The self must be protected. This defensive stance under threat, however, is exactly the reverse of what is needed for effective learning and helping. Helpers want their clients to change their self-perceptions, not defend them! Events that force people into strongly defensive positions are directly contrary to what we are trying to accomplish in the helping professions.

The effects of threat on perception are especially important for members of the helping professions who are expected to help persons in trouble. The degree of threat experienced by a person is directly related to feelings of personal adequacy. People with highly positive feelings about self are less likely to feel threatened by any given event than those with inadequate self-concepts. Persons with low self-esteem are likely to be highly sensitive to threat. The persons most in need of the helping professions are thus also the most sensitive to the experience of threat.

Challenge

Some people do not react to threat in the ways we have been describing. Some people, instead, seem to be challenged to do better work. What is the difference between threat and challenge?

People feel threatened when confronted with situations they do not feel adequate to cope with. People feel challenged by problems that interest them and which they feel reasonably able to handle. The behavior of persons who feel threatened is likely to be tenuous, unsure, inaccurate, and inadequate. They may even attempt to escape from the situation. In the same situation, another person who feels adequate to deal with the problem may not feel threatened at all. The situation may be perceived as a challenge with important opportunities for self-enhancement. It may even be greeted with joy as a new test of adequacy.

Again, it is necessary to remind ourselves that the distinction lies not in the eyes of the outsider but in the eyes of the beholder. The teacher encouraging the shy child to "share and tell" may feel she is offering a challenge. From the child's point of view it may only seem a terrifying possibility of humiliation. The differences between threat and challenge are so important and the effect of these diverse experiences so great that every person in the helping professions needs to be keenly aware of them. A very large part of the helper's efforts will be devoted to finding effective ways for challenging persons they are trying to help, without threatening them.

RELATION OF MEANING TO MEMORY, EMOTION, AND FEELING

Memory

The importance of personal meaning extends far beyond its significance for human learning. It is also important for memory, feeling, and emotion. When a person looks back at some event in the past, what he remembers is not what really happened but the meaning it had then or has now. He remembers what seemed to be happening at the time, or, even more inaccurately, what now seems *must* have happened! The memory of an event is a belief about it, not an accurate record. Any teacher who has ever given an examination is familiar with the maddening and sometimes hilarious meanings students retain from the most carefully planned lesson. Students do not recall what was said. They recall what they comprehended. The crucial character of meaning in remembering may also be observed in counseling. Clients may spend long periods exploring memories of early life in the counseling hour and in the course of these explorations may often change their minds. They exclaim, "You know, I don't believe it ever really happened like that at all!"

Additional errors in remembering may be produced by the selective effect of need, self-concept, or the existing field of meanings. Memories may be distorted in ways more advantageous to the reporter. Who has not been guilty of reporting what happened in the best possible light? And who has not embroidered his tale in a way that made him appear blameless, more righteous, brave, or smart? Memories may also be distorted in ways to make them fit the existing field. This occurs when persons remember what *must* have happened. Magicians make good use of this characteristic by purposely establishing in the observer a reasonable "set," so that what is seen later is interpreted in terms of what seems to the observer must have occurred.

In courts of law, the notorious inaccuracies of human memory make the "credibility of witnesses" an ever-present problem for defendants, lawyers, judge, and jury. Many courtroom rules of procedure, puzzling to the layman, were established as devices to assure the most accurate possible reports of exactly what happened in a given case. Even under oath the story told by the most well-intentioned witness may be in error for any of the reasons we have reviewed.

Emotion

For the psychologist, emotion is a state of acceleration. It is the response of the organism that makes it ready to act. Ordinarily, emotion is very low when one is sleeping with his "motor barely turning over." On awakening, more energy is required, and body processes accelerate to adjust to greater demands. Emotion reaches its greatest heights in emergency situations where the self is in danger, as in anger or fear, or when it is engaged in important enhancing experiences such as ecstacy or triumph. At such times the organism is capable of tremendous bursts of energy for short periods of time.

Emotion is an artifact of the meanings existing for the individual at any moment. Generally speaking, the closer the event is perceived to self the more intense the behavior and also the emotion experienced by

Figure 4.2. Personal Meaning and Emotion.

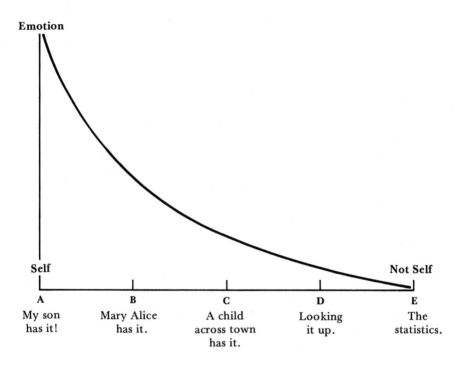

the behaver. In the pulmonic stenosis illustration used earlier, we observed that effects on a person's behavior increased with the closeness of meaning to self. The experience of emotion is also affected by the degree of personal meaning. As shown in Figure 4.2 the degree of emotion experienced is a consequence of the relationship of the event to self.

Feelings

The descriptions we give to emotional experiences are called feelings. They might also be called personal meanings for that is what a feeling is—a description of the personal meaning of something to the behaver. When one says, "I love Mary," "I hate John," "I detest dogs," "I like good movies," "I feel hurt, disappointed, proud, amused, delighted," one is expressing the personal meaning of those people or events.

Actually, no one can ever express the full meaning of an event to self. The full meaning of the event involves the entire perceptual field of the speaker at the moment, and only a portion of that can ever be translated into words. We are all keenly aware of how poorly words express the full import of what we feel. What lover has not complained at the inadequacy of words to say all that he or she wished. While feelings are personal meanings, their verbal expression is no more than an approximation, a representation of the meaning itself, a kind of shorthand to express a complex notion.

An understanding of this relationship between feeling and meaning is important for workers in the helping professions, for there is a common belief that cognition and emotion, knowing and feeling, are unrelated entities. In the light of our discussion here, it must be clear that whatever meaning a person has must possess both cognition and emotion in some degree. There can be no feeling except about something, and no knowing without some personal reference. So the counseling client who says, "I know it intellectually, but I can't do it" is telling us simply that his knowledge is ineffective because he does not relate it meaningfully to himself. To solve this dilemma, he does not have to know something else; he needs to discover deeper meaning of what he already knows. When he does, he will express it in feeling terms: "I feel that's what I should do," or "I believe I'll try that," or "I think that would be fun."

SOME IMPLICATIONS FOR HELPERS

The Fetish of Objectivity

Workers in counseling and education often refer to "the affective domain" as though emotional aspects of human experiences were somehow separate from cognitive ones. Critics of education, for example, have sometimes asked, "Do you want to educate for knowledge or adjustment?" The attempt to separate these matters in such an either/or fashion damages our understanding of human dynamics. Truly intelligent behavior cannot be so neatly segregated. It requires both the knowledge to cope with life, and the personal discovery of meaning to make it viable. Feeling and emotion are indicators of personal relevance. As students and clients talk about events, they reveal the degree of importance they attach to those events by the levels of feeling and emotion they express. The relationship is so close, in fact, that attending to levels of feeling can give observers significant clues to the personal involvement of students and clients in helping relationships. It is possible, for example, to gauge the involvement of members in a group experience by listening to levels of talk. Early in a group experience with little or no commitment yet established, people talk to one another at finger-tip lengths. Their talk is mostly descriptive, usually pertaining to events outside themselves: "There was this man and . . . ," "Did you read where . . . ?" "My cousin once. . . ." As commitment begins, one is likely to hear occasional references to self: "I read that . . . ," "Can you tell me if . . . ?" "I went to see. . . ." Such comments are still likely to be highly descriptive. With still greater commitment, tentative involvements of self begin to show themselves: "I don't know about that . . . ," "I am not sure about this, but . . . ," "It seems to me. . . ." Much closer to self are comments like "Well, I thought . . . ," "I don't really care for . . . ," "I enjoy. . . ." At deepest levels of commitment one may even hear what some psychologists call "gut" talk: "I hate . . . ," "That makes me so mad!" "I love."

The attempt to treat knowing and feeling, or cognition and emotion, as though they were unrelated matters obeying different laws can only lead to failure. We do not experience cognition and emotion as separate entities. Things that have no personal meaning arouse no emotions. In light of these facts, the fetish that some persons make over the necessity for objectivity becomes ridiculous. Complete objectivity is an illusion. Whatever is experienced is experienced in a person and that fact inescapably influences what is perceived. One can only "be objective" about events with little or no personal relevance. What is not relevant to self in turn is unlikely to affect one's behavior. If learning is not affective, it is probably not happening at all. The practice of education, counseling, social work, or pastoral care that rules out feeling makes itself ineffective.

Our society is properly impressed by the enormous contributions made by science through the application of objective methods sometimes called the *scientific method.* Because of these successes many people have attempted to translate such methods directly to problems of dealing with people. Unfortunately, the answers to human problems arrived at through complete objectivity frequently apply only to persons operating under laboratory conditions. They do not hold up for the man in the street, the child in the classroom, or the client in the counselor's office. For the helping professions, the attempt to deal with people in purely objective terms may only result in making the helper ineffectual. Some research on the helping professions found that objectivity on the part of teachers, counselors, and priests correlated with ineffectiveness!

Discovering Meaning Takes Time

It takes time to discover meaning. It is easy to forget this fact in the desire to help someone. The teacher who studied a subject for twenty or thirty years and now believes it can be taught to a student in a few weeks or months has embarked on a frustrating course. The maximum speed for the discovery of meaning depends upon a number of factors having to do with the nature of the individual, the subject under investigation, the student's previous experience, present circumstances, and so forth. The attempt to push discovery of meaning too fast may actually destroy the possibilities of the person's discovery of meaning at all. When people are pushed beyond the point where they believe they can effectively cope with events, resistance sets in and destroys the possibilities for effective learning. Generally speaking, the more important the meaning to be grasped, the slower the discovery of its significance is likely to be.

A major requirement for helping is the quality of patience. Many a helper has made himself ineffective in his zeal to move too fast in carrying out the helping function. Persons being helped are also understandably anxious to get on with finding the solutions to their particular problems. They are often likely, therefore, to put great pressure on helpers to speed things up. Since the helper, too, is anxious to help the client, it is easy to succumb to temptation, and attempt to direct and control the process of learning with firmness and dispatch. This usually slows the process of meaning discovery if it does not defeat it altogether. It is incumbent upon helpers to aid in the quickest possible manner; but it is also necessary that helpers have clear conceptions of the goals, purposes, and dynamics of the processes they are engaged in. There are limits to how much learning can be accelerated. There is a vast difference between merely possessing information and being so aware of its meanings that one is able to behave in terms of it. Attempts to bypass the discovery process may only provide an illusion of aid, which quickly breaks down when subjected to the test of application.

Truly significant changes in human beliefs are rarely made suddenly. More often than not, they occur in step-by-step fashion over considerable periods of time. Accepting intermediate steps as sufficient objectives can even block a helpee's further search for adequate solutions to problems of growth and development. Early in the history of client-centered counseling, for example, treatment was comparatively short, often lasting for only seven or eight interviews. Modern counselors now find the number of interviews spent with clients is very much larger, sometimes going on for a year or more. Clients seeking counseling frequently do so to deal with some annoying symptom of deeper problems. Often they find effective ways to handle such surface manifestations in a comparatively short time. Looking back on the early days of the client-centered movement, it now appears that many counselors were probably accepting such solutions as indications that the case was closed. Today they are more likely to recognize such solutions as tentative steps toward more significant objectives.

More often than not, the very best clues to maximum speed are provided by the persons being helped. As already seen in previous chapters, the individual's need for adequacy provides the motivation to move with dispatch when the way seems open to do so. Experts in the helping professions discovered this fact long ago and have learned to work with, rather than against it, by following the lead of their subjects. They have learned that aiding the discovery of meaning most efficiently is not so much a question of manipulating people as a matter of guiding them towards discovering alternatives.

Discovery of meaning comes about through a process of increasing differentiation of experience. Usually this occurs as a consequence of a series of slow steps in which one differentiation is followed by another and another until the new event is learned or its personal meaning discovered. This is true even in those instances where insight seems to come about in a sudden flash of recognition—what the French call the "aha moment." Even in such instances, however, what appears to be a sudden flash of meaning usually turns out on closer examination to be but the final differentiation in a whole series of previous, almost imperceptible, stages leading to the final denouement. This is somewhat like finding the key piece in a picture puzzle that makes all of the surrounding parts comprehensible. Without the discoveries preceding it, finding the key piece would have been of little or no consequence. Its extraordinary value is dependent upon the hard work that went before. So it is with personal meaning; the fruit only comes when the ground has been plowed, when the seed has been planted, and when conditions favorable for growth have been established.

Helping: A Problem in Learning

Learning, we have seen, always has two aspects: the acquisition of knowledge or experience and the discovery of its meaning. Professional helpers provide their subjects with information and experience in their particular area of concern. The teacher provides the student with information about a subject. The social worker introduces a client to a new group setting and so provides new experiences of other people. Similarly, the counselor interprets a psychological test for a client, a nurse shows a new mother how to bathe a baby, and the priest or rabbi interprets the Bible for his flock.

Helping does not stop with the provision of information. Almost anyone can provide other people with new information or experience. You don't need a professional just to give information. In fact, with our shiny new hardware we can often do this better without any human intervention at all. Problems of humanization and personal discovery must be solved in the final analysis by human commitment and involvement, in the interaction of persons with persons. This is what the helping professions are all about.

Helping clients learn new ways of perceiving themselves and the world generally involves the helper in three important steps:

1. Creating atmospheres that make exploring possible.
2. Providing new information and/or experience.
3. Aiding the personal discovery of meaning.

In later chapters we will explore these essential phases in greater detail.

Selected Readings

Starred entry indicates appearance in Donald L. Avila, Arthur W. Combs, and William W. Purkey, *The Helping Relationship Sourcebook*, Boston: Allyn and Bacon, 1977.

Beard, R. M. *An Outline of Piaget's Developmental Psychology for Students and Teachers.* New York: Basic Books, 1969.

Combs, A. W. *Myths in Education: Beliefs that Hinder Progress and their Alternatives.* Boston: Allyn and Bacon, in press.

De Charms, R. *Personal Causation: The Internal Affective Determinants of Behavior.* New York: Academic, 1968.

Jones, R. L., ed. *Black Psychology.* New York: Harper & Row, Publishers, 1972.

Kelley, E. C. *Education for What Is Real.* New York: Harper, 1947.

Kohlberg, L. Stage and Sequence: The Cognitive-Developmental Approach to Socialization. In D. A. Goslin, ed., *Handbook of Socialization Theory and Research.* Skokie, Illinois: Rand McNally & Co., 1969.

*Rogers, C. R. The Interpersonal Relationship in the Facilitation of Learning. In R. R. Leeper, ed., *Humanizing Education: The Person in the Process,* pp. 1–18. Washington, D.C., Association for Supervision and Curriculum Development, National Education Association, 1967.

Rogers, C. R. *Freedom to Learn.* Columbus, Ohio: Charles E. Merrill Publishing Co., 1969.

Rosenthal, R., and Jacobson, L. *Pygmalion in the Classroom.* New York: Holt, Rinehart and Winston, 1968.

5

The Range of Human Potential

Whatever helpers believe about the nature of human capacity inevitably affects the goals they seek, the methods they employ, the respect they have for their clients, and even the amount of effort they are likely to expend in trying to be helpful. Research has shown, for example, that effective helpers believe their clients are able to cope with life, while ineffective ones doubt the capacities of the persons they work with. Teachers who believe children are able can let them. Teachers who don't, do not dare give students freedom. People do what seems to be possible. They do not try very long to achieve what seems beyond their capacities. What do we know about the range of human potential?

CAPACITY AND THE PHYSICAL MODEL

When we think about what is possible for people, it is natural to do so in terms of experience with our physical bodies. We are obviously limited by the nature of our physiology. There are limits to how far and how fast we can run, and these usually become more limited as we grow older. We need only get sick to observe how illness may impair effectiveness. Clearly, we cannot make our bodies do what our physiology will not permit. Our physical capacities are dependent upon our hereditary characteristics and the condition we have managed to keep ourselves in to the present. With the physical model constantly before us, it is easy to assume that the capacity for behavior or misbehavior is similarly limited. This concept of human capacities was commonly held for generations. Until very recently it was also held by most psychologists. Today we must take quite a different view.

One of the most exciting discoveries of this generation is the idea that human capacity is far greater than anything ever thought possible. The fascinating thing about human beings is *not* their limitations, but their immense capabilities. For years we have believed that people are born with strictly limited potential and that there is little or nothing anyone can do about it. Now we know that intelligence can be created. Let us see why this is so.

It is true that physical condition controls our physical prowess. But, most of the behaviors required for getting along effectively in the world have little to do with the state of our physiology. Behaviors like thinking, loving, hating, wanting, creating, hoping, searching, and understanding or misunderstanding each other are matters of perception. They have little to do with the nature of the physical organism in which they occur.

The body is the house in which we live. It provides the vehicle for much behavior, but it does not explain it. It is true that we must have eyes to see. Thereafter, what is seen, what has been seen, and what will be seen in the future is no longer a question of the structure of the eyes alone. A study of physiology will not provide us with the full understandings we need about persons. The capacity for behavior or misbehavior transcends the organism in which it occurs. The body is not the controller of behavior, but the vehicle in which it occurs, and capacity lies not in the structure, but in the use to which it is put.

Human Beings Are Overbuilt

The outstanding thing about the human organism is not its limitations but its potentials. It is characteristically overbuilt! When an engineer builds a bridge, he designs it with a built-in "safety factor"—a degree of sturdiness many times stronger than he expects the structure will need to withstand. People are like that, too. Most of us, in the course of our daily lives, use but a small portion of what is possible for the physical organism. Some years ago one of the authors left his disabled car on the side of the road and began to walk along the edge of the highway for help. In the distance he saw a car approaching at great speed weaving back and forth across the road. A moment later he realized with horror the car was coming straight for him. In a flash he jumped the ditch beside the road and fled into the adjoining field. Brushing himself off he walked back to the ditch verbally venting his wrath on "that crazy driver." The ditch looked pretty wide when he reached it, but he thought that having jumped it one way, the ditch should be no problem on the return trip. So, taking a mighty leap he jumped—landing in the middle of the ditch in water up to his waist! With the danger gone he was back to his normal expenditures of energy.

Such feats are really a matter of need and concentration. There is a fictitious belief, for example, that psychotics have superhuman strength. This is because, in states of desperation they have performed acts that appear to be beyond most people's capacity. One of the authors once witnessed such an act while working in a sanitarium. A small, frail female patient in her early twenties was asked to take a bath. No one knew why, but taking a bath was one of the things this girl most hated to do. When asked, she always became extremely angry. The room where she had to bathe was at the end of the corridor where her room was located. One day the sanitarium attendants entered her room and told her it was time to bathe. She immediately bolted from her room, ran the length of the corridor and disappeared into the bathing room. The attendants, knowing she had nowhere to go, began to walk slowly down the hall, but before they could reach the end the young girl reappeared, flinging an entire wash basin toward them! She had ripped it from the wall!

This young woman did not suddenly acquire superhuman strength. She had just reached her breaking point, accumulated enough need for revenge, and concentrated her entire being towards finding some way to pay back her tormentors.

In less physically related behavior the scope of human potential is even more impressive. People can learn to read a page at a glance and to perform prodigious feats of memory and perception. Human creativity goes on and on. Scientists continue to discover, painters paint, and poets write. There seems literally no limit to the possibilities for thinking, feeling, loving, hoping, seeking and the behaviors they produce. People are always rising to new occasions. It is commonplace to find that an individual's behavior lives up to the promotion to which the person has been raised. From everything we can observe, it seems clear that few of us ever remotely approach the potentialities for effective behavior that lie within us. Most of us use but a small fraction of our capabilities. Indeed, it had to be so throughout human history. The human organism could only have survived the course of evolution if it had within it the capacity to rise to emergencies.

INTELLIGENCE AS FUNCTIONAL CAPACITY

Intelligence is the capacity of an individual to behave effectively and efficiently. This capacity may be looked at in two ways: ultimate capacity and functional capacity. *Ultimate capacity* is the maximum potential permitted by the physiologic make-up with which the person is born; it is what the individual could deliver if every condition of his life was maximally operative. *Functional capacity* is the behavior that a person can normally deliver when necessary. This concept refers to the person's current capacity for effective and efficient behavior. It is also what we mean in this book when we speak of intelligence.

Ultimate Physical Capacity

Every animal is ultimately limited by its physical structure. Persons, too, can do only that which inherited structure will permit. Physiologically, these limits are comparatively narrow; psychologically, they are far greater. We need, therefore, to distinguish between physiological and behavioral ultimate capacities. In Figure 5.1 we have done this. We have represented the potentials for physical activities by a dot-dash line rising in a fairly smooth curve at one end of the continuum, and leveling off at a height fairly well above the base line. The levels at which

Figure 5.1. Diagram of Physical and Behavioral Potentials of Human Beings.

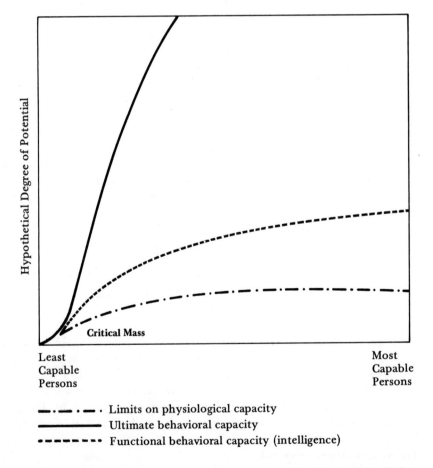

Least Capable Persons

Most Capable Persons

— · — · — · Limits on physiological capacity
————— Ultimate behavioral capacity
• — — — — • Functional behavioral capacity (intelligence)

people are able to engage in their day-to-day activities lie somewhere between this line and the base of the chart. While persons may occasionally, under extraordinary circumstances, come close to the ultimate level, usually their physical activities are much lower.

Ultimate Behavioral Capacity

The curve for behavioral potential is quite a different shape. There are, of course, a comparatively small number of pitiful souls born into the world with such inadequate physiology or nervous systems as to be severely handicapped behaviorally as well. Some of these, such as the "crib cases" in our institutions for the mentally retarded, are destined to live out their lives as little more than human vegetables. Others, like those less severely limited by brain damage or in-utero or postnatal failures of organ development, manage to cope more or less successfully with life but are destined to limited success because of their physical problems. They are represented on our diagram at the extreme left of the ultimate behavior curve. For most of us, fortunately, the picture is quite different.

Earlier we described human behavior as the product of the person's perceptual field. Given the machinery for perceiving, even with limitations, behavioral possibilities are almost astronomical. Once a person possesses eyes or ears in reasonably workable condition, the possibilities of what he may see and hear are no longer restricted by physiologic endowment. The situation is similar to the critical mass required for an atomic explosion. Up to a point the atomic pile reacts in smooth predictable fashion until the critical mass is reached; then a whole new set of conditions comes into being. Something like this happens with our ultimate capacity for behavior. Given the critical mass to make perceiving possible, what the organism makes of it after that is no longer a function of physical conditions. Ultimate capacity to behave is represented in Figure 5.1 by the unbroken line, which begins to rise smoothly to the critical mass, then zooms off the chart to heights unknown. Perception transcends the physical structure in which it occurs.

Intelligence: The Capacity for Effective, Efficient Behavior

Intelligence is the person's functional capacity—the ability to behave effectively and efficiently, when it is necessary. This functional capacity is represented in Figure 5.1 by a dotted line that begins at a very low level for the severely handicapped at the left-hand side of the diagram and rises to the heights achieved by the most brilliant persons on the right-hand side. Due to the limitless possibilities for human perception, none of us ever achieves more than a small part of what is possible. Since

The Range of Human Potential 73

none of us ever approaches the limits of perception, ultimate behavioral possibilities are an academic question of practical significance.

Historically, psychologists used the term *intelligence* to refer to ultimate capacity. Used in this way, intelligence was regarded as fixed and immutable, derived primarily from one's heredity and only minimally influenced by change from outside forces. More recently many psychologists define intelligence in terms of functional capacity. This is a much more useful concept for the helping professions. A person's current capacity for effective and efficient behavior is what most people mean by "intelligent behavior." It is also what intelligence tests are designed to measure. The production of intelligent behavior is the goal of education and of the helping professions.

Defined as the capacity for effective and efficient behavior, intelligence is not an hereditary problem nor is it a static, unchangeable potential. Rather, it represents a comparatively low level of achievement with vast possibilities for improvement. It is interesting that this was the position taken by Alfred Binet, originator of the first intelligence tests. He declared:

> Some recent philosophers appear to have given their support to the deplorable verdict that intelligence of an individual is a fixed quantity—we must protest and act against this brutal pessimism—a child's mind is like a field in which an expert farmer has advised a change in the method of cultivation with the result that in place of desert land we now have a harvest. It is in this particular sense, the one which is significant, that we say that the intelligence of children may be increased. One increases that which constitutes the intelligence of a school child, namely, the capacity to learn, to improve with instruction.[1]

Unfortunately, Binet's warning was largely overlooked for a good many years after his death, and it is only recently that intelligence is once again being regarded as a broader human function capable of change. We will not stop here to review all the research that leads to the conclusion that capacity for behavior can be created. The evidence is so extensive and varied as to call for a book in its own right, which J. McV. Hunt has already done superbly well in a volume called *Intelligence and Experience*. We heartily recommend this book to readers interested in pursuing the evidence for intelligence change in greater detail. In concluding his scholarly review of the data, Dr. Hunt has this to say:

> It is highly unlikely that any society has developed a system of child rearing and education that maximizes the potential of the individuals which compose it. Probably no individual has ever lived whose full potential for happy intellectual interest growth has been achieved . . . .

1. A. Binet, *Les Idees Modernes sur les Enfants* (Paris: Ernest Flammarion, 1909): 54–55.

The hope of increasing the average level of intelligence by proper manipulation of children's developmental encounters with their environments, a hope which becomes reasonable with the evidence surveyed here and with relinquishing the assumptions of fixed intelligence and predetermined development, provides a challenge of the first order. It has great implications for human welfare as the growth of technology in western culture demands a higher and higher percentage of people who can manipulate symbols and solve complex problems. In this challenge the theory of man's nature and the fate of his welfare are obviously intertwined.[2]

The idea that human capacity is not so fixed and immutable as we have thought in generations past is a concept of tremendous significance for the helping professions. Later in this chapter we will explore its implications further.

WHAT INTELLIGENCE TESTS MEASURE

For many years intelligence tests have been used for the determination of human potentialities and are often regarded by the public and some users of tests as infallible indications of a person's possibilities. Most of the early intelligence tests were manufactured by persons who regarded intelligence as a capacity of the organism, primarily obtained from heredity. People might fall short of their possibilities; they could never rise above them. The early testmakers tried to measure that ultimate potential.

Since ultimate capacity is not open to direct measurement, intelligence testmakers had to find another way of estimating it. They did this by making the assumption that all persons taking the test had had an equal opportunity to learn the material it contained. If everyone had an equal opportunity to learn the material, they reasoned, then those persons who did better must have already possessed greater innate capacity. Over the years we have come to understand that that basic assumption is rarely tenable. If behavior is truly a function of the private world of perceptions for each individual, there can never be common experience for any two people even in the same externally observed situation. Even in a family of identical twins, apparently treated identically, twin A's experience is largely created by twin B and twin B's is supplied by twin A!

A great deal of mischief has been done over the years through the misuse of intelligence tests. This is especially true when they have been used to label people or establish expectancy levels. We have already seen in Chapter 3 how important the self-concept is in determining a

2. J. McV. Hunt, *Intelligence and Experience* (New York: The Ronald Press Company, 1961): 346. Copyright © 1961 The Ronald Press Company, New York. Reprinted by permission of the author and publisher.

person's behavior. Labeling persons, therefore, as "dull," "moron," "below average," "average," and the like, especially when such labels are backed up by "scientific" tests of intelligence can have devastating effects upon the performance of persons who come to believe them. Sometimes the results of intelligence tests assume a position of such unquestioning authority that school children are described as "overachievers," as though it were possible for a person to exceed his potential! It would be more accurate to describe such children as misjudged or underestimated. In a similar vein, counselors and administrators have been known to advise students and clients not to go to college or try some new experience because intelligence test results show "they would never make it." Such use of tests as infallible indicators of potential is totally unwarranted.

Intelligence tests measure the degree to which a person's cultural milieu fits the sampling of items selected by the test's constructors. If a person's life experience does not include the type of behavior demanded by the test he probably will not do well. Yet, the same person may behave "brilliantly" in a situation with which he is familiar. This is why so many minority group members and champions of lower socioeconomic groups argue so fervently against I.Q. tests. They state, and rightly so, that the experiences of these people are so different from the normalization samples of the test, that their true ability is falsely judged. Typical middle-class children often do well on standardized tests, but how intelligently would they behave or how long would they last on the inner-city streets of New York, Chicago, or Los Angeles? The ability to survive and live effectively in the world is, after all, what intelligence is all about, and different worlds call for different kinds of knowledge and skills.

Although we have rejected the basic premise of intelligence tests, it should not be supposed that such tests are totally without value. As tests of achievement, they can locate a person with respect to a given body of information. In the degree to which they have been carefully constructed, they can also give us an indication of a person's current level of functioning. That, of course, is valuable information. The use of intelligence tests as indicators of what persons either can or will do in the future, however, is a highly invalid assumption.

DETERMINANTS OF INTELLIGENCE

A person's functional capacity interests the professional helper for two reasons: It is a far more useful concept, and there is something we can do about it. Given a reasonably adequate physiology to start with, the capacity for intelligent behavior will depend upon two things: the meanings a person possesses and his freedom to use them.

Elsewhere, Combs has stated: "How intelligently a person is able to behave at any moment will be dependent upon the richness, extent, and availability of meanings in his perceptual field."[3] This is to say that the capacity to behave effectively and efficiently requires, in the first place, that a person possess the necessary or appropriate meanings for the situation that confronts him. The richer the field of meanings, the greater the potential for effective behavior. But mere possession of a rich and extensive perceptual field alone is not enough. It is also necessary that meanings be available for use when they are needed.

In earlier chapters we have already discussed the effect of need, self-concept, and the existing field of meanings on the determination of behavior, and so on intelligence. But there are other factors that must be added.

Physical Condition

The acuity of sight, hearing, touch, smell, and taste certainly have their effects upon the nature of a person's experience. These are our "windows on the world" through which interaction occurs. The physical vehicle we ride around in also has its effect through the feedback it produces in the reactions of other people. The experiences of a beautiful young woman are different from those of her less attractive sisters. Similarly, the physical prowess that makes a young man a football hero may bring him vastly different meanings than those he might have had without his magnificent physical condition. Feedback of a less happy nature is received by adolescents with acne or handicapped persons. Their physical conditions may impede full participation in the life around them and distort others' reactions to them.

Whatever reduces body vigor may also impair the possibilities of experience. Because a sick and lethargic child does not get involved in school or play with his peers, the meanings he develops may be limited. Almost everyone has had the experience of feeling "too tired to care" or so ill that all he wanted to do was sleep. So, almost anything that reduces the body's readiness and capability for involvement may reduce experience. Reducers may include such things as malnutrition, focal infections, illnesses of various kinds, glandular disturbances, injuries, or the like. Some persons with severe impediments, like Helen Keller, manage to develop great breadth and depth in their field of meanings despite physiologic limitations. It is conceivable that some handicaps might enrich a person's field of meanings, making him more accomplished in some ways than his more fortunate fellows, such as Beethoven playing and writing music, Jose Feliciano reaching stardom, and a man with one

---

3. A. W. Combs, A. C. Richards, and F. Richards, *Perceptual Psychology: A Humanistic View of the Study of Persons* (New York: Harper & Row, Publishers, 1976).

hand and only half a foot setting a record for the longest field goal in the history of professional football.

Age

Developing a field of meanings takes time. People have to have lived long enough to have had some kinds of experiences, especially those dependent in sequential fashion on earlier ones. Despite the doubts of young people, there really is some advantage in experience. The mere fact of living longer means more possibilities for experience but does not guarantee them. Existing meanings may restrict further possibilities for perceiving. This often happens when older persons become unable to accept new meanings, and often produces the generation gap so distressing to young and old alike.

The authors are also aware that persons can be so closed to experience that they fail to benefit from it, and others so open that they get much more out of each experience than most people do. Thus, we have some twenty-year-olds who are more mature and wiser than others in their forties and fifties. We also know that it is possible for one person to live through what should have been a significant experience and not benefit from or even understand it.

Opportunity

People's meanings are affected by every aspect of environment, particularly by the persons with whom they come in contact. Meanings for people in the North and South are by no means the same. People who live in the mountains, the plains, the seashore, valleys, desert, or woods have different kinds of experiences and different kinds of meanings as a consequence. Such interactions with the world and the people in it create private worlds of meaning and feeling and determine the intelligence with which each person may operate. The effect of opportunity on personal meaning begins at birth and continues as long as a person lives. Because of the selective effect of existing meanings upon subsequent ones, the earliest development of meanings is particularly crucial for development of intelligence.

Many children in our society are raised in poverty-stricken areas where there is little opportunity to broaden experience beyond the deadly, daily grind of keeping body and soul together. These children have no opportunity to experience even the most common events in the lives of others, like seeing a cow, using a telephone, learning to swim, riding a bicycle, writing a letter, or counting money. They grow up with restricted meanings and are often inadequately prepared to cope with the world in which they have to live. This can result in a vicious circle that continually corroborates itself. Because they are ignorant, they cannot cope with life. Because they cannot cope, they continue to be deprived and produce for their children in turn the same dreary existence that so warped them in the first place. With a new awakening of conscience, we are beginning to find ways of breaking into this vicious cycle. Federal, state, and privately supported programs designed to fight poverty, improve education, provide employment, and eliminate prejudice are increasingly being instituted to enrich the lives of children caught in such traps. In doing so, we are also increasing the capacity of children for more intelligent, and efficient behavior in the future. Without opportunity, meanings may be restricted or distorted so that effective behavior becomes nearly impossible. The principle is nicely illustrated in the report of a colleague about his experience working with children from upper-middle-class homes compared with those in a poverty-stricken slum area. One of the problems he presented to these children went as follows: "You are all alone in an empty room of a deserted house. Up against the ceiling out of your reach is a balloon with a ten-dollar bill attached to it. How would you get it down?" Many of the children from upper-middle-class homes had great difficulty in finding a solution to the problem and gave up. Children from slum neighborhoods, on the other hand, frequently solved the problem with great dispatch. "I'd break the window," they said, "and throw the glass at the balloon!" For these children, windows were not inviolate. They were something to be broken if need be. For the upper-middle-class child, windows had quite a different meaning, which did not make them available for solving the problem.

Significant research has been carried out in recent years by psychologists investigating the effects of enriched experience on the growth of intelligence in very young children. In one of these, Ira Gordon taught new mothers how to stimulate their babies by using ordinary materials that might be found in even the most poverty-stricken home. At the end of a year, he was able to show that these efforts did, indeed, raise the intelligence levels of children. Samuel Kirk demonstrated that important gains in intelligence levels could be brought about for many children originally diagnosed as mentally retarded by means of broadening opportunities provided by experience in nursery school. The work of these researchers, corroborated by many others, clearly demonstrates enriched opportunity can create markedly improved capacities for effective behavior.

Effects of Values and Goals

The goals we seek and the values we ascribe to, have inevitable effects in determining the nature of the field of meanings and, thus, possibilities for intelligent behavior. The decision to go to college opens a whole new world of possibilities for the student on one hand; on the other, it closes doors and makes certain kinds of experiences more unlikely. Similarly, the decision to become a fisherman takes a man out to sea. This will bring him very different kinds of experiences from those of his brother who becomes a coal miner. People's interests will also affect the extent and character of meanings they acquire. Persons interested in baseball go to baseball games; those interested in art go to museums. Interests even determine such simple matters as the pages one reads in a newspaper.

SOME IMPLICATIONS FOR THE
HELPING PROFESSIONS

Variations in the breadth and depth of meanings people possess fluctuate widely. At one end of the scale is the severely mentally retarded patient who spends his life in the fetal position in which he was born. Further up the scale are persons able to "get by." That, in itself, is no mean feat in today's world. The richness and extent of meanings needed just to navigate safely in a city like New York or Los Angeles, for example, are considerable. Most people, fortunately, manage to develop meanings taking them far beyond such minimal levels, and some, like our most gifted citizens, become truly remarkable. The perceptual fields of some persons become more fertile and extensive throughout their lives. For others, unhappily, the field of meaning may become less rich with time.

The importance of our new conceptions about human capacity can hardly be overestimated. The world can never be the same for having come to understand it is possible to create intelligence. For many years athletes believed the four-minute mile was impossible until Banister showed it could be done. Since then, what previously was considered impossible, has been repeated by dozens of others. With the shackles off our conceptions of human potential the way is open for undreamed of heights of human achievement.

A Personal Check List

A glance back to the determiners of effective behavior we have been discussing in the last few pages will make it clear that all, except one (time), are open to considerable change. One can do little to manipulate age. The rest of the determiners, however, lend themselves to manipulation. This means intelligence can be created, and these are the variables through which it can be accomplished. They are also the factors through which helpers may contribute effectively to the growth and fulfillment of clients, students, and patients. By converting factors determining intelligence to questions for selecting practice, helpers may discover for themselves more effective ways of operating in their respective relationships. Here are a few examples:

1. Physical condition: What can I do to assist my helpees toward maximum health and vigor?
2. Opportunity: What kind of environments can I create to provide my students, clients, or patients with rich extensive fields of meaning? What can I do to provide information and experience likely to free and expand potential?
3. Need: Can I help my client to achieve more satisfying fulfillment of his basic need for self-actualization? What can be done to help him feel more adequate and less deprived?
4. Self-Concept: What can I do to help my client feel more positively about himself? (Much more about this in the next chapter.)
5. Goals and Values: How can I help my clients or students explore and discover new values and goals?
6. Effects of Threat: What can I do to free my clientele from inhibiting effects of threat on their experience?

A systematic search for answers to questions like these may provide important clues to what helpers can do to free human potential and assist their clients toward greater personal fulfillment.

Keeping Perspective

Knowing that capacity can be created does not mean it can be done either quickly or easily. A child growing up with a restricting self-concept is just as severely limited as though he had been born that way. We have also seen that, once established, the self-concept tends to resist change, and the circular effect it exerts upon selection of perceptions causes it to corroborate itself. Similarly, inadequate physical bodies, impoverished environments, lack of opportunities, inhibiting goals and values, or the effects of threat upon perception can all produce seriously limiting effects upon intelligence. What is more, these limitations may be so difficult to eliminate that people do not have the time, energy, or economic wherewithal to deal with them. There are, indeed, limits upon the growth of intelligence, and functional limits can be as formidable as hereditary ones. They have the advantage, however, that in being functional there is something we can do about them.

There is a great deal of difference between approaching a job believing that it is only a holding operation with little or no likelihood of success, or believing that it offers vast possibilities. For generations many teachers believed that there was very little they could do to increase a child's capacities. The beliefs they had about the children they worked with severely limited their expectations both for the children and for themselves. All too often, both parties fulfilled those expectations. A point of view about human capacities that places many of the determiners within the helper's hands, therefore, opens whole new vistas. They can approach their jobs with hope, and rest assured that what they do is significant. This knowledge can provide great challenge and satisfaction. It can also be deeply threatening. It means that failures cannot be blithely charged to heredity or the will of God. Failures, instead, must be confronted as the lack of will of helpers. To this point we still do not know the ultimate levels to which intelligence can grow. Whatever those limits are, the attainment of them will be brought about through learning how to deal with the determiners of behavior we have listed above and such others as we may yet discover. We are still a long way from knowing how to create intelligence with skill and certainty, but there is much we can do with what we already know. A great deal more research is necessary to help us better understand these determiners and to find effective ways of putting that knowledge to work.

One place we can look for clues to that research is in the lives of gifted persons. We have been accustomed to looking at such people as happy accidents of heredity. If it is true that intelligence can be created, however, these are no happy accidents. Rather, they represent our crowning achievement—the people with whom we have already been especially successful! Our problem is not to find and coddle them. It is necessary to find out how we produced them so that we can set about producing many more of them as rapidly as we can!

To make full use of our new understandings of human potential, effective helpers will need to be knowledgeable about the determiners of capacity we have been discussing. These will become the tools of their trade. Helping people develop richer and more extensive fields of meaning will make it possible for them to cope more effectively with life and to behave in more intelligent fashion. But the mere possession of such a field is not enough. There must also be freedom to use the meanings people have. That is the problem of the next chapter.

Selected Readings

Starred entries indicate appearance in whole or in part in Donald L. Avila, Arthur W. Combs, and William W. Purkey, *The Helping Relationship Sourcebook*, Boston: Allyn and Bacon, 1977.

*Combs, A. W. "Intelligence from a Perceptual Point of View." *Journal of Abnormal and Social Psychology* 47, 1952, pp. 662–673.

Henry, J. *Culture Against Man.* New York: Random House, 1963.

Hunt, J. M. *Intelligence and Experience.* New York: Ronald Press, 1961.

Hunt, J. M. The Role of Experience in the Development of Competence. In J. McV. Hunt, ed., *Human Intelligence.* New Brunswick, New Jersey: Transaction, 1972.

Jourard, S. *Disclosing Man to Himself.* New York: Van Nostrand, 1968.

Kelley, E. C. *In Defense of Youth.* Englewood Cliffs, New Jersey: Prentice-Hall, 1962.

*Maslow, A. H. "The Creative Attitude." .*The Structuralist* 3, 1963, pp. 4–10.

Piaget, J. *The Child and Reality: Problems of Genetic Psychology.* Translated by A. Rosin. New York: Grossman, 1973.

6
Dimensions of Self-Fulfillment

Human beings strive for personal fulfillment every moment of their lives and a primary goal of helping professions is to aid them in this search. Maximum attainment of personal fulfillment requires both rich and extensive fields of perception and the achievement of personal growth characteristic of self-actualization. To help students and clients towards self-fulfillment, helpers need to understand the nature of self-actualization, what highly self-actualizing persons are like, and the dynamics involved in growth toward personal fulfillment.

WHAT IS SELF-ACTUALIZATION?

In recent times scholars have devoted attention to the study of self-actualization, what persons could become if they were maximally free to use their potentialities to the utmost. They ask, "What would such a person be like?" and "What can we do to help people achieve these exalted ends?" Some scholars have described self-actualizing persons objectively, in terms of typical behaviors or personality traits. Maslow, for example, described a long list of characteristics including: more efficient perceptions of reality and more comfortable relationships with it; acceptance of self, others, and nature; spontaneity; problem centering; the quality of detachment; autonomy; independence of culture and environment; freshness of appreciation; the "mystic" experience; feelings of oneness with others; democratic character structure; clear discrimination between means and ends; an unhostile sense of humor; creativeness; and resistance to enculturation. Carl Rogers has added additional traits of self-actualizing persons as: openness to experience, living in a more existential fashion, being and becoming a process, an increasing trust in the organism.

Listing the traits of self-actualizing persons is helpful and informative, but still essentially descriptive. Knowing that self-actualizing persons are creative, trust their organisms, have freshness of appreciation, or an unhostile sense of humor still leaves us with the problem of how to facilitate growth and development of these traits. Trait descriptions, however accurate, do not in themselves provide us with guidelines to effective action. We need to understand self-actualizing persons in dynamic terms that tell us how such traits come into being. To this end some writers have chosen to examine self-actualization in subjective terms. Earl Kelley, for example, described the fully functioning personality in the following terms: thinks well of himself, thinks well of others, sees his stake in others, sees himself as a part of a world in movement, in process of becoming, sees the value of mistakes, develops and holds human values, knows no other way to live except in keeping with his values. Approaching the matter in perceptual terms, Combs, Richards, and Richards have described three factors especially characteristic of self-actualizing persons. These are a positive view of self, openness to experience, and identification with others.

POSITIVE VIEW OF SELF

Scientists who have written about the nature of self-actualization generally agree that one of its characteristics is a high degree of self-esteem. Highly self-actualized persons see themselves in essentially positive ways. It would be hard to overestimate the importance of a positive view of self for effective behavior, for the self is the center of a person's existence, one's frame of reference for dealing with life. With a positive view of self one can dare, be open to experience, confront the world openly and with certainty. Negative views of self may lock a person in a vicious circle in which efforts to deal with life are always too little, too late, or inappropriate.

Bolstering Effect of a Positive View of Self

The self is involved in every interaction with the world. Whatever its nature the self-concept goes along. Even a poor, ragged, unhappy self must be dragged by its owner into everything he does. A positive self has vital effects on a person's efficiency and on a person's freedom to confront new matters. Having a positive view of self is like owning a stout ship. With a sturdy vessel under foot one may go sailing far from shore. When one has doubts about his ship and concern about its seaworthiness, he must play it safe and stay close to harbor. A positive self is like that. It provides a firm foundation from which to deal with the problems of life with security and confidence.

Self-actualizing people, studies show, see themselves as liked, wanted, acceptable, able, dignified, and worthy. These deep feelings of personal security make it much easier for them to confront the emergencies of life. They feel they are people of dignity and worth, and they *behave* as though they are. Rogers has pointed out that one of the characteristics of healthy personalities is trust in the organism. With greater feelings of certainty about themselves, people can trust their impulses more. They experience their selves as trustworthy and dependable.

Whatever demeans the self, on the other hand, undermines confidence and produces fear and withdrawal. Persons with a long history of success are best able to cope with trauma. Those with a history of failure are unable to handle emergency situations. This assurance-producing character of a positive view of self can be observed in the behavior of children with positive and negative views of self as they confront the problem of what to do about poor schoolwork. When examiners asked children with positive views of self and histories of success in school, "What can you do about it if you have a bad grade in spelling?" (arithmetic, social studies, or whatever) the children suggested all kinds of possibilities: "Study harder," "Ask my teacher," "Ask my mother to help me," "Practice," "Try to find out what I'm doing wrong," etc. When the same questions were asked of children with negative self-concepts and histories of failure, the reply was, almost without exception, "Nothing!" They regarded the matter as hopeless, the problem insoluble.

People with high self-esteem are more likely to be independent, autonomous agents. They do not need to go with the crowd. Because they have "trust in the organism," they can stand on their own two feet. They resist the surrender of integrity involved in dependent relationships. They depend on themselves. If the self is sufficiently strong, there is no need to rely on the decisions of others when such reliance is not appropriate. With trust in self, a person can afford to depart from group norms and ignore group pressures. The same feelings of self-esteem also make it possible to be a more effective cooperator when that is appropriate, for such relationships can be entered without a feeling of self-surrender. Cooperation is not capitulation, but self-investment, a manifestation of psychological freedom.

The Rich Get Richer

The self-concept as we have seen, tends to corroborate itself. The feeling of "can-ness" loads the dice in favor of its owner and makes success more likely. It is notorious, for example, in the field of athletics that once a record has been broken it is quickly equalled by others. Coach Darrell Mudra reports an amusing example of the effect of a positive view in the following incident:

We had a wrestler at Adams State College when I was there who was confused about the quality of his opponent. There were two boys named Martinez in one of our meets. One was a great wrestler and one was a poor wrestler. The one our boy was wrestling was really the good one, but he thought he was wrestling the poor one. Our boy was just an ordinary, average wrestler but he went out there and tore the boy up. After the match, we rushed down to the locker room to congratulate him. He was standing on the bench there and we were telling him about how great it was. He was really puzzled. When he finally became aware of what had happened, he fell off the bench! Now, if he had really known, I am sure he would have been pinned in the first period. But because he didn't know he performed at a level that was not thought possible. Think of how surprised the other wrestler was to have this boy come out there like a tiger![1]

We have already observed how the experience of challenge or threat is a question of feelings of personal adequacy. People who see themselves in positive ways live in a less threatened world. More of their experience is likely to seem challenging. They can risk involvement. They can dare to try. They may even find joy in the confrontation of problems.

Persons with positive views of self tend to behave in ways that result in experiences of success with the world and with the people in it. The feedback they get from the world in turn makes them far more likely to be happy and effective in their personal and public lives. This success serves to build a person's feelings about self still higher. The circular effect is equally true in the opposite direction. Persons feeling inadequate behave in ways that tend to confirm their own inadequacy. Fearful, tentative approaches to life are more likely to result in failure and inefficiency. People who expect to be inadequate behave in ways that guarantee their expectations. What contributes to self-esteem makes intelligent behavior more likely; what destroys or "derogates self is stultifying and stupefying."

The Fallacy of the Value of Failure

Many people believe that failure is good for people, a valuable stimulant for growth. This idea seems to have arisen from the observation that people are often strengthened by confrontation with problems. That, of course, is true. Many people also believe failure is a strengthening thing. They adopt the attitude "if it's hard, it's good for them," and honestly believe that the experience of failure builds character, courage, and stimulation to succeed. That belief is a fallacy. From what we know about healthy people, such an assumption is not only false but downright destructive!

1. Reprinted by permission of Dr. Mudra from a manuscript unpublished at the time this volume went to press.

Earlier in this volume we described psychological illness as a problem of deprivation, a failure of the organism to be able to achieve fulfillment. Psychological failure is like physiological disease. We do not say about diseases, "Let us give these diseases to children as soon as possible!" Rather, we say, "Let us keep this child from getting diseases just as long as we possibly can." Or, alternatively, we may say, "Let us give him the disease in such an attenuated form that we know he will be successful with it." This is what we do with an innoculation or a vaccination, because we know that the body is strengthened by *successful* experience with the disease. The same principle holds true psychologically. A diet of failure is destructive to human personality. People learn they are adequate and able from success experience. The best guarantee we have that a person will be able to deal with exigencies in the future is that he has been successful in the past. Even the self-made man who beats his chest and proclaims to the world that he came up the hard way overlooks the fact that he became a self-made man by being successful. He became what he is today, precisely because he successfully avoided failure!

Positive effects of feelings of success and negative ones from experiences of failure are beautifully illustrated in the following report from a nursing supervisor:

> Louise was in her second year as a sophomore in our College of Nursing program when she was assigned to my instruction. She was the motherless daughter of a small town general practitioner. Her older brother was a medical student and progressing well.
>
> Her intellectual test scores placed her as "barely able" to achieve in college. The previous year she had failed the first semester of the sophomore year. She decided to repeat that semester the following year. She attained a "D" grade. Her evaluation gave little hope for her success. The instructor in effect was saying, "I tried, but I couldn't find enough evidence on which to base a grade of 'F.'"
>
> Louise was very plain, the only student who insisted upon wearing her mousey brown hair in a net. She had "I can't succeed" written all over her face. She trembled when asked to recite formally or when asked a question informally.
>
> I felt, as her clinical instructor, that the patients would suffer if Louise's assignments were too difficult. I felt she would make mistakes, possibly drastic ones, and I did not want that burden. Looking back, I never thought I was providing success for Louise by giving her patient assignments she could handle. I never thought of Louise in that way at all. I was concerned with myself and the patients for whom my students were caring.
>
> The other instructors were interested in Louise's progress. As the weeks passed, I proudly related how well she could perform with her simple assignments (four to six months behind) and that her trembling had stopped. She could smile and relate to others more freely.

I was told by my superiors, however, that I was handling the situation terribly. (This was damaging to my self-concept, I realize.) The only way to approach extremely weak students like Louise, they said, was to give them the roughest assignment possible for that level students, supervise them heavily, collect the data to fail them, show them where they have failed, write it up and put an "F" on the evaluation.

They convinced me! I did a bang-up job and you know what? Louise behaved true to her perceptions. She blundered miserably, made hair-raising mistakes and failed.

I did such a good job. I was praised highly. Louise did not return this past September. And I feel like a failure knowing that I am a part of Louise's nightmare of failure.

It is dismaying to observe how our society believes in the value of failure. When modern educators suggest eliminating failure from the classroom, they are often met with storms of protest from parents and community who fear that this would destroy the very basis of our public schools. There is no word in the vocabulary of the English language that distinguishes between the act of failing and judging it "non-negatively" and non-critically. The very word *failure* is derogatory, implying a sense of "no goodness"; that one is vanquished, defeated, and inadequate. A person learns very early that if act does not reach its expected or desired outcome, then he or she is a failure. A society that does not distinguish between "non-accomplishment" and "failure" runs a serious risk of demoralizing and discouraging vast numbers of its populace.

By rejecting the value of failure, we do not mean that people must be protected from difficult kinds of experience. People like to work hard when tasks provide a feeling of self-accomplishment and goals are perceived as possible. People enjoy being challenged. It is the experience of long-continued failure that produces destructive outcomes and feelings of inadequacy. Failure is debilitating and weakening.

Implications of a Positive Self for Helping Practice

A major goal of helping is the development of a more positive self, and every act of the helper must contribute to this end. How can the helper do this? The answer is to be found in the perceptual organizations of self-actualizing people. They see themselves as persons who are liked, wanted, worthy, dignified and able, among other things. But these are qualities learned from experience and it is here we can look to find clues for the helper's behavior. The "how to" guides for helping lie in the answers the helper finds to the questions:

- How can a person feel liked, unless someone likes him?
- How can a person feel acceptable unless somebody accepts him?
- How can a person feel able unless somewhere he has some success?

- How can a person feel he is a person of dignity and integrity unless somebody treats him so?
- How shall a person feel that he matters unless someone cares?

In the answers helpers find to these simple questions, guides to effective practice may be found. These are not easy answers, however. The kind of experience that produces these feelings in the client is not simply a matter of manipulation. Helpers cannot produce them unless they believe them. Helpers contribute to a positive view of self, not by what they do *for* the client or *to* the client, but through what their behavior conveys about their real feelings and beliefs about students and clients. The criteria for self-actualization thus also provide definitions for the nature of the perceptual organization that must characterize the helper himself.

OPENNESS TO EXPERIENCE

A second characteristic required for maximum self-actualization is openness to experience. This has to do with a person's ability to perceive the world. It is the capacity to confront what is, to enter into transaction with it, and develop new meanings as a consequence. Highly self-actualizing, fully functioning personalities seem able to deal with the world with a minimum of distortion. They see themselves more accurately and realistically.

Psychologists call openness to experience "acceptance," by which they mean the ability to confront what is—whether it be in self or the outside world. It should be understood that the word *acceptance* used in this way does not mean "giving in to" or "being resigned to." It is possible for persons to accept the fact that someone dislikes them, for example, without necessarily agreeing that they are, therefore, totally inadequate. Persons in the helping professions are often called upon to accept the fact of a client's misbehavior without rejecting the client.

The first requirement for being able to deal with the world or with one's self must be the capacity to perceive it, to enter into a dialogue with it. Whether this is possible will depend in large measure upon a person's feelings of self-esteem. Highly self-actualizing persons find acceptance easy. Deeply deprived and maladjusted people often find it difficult or impossible to achieve. This relationship of openness to positive views of self was measured in a simple experiment carried out by one of the authors. All of the sixth-grade children in a school were given standard tests of adjustment. On a list of things "Boys and Girls Sometimes Do" they were asked to indicate those items that were true of themselves. All of the items on the list consisted of behaviors chosen because they were probably true of every child, but somewhat unflattering to admit. Some samples: "Sometimes I have lied to my mother," "Sometimes I forget to brush my teeth on purpose," or "Sometimes I have been unkind to animals." When the results of the two tests were compared, it was discovered (as predicted) that better-adjusted children said more of the unflattering things were true of them than did the maladjusted ones. One little boy, with the highest adjustment score in the group, agreed that nineteen of the twenty unflattering items were true of him.

Highly self-actualizing people have such a degree of trust in themselves that they are much more able to look at any data without the necessity for defending themselves or distorting events in ways they would like them to be. Lack of acceptance, on the other hand, is a major characteristic of neurosis and shows itself in myriad forms—in the inability of the young child to accept his baby brother, in the failure of prejudiced persons to accept members of minority groups, in the resistance of males to accept the principles of "women's lib" and many more. Persons with extreme inabilities to accept reality end up in our mental hospitals and are described as "out of touch with reality."

Openness and a Positive View of Self

The walls people build to keep others out also keep themselves in. Protections set up to avoid injury can also destroy openness to new experiences. Persons who reject themselves are very likely to reject other people as well, and so contribute to closing themselves off from the very experiences that might eventually result in personal fulfillment. It has been repeatedly demonstrated in research and in clinical practice that feelings of self-acceptance are a prerequisite to the acceptance of others.

The interdependency of self-acceptance, acceptance of others, and openness to experience was beautifully illustrated by two severely handicapped young women known to one of the authors. Two women, each seeking entrance into a graduate training program in clinical psychology, came to the author's office on successive days. Because the office was on the third floor, each had to be carried up for an interview. The first woman was a hard and bitter person. She had an attractive face, but her dour, angry, defiant stance spoiled what good possibilities she had, and her attitude at once repelled her audience. In the course of conversation the author said, "I wonder if you have given any thought to the degree to which your handicap . . ." That's as far as he got. She snapped, "I don't have a handicap!" Unable to accept herself, she was also unable to deal effectively with herself or others. The second candidate had the same condition, but what a difference! She was not as physically attractive but had a much more open, friendly personality—a person one felt immediately drawn to. The author said the same thing he had said to the first young woman, but this time was allowed to complete his sentence: "I wonder if you have given any thought to the degree to which your handicap might make it difficult for you to work in this field?" This is what she replied:

"I have thought a lot about that. You know, in addition to polio I had TB some years ago. At that time I laid on my back for two years in a hospital and had lots of time to think. It seems to me that experience could be helpful. You know, I kind of feel that somebody who has gone through this much will be better able to understand other people who have suffered."

People open to experience enjoy exploring. They are freewheelers able to move off in new directions, which is what creativity means. They are neither thrown by their experience, nor defensive against it. Being more open, they have a wider selection of data from which to draw solutions to problems. With more data they are likely to find better answers, and this in turn makes possible more effective and efficient behavior, which is what we mean by intelligence.

The need for self-enhancement generally keeps the individual continuously searching his world for new ways of achieving greater self-actualization and has the effect of opening him to experience. The same need may also operate to discourage openness.

Values and Openness

Values have the effect of opening and closing avenues of experience, and some values are more likely to produce openness than others. For example, the attitude that it is good to look and fun to try, is almost certain to lead an individual into circumstances where his experience will be broadened and deepened. One of the characteristics of persons who have achieved a high degree of self-actualization seems to be what psychologists call a "toleration of ambiguity." That is to say, such people seem to have an attitude that it is "all right" to live with an unsolved problem. Less fulfilled persons often find confrontation with problems that do not have immediate solutions unbearable and so may be led to adopt any solution, even a bad one, to avoid discomfort.

Some Implications of Openness for Helping Practice

A large portion of the time and efforts of persons in the helping professions will be directed toward aiding clients, students, and patients to develop greater openness and acceptance. Much human maladjustment is a consequence of the inability of persons to accept experience. Few of us misbehave because we do not know what we ought to do. Maladaptive behavior occurs because we are unable or unwilling to accept the implications of the knowledge we possess. Much of the work of counselors, psychiatrists, social workers and all those persons who work with the mentally ill will, of necessity, be oriented to aid their clients toward greater openness to experience. Professional helpers working with well-adapted persons also spend much effort on this matter.

Encouraging openness, of course, is a two-way street. That is, both the helper and the helpee must be open to experience and *aware*. A hundred pound nurse, for example, who tells her two hundred and fifty pound patient that it is *easy* to lose weight "if you only stay on your diet" is a case in point. It is easy for the nurse who has eaten pretty much what she pleased most of her life. For her patient on a 1200 calorie diet, it is quite another matter.

The search for meaning is an active process; it cannot be accomplished standing still. The helping encounter must actively encourage the process of searching. This condition is achieved in part by an attitude of fearless looking, that "it is good to look and fun to try." It may be provided in the form of success experience or the discovery of challenging problems. It may be acquired "by osmosis" from the attitudes and behavior of the helper. Whatever contributes to the feeling that anything can be looked at is likely to be helpful. On the contrary, whatever prevents such an attitude gets in the way of effective learning.

We have succeeded, almost everywhere in our institutions and child rearing practices, in erecting an incredible number of barriers to involvement—attitudes that say to people: "Watch out!" "Don't look at that." "That is forbidden" (or inappropriate, or nasty, or unacceptable). Teachers do this when they say to the child, "I'm not interested in what you feel about that. What does the book say?" We do it with children in our families when we teach them the "right," "nice," "proper" things to do, think, and feel. We do it with each other when we change the subject because "we would rather not think about that." Even as a society, we become highly skilled in simply not seeing what lies before our eyes —for example, the sick, the slums, unfair treatment of minorities, the prisoners, or the fact that other countries and other cultures do not see things as we do. A major task of the helper, no matter what branch of the profession he may be engaged in, must be to overcome the negative effects of such built-in resistance to looking.

The dynamics of self-actualization provide guidelines for helpers. By understanding those dynamics the helper may determine clues for practice by asking such questions as:

• Do the methods I am using assist my students or clients to accept themselves and the world?

Dimensions of Self-Fulfillment   **93**

- Is the atmosphere I am creating truly encouraging my clients to be more open to their experience?
- Am I demonstrating by my own behavior a willingness to look at any and all events?
- Am I teaching my students or clients acceptance of themselves?
- Am I providing experience of successful confrontation with themselves and the world?

FREEDOM AND IDENTIFICATION

A third major quality of self-actualizing people is identification, the feeling of oneness with others. Humans are social beings. The degree to which they are able to attain fulfillment is dependent upon how successful they are in working out effective relationships with other people who make up the society or culture in which they live. We are so dependent upon other people that some measure of successful interaction with them is essential to life itself. Experiments with monkeys deprived of opportunities to interact with other monkeys demonstrate that such isolation causes them to grow into distorted, maladjusted personalities. Raised out of touch with each other, they frequently cannot even be induced to mate. Apparently, they do not know they are monkeys without experience that helps them discover who and what they are. Similarly, people become human through human interaction. Feelings of identification contribute to that process and so to the humanization of persons. People are the most important aspects of our world, the sources of most of our satisfactions and frustrations. In fact, other people are the only really important ingredients of life. Material possessions, whether they be money, cars, or clothes, only gain meaning and importance when they are shared with other human beings. The nature of our relationships with others determines our freedom and personal fulfillment.

Identification with Ideas

Identification is equally significant with respect to ideas. We have already observed the intimate relationship between the self-concept and learning. Whether any information is likely to result in changed behavior will be dependent upon the closeness with which that information is perceived to the self. Ideas incorporated into the self-structure can be counted on to determine future behavior. There is simply no learning of consequence without involvement of the person in the process. Ideas by themselves are mere illusions. It is only in persons that they come alive, and only through the personal discovery of their relationship to self that they affect behavior.

Real learning and the richness it bestows upon life comes about only with self-involvement. Persons who will not or cannot enter into dialogue with ideas are cut off from experience. This principle was vividly brought home to one of the authors of this book while visiting a museum with an artist friend. The author was working hard at trying to understand some modern paintings, but getting absolutely nowhere. Then his friend said to him, "Stop working at it. You are looking at it from afar, groping for it with your fingertips. Let it come to you. Try to be with it. Let yourself get involved. Let it flow into you." Looking at the painting in this way, the author almost at once experienced a whole new relationship with paintings. He discovered a new beauty, meaning, and sensual delight as he let himself "be with it." Instead of *looking at* the painting, he learned to enter into a *dialogue with it* and so opened a whole new world of experience for exploration. The self at war with experience is shutting itself off from meaning, reducing psychological freedom. The self capable of entering interaction with ideas or concepts is opening and expanding its world, simultaneously broadening its base of operations and increasing its chances for the achievement of self-fulfillment.

Nowhere is this relationship between the self and ideas so important as in education. A major purpose of schools is to bring students into effective relationships with the accumulated experience of other human beings. The success of schools in accomplishing this task will depend on their degree of success in inducing students to invest themselves in the processes of learning. We have all had the experience of being or not being "with it" in school. We learned little or nothing in those classes where, for some reason, we refused to invest ourselves in the learning process. On the other hand, we can remember that in those classes where we worked hard and interacted with our classmates we learned a great deal. It made no difference whether our interest came from within or was the result of an inspiring teacher or exciting subject matter. Once invoked, we were with it, and we learned. What was learned was also far more likely to be retained and acted upon. People do not sabotage their own projects.

Identification and Self-Actualization

Deep feelings of identification with other people is a major characteristic of highly self-actualized persons. The possession of such feelings in turn produces interactions with their fellows that corroborate and strengthen existing beliefs. Broad feelings of identification, for example, make it possible to place more trust in others. Relationships with others can be entered into much more openly and freely. When one is certain of being welcome, one is free to walk more boldly and dare to do or say what others less certain could not risk. Interactions with others can thus be entered with an *expectancy* of success. Because they feel they belong, broadly identified persons establish relationships with other people as though they were members of the family rather than strangers. Fulfillment comes much easier to persons capable of such involvement. The feedback they experience from these interactions is also more supporting and enhancing than that of less self-actualized persons.

Those who identify strongly with others are likely to experience deep compassion for people. Others quickly discover this fact and respond in kind. They also discover that deeply identified persons are highly responsible and trustworthy, for what they do for others, they do for themselves and vice versa. As a consequence they respond to them warmly and openly. Because broadly identified persons are less threatening, other people can afford to relax their defenses and enter into more responsive relationships with them. This was so frequently true in the lives of some of the self-actualizing persons Maslow studied as to sometimes become an embarrassment. Because they were warm, open, compassionate, and understanding, they tended to attract people with problems and so found themselves at times surrounded by unhappy persons in need of help!

Deep feelings of identification are also likely to contribute to more intelligent behavior. With positive feelings toward others, persons can approach relationships with the expectancy of success. With a feeling of oneness they have little to fear and so can commit themselves wholeheartedly to interactions. Persons without such feelings operate under great handicaps. They must deal with others defensively as strangers or enemies, rather than as possible friends. Accordingly, they tend to approach interactions with hesitation. Expecting resistance, they are very likely to get it and so defeat themselves almost before they begin.

Identification and Psychological Health

Many of the great social and personal problems of our time have been brought about by the terrible dehumanizing forces we have set loose in our midst. The net effect of many of our technological innovations has been to depersonalize the individual and make satisfying human interrelationships increasingly difficult to achieve. We have created a society in which millions of people feel they are of little account. In his book, *Working,* Studs Terkel quotes more than a hundred persons as they express their feelings about the work they do. With only a few exceptions, the overwhelming theme that comes across to the reader is that most people do not like the work which they believe they *have* to do. They do not feel good about it, think it is unrewarding and unimportant, and see their job's importance as mainly one of survival. A large part of the activities of persons in the helping professions will be directed toward helping people discover and enter into new and more satisfying relationships between themselves and other people.

The problems of alienation and loneliness, of course, exist at every level of our social structure. They are especially poignant with respect to the young. It is probably no accident that the best cure for juvenile delinquency seems to be marriage. Of all the things associated with delinquents who improve, getting married seems more effective and more certain than any other one thing that we know about. When you have somebody who cares, somebody to live for, somebody to share things with, you are provided a measure of relief from the boredom and feelings of alienation that lie at the basis of much delinquent behavior. Many young people grow up with deep feelings of alienation from the society they live in. Many are desperately lonely and find themselves at loose ends without satisfying commitments. We cannot afford this waste. On humanitarian grounds the loss in human potential involved in such rejection is tremendous. The loss in human happiness is even greater. If it is not enough to be concerned about the matter because we love and respect our young people, there is another very practical reason why we had better be interested. It is downright dangerous not to be concerned. These are the citizens of tomorrow.

Some Implications of Identification for Helping Practice

Identification and Discovery of Meaning

Since learning is essentially a social process, our most important learnings are a consequence of some kind of interaction with others. Despite the admonitions of generations of teachers that children should "work alone," students show great ingenuity in finding ways to work together, because they know it is more effective that way. It is a mistaken notion that learning is a solitary matter best achieved in isolation. The most important aspect of our world is people, and it is with and through people that our most important learnings are achieved. This is true even for the learning of highly abstract intellectual concepts. It is far more true with respect to learning the things we need to know about getting along with each other and achieving maximum fulfillment.

The feeling of oneness has important implications for the behavior of helpers in the helping process. Identification is learned from successful encounters with other people. When a helper is able to give of himself he does much more than provide a warm atmosphere. He is, himself, a demonstration of commitment, a living invitation to students and clients to join the human race. Empathy is an invitation, a holding out of the hand, an indication that someone cares.

Dimensions of Self-Fulfillment　　　　　　　　　　　　　　　　**97**

To serve as significant others in the lives of those they seek to aid, helpers must commit themselves to the process. They must care. Carl Rogers has postulated that an essential characteristic of the helping relationship is "unconditional positive regard." The importance of this factor has been demonstrated repeatedly in research. A feeling of oneness with others is associated with effective helpers, while feelings of alienation are attitudes of ineffective helpers. People do not identify very long with those who reject or are indifferent to them. Being loved is immensely releasing, and the loving and caring attitude of helpers, in itself, provides an important ingredient for aiding the discovery of meaning.

The importance of love as a major factor in successful human relationships has been universally recognized by artists, poets, novelists, philosophers, psychologists, anthropologists, and the clergy. Yet the place of love in the helping professions is often ignored in favor of "being objective." Love is approached, if at all, with apologies, fear, or shame. Even to talk about "liking" is sometimes regarded as not really relevant to the helping process. This was beautifully expressed in a letter written by a fifth-grade boy after his teacher permitted the class to hold a free discussion that got around to the question of love. Next day the little boy wrote:

Dear Miss Jones:

It sure surprised me when we talked about love in our class yesterday. I learned a lot of things. I learned how people feel about each other. It sure surprised me when we talked about love. I never knew you could talk about things in school that you didn't get grades for!

What a pity that such an important factor in human life is often not regarded as part of the curriculum!

If helpers do not care, they run a grave risk of defeating themselves as professional workers or, worse yet, of interfering with the growth of those they seek to help. This does not mean that helpers have to love everyone. Some people are not very lovable and no one can turn feelings on and off at will. The authors have seen teachers and counselors ready to quit the profession because they felt guilty for not liking a particular child or client. Helpers are required to deliver the very best professional relationship they are capable of. That, in itself, is a kind of caring. But, if a helper has such strong negative feelings toward a helpee that he or she can't do a good job, then something should be done. Quitting, however, is not the answer. The helper is only human, and disliking others, if a crime, is one all helpers will be guilty of at some time or other. In such cases, accepting the situation and making arrangements for the helpee to work with someone else is an honest, healthy, and simple solution.

FREEDOM AND SELF-ACTUALIZATION

Individual freedom may be curtailed by lack of a rich, extensive, and available field of perceptions or by failure of the person to achieve a positive self, openness to experience, or identification. Freedom and self-actualization move hand in hand. Generally speaking, the greater the degree of self-actualization, the greater the psychological freedom with which a person may live. Self-actualizing persons can operate with maximum degrees of freedom and often seem to be moving through the world like smooth running machines operating at peak efficiency. They are no less human than the rest of us. They hurt and bleed and die like everyone else, but over the long run confront life's problems with more confidence and success than the rest of us.

In his studies of self-actualizing persons, Maslow observed that such people show more expressive behavior than coping behavior. That is to say, much more of their behavior is directed toward simply being who and what they are rather than directed toward "dealing" with life. What is more, the expressive behavior of such people is much more effective in coping with life than the coping behavior of less fortunate persons. They cope simply by expressing themselves. Such a relationship with the world is the very essence of psychological freedom. It is also the essence of creativity. We have already observed that a positive view of self makes daring and personal involvement more likely. These things, with the tendency to expressive behavior that Maslow reports, lie at the very heart of creative behavior. Self-actualizing persons can afford to be free spirits. Indeed, anything less would be a negation of themselves. Creative is what they are; it is not a problem to be worked at.

The freedom enjoyed by self-actualizing persons is not mere self-indulgence. Because such persons have deep feelings of identification with others their activities are likely to be characterized by high degrees of responsibility. Indeed, it is probable that the capacity for responsible action varies directly with the degree of self-actualization a person has attained. We do not expect great demonstrations of responsibility from our criminal, mentally ill, or retarded citizens. We view them as ill and incapable of the kind of responsible action required for effective living.

In this chapter we have scarcely scratched the surface of the full implications current concepts about human fulfillment and actualization may have for human existence. The little we do know, however, provides important guidelines for the efforts of helpers in working with students and clients. We need to explore these concepts much further while at the same time inventing new ways of putting them into action. We cannot turn back. Now that we know that it is possible, we must get about the business of producing more fully functioning people in every way we can. Now that we know the limitless possibilities of human capacity we need to exploit our understandings to the limit. Not to do so is to fail ourselves, our students, clients, patients, and society itself.

Selected Readings

Starred entries indicate appearance in whole or in part in Donald L. Avila, Arthur W. Combs, and William W. Purkey, *The Helping Relationship Sourcebook,* Boston: Allyn and Bacon, 1977.

*Combs, A. W. "What Can Man Become?" *California Journal for Instructional Improvement* 4, 1961, pp. 15–23.

Combs, A. W., ed. *Perceiving, Behaving, Becoming,* 1962 Yearbook. Washington, D.C.: Association for Supervision and Curriculum Development, 1962.

Eisner, W. W. *Think with Me about Creativity.* Dansville, New York: Owen Publishing Co., 1964.

Goble, F. G. *Third Force: The Psychology of Abraham Maslow.* New York: Grossman Publishers, 1970.

Harlow, H. "The Nature of Love." *The American Psychologist* 13, 1958, pp. 673–685.

Jourard, S. M. *Health Personality: An Approach from the Viewpoint of Humanistic Psychology.* New York: Macmillan Publishing Co., 1974.

Maslow, A. H. *Motivation and Personality,* 2nd ed. New York: Harper & Row, Publishers, 1970.

Maslow, A. H. *The Farther Reaches of Human Nature.* New York: Viking, 1971.

May, R. *Love and Will.* New York: Norton, 1969.

Toffler, A. *Future Shock.* New York: Random House, 1970.

Richards, F., and Richards, A. C. *Homonovous: The New Man.* Ft. Collins, Colorado: Shields, 1973.

7

Two Frames of Reference for Working with People

Two fundamental choices are available to helpers for dealing with human problems: closed or open systems. Each is a way of thinking about working with human beings with inevitable consequences for action. Each system is also accompanied by characteristic psychological theories and implications for practice. Careful examination of closed and open systems can contribute much to the development of a helper's personal frame of reference for approaching the helping task.

CLOSED AND OPEN SYSTEMS OF THOUGHT

The closed system proceeds by defining a final objective in the clearest possible terms, then establishes the machinery to reach that objective. This is the technique one would use to plan a trip. It is also the system used in industry for the production of products or by teachers who desire to teach a child a specific skill. One defines the goals to be reached, establishes procedures to reach them, then assesses the outcomes to determine if, indeed, the objectives were achieved. An open system, on the other hand, may begin without a manifest objective. It proceeds to confront a problem, then searches for solutions, the nature of which cannot clearly be discerned in advance. This is the approach that counselors or social workers use in assisting a client to explore a problem. It is also the system employed in a legislature debating an issue, or in modern "discovery" approaches to teaching.

Each system of thinking has advantages and disadvantages and each is especially appropriate for certain kinds of problems and conditions. Whichever system is chosen inevitably commits the helper to a whole series of consequences including the problems selected for attention, psychological theories to be used as guides to action, ways of regarding participants, techniques for dealing with them, responsibilities for action, and philosophical and moral implications. Helpers use these systems whether they are aware of them or not. Clear understanding will increase the options available to helpers and so improve their chances of success.

The Goals of Closed and Open Systems

In a closed system of thinking outcomes are known in advance. Goals can be clearly defined, often with high degrees of precision. Problems have clear beginnings and ends, and goals can be stated as "oughts" or "shoulds." Objectives can often be expressed in terms of specific acts or behaviors and subjected to precise methods of measurement or assessment. This objectivity and precision seems so straightforward and business-like that closed systems are often especially attractive to legislators, managers, tax-payers, and the general public.

The goals of open systems cannot be so precisely defined. Outcomes will often be unknown in advance or may exist as holistic objectives capable of statement only in general terms. In counseling, for example, client and counselor goals may be to help the client become more clearly aware of himself or to improve his marital relationship. Precisely what that will mean or how that will come about neither counselor nor client can perceive at the start of the process. Open systems are discovery-oriented. Sometimes explorations involved in the process may be even more important than outcomes. Open system goals may even change in the course of operation as, for example, when students pursuing one line of study discover fascinating new problems for exploration not foreseen in the beginning. Open systems are especially useful to helpers having to deal with internal, subjective matters like feelings, attitudes, beliefs, values, fears, loves, and aspirations.

Techniques in Closed and Open Systems

Kurt Lewin discussed what he called "Aristotelian" and "Gallilean" approaches to the building of psychological theory. Aristotelian theory he described as a systematic attempt to build basic principles one on another much in the fashion of a mason building a house. The process begins with establishment of precisely described items, then fits these together in larger and larger patterns. The Gallilean approach is more applicable to problems like the opening up of a new territory. Explorers arrive on an unknown shore and penetrate tentatively into the interior. As exploration proceeds, first trails become paths, paths become roads and eventually highways, until the new territory has been mapped and understood in all its ramifications. These two positions are much like the closed and open systems we are discussing.

Closed systems proceed in highly objective ways to deal with problems in precisely defined, orderly, step by step, logical sequence. Open systems operate in more subjective ways. Ends are unknown in advance, so machinery cannot be so neatly designed to reach them. Open systems must rely on the intelligence and motivation of helpers and clients to confront problems and discover appropriate solutions. If one is not certain about specific outcomes, guidelines for seeking must concentrate on processes governing the confrontation of problems and the facilitation of exploration. Helpers in open systems, therefore, concentrate on creating conditions conducive to effective problem solving.

The process orientation of open systems causes them to be grossly misunderstood in a society like ours, which worships objectivity, production, and scientific method. Compared to the neat, straightforward, business-like efficiency of closed systems, the operations of open ones seem dreadfully vague and imprecise. As a consequence, open systems are often citicized as mystical, unsystematic, or unscientific, and practitioners may be described as irresponsible dreamers. Ask a closed system worker what he is up to and you get nice, neat statements for answers. Ask an open system worker what he is after and he confuses you with talk about processes, conditions, and thoughts and feelings. Closed systems have comforting illusions of certainty, while open approaches may seem dangerously permissive or devious.

Few people understand that a system is not good or bad in its own right. A system is only a device for assuring the achievement of objectives. Applied to the wrong objectives a system may only guarantee that one's errors will be colossal! Unfortunately, the general public continues to regard events that provide the illusion of neatness, order, and system as practically synonymous with goodness or rightness.

Regard for Persons in Closed and Open Systems

Closed systems are product-oriented. As a consequence persons involved tend to be regarded as part of the machinery by which the product is produced. Behavior is paramount, and persons are likely to be treated as objects to be moulded or shaped. Such a view of human beings is a natural outgrowth of the objectivity characteristic of our society. We are controlled and managed throughout our school years. We live in an industrial society and admire the efficiency and precision with which our manufacturing giants provide us with countless goods and services. We worship science and objective "scientific method" as a sacred cow. Even our religions have taught us to treat ourselves as objects when they exhort us to "make yourself be good." In a closed system of thinking the important thing about people is not personality but behavior, what they do, and how they can be so managed to achieve desired outcomes with the greatest possible efficiency.

Open systems have a different view of persons. People are regarded as dynamic rather than static processes. Problems confronted and solutions accepted are judged in terms of the persons involved. Success or failure is measured in terms of human satisfactions, values, feelings, and interrelationships. Persons are not the machinery by which the product is produced; persons are, themselves, the product. Failure to understand this fact has caused enormous mischief throughout our society as we have tried to apply objective industrial models to human institutions. Education, for example, is currently suffering from well-intentioned efforts to increase efficiency by the application of methods that have worked well in the production of goods in industry. The effort is doomed to failure because the model is not appropriate. If industry were truly organized for the welfare of the worker, our great corporations would not be organized the way they are. Open systems call for patterns of organization based on a view of persons as being and becoming.

The ways in which persons are regarded in closed and open systems have inevitable effects upon the ways participants react. Regarding people as objects results in a lack of commitment and the separation of persons into categories of managers and workers, teachers and students, doctors and patients, and the like. Being regarded as objects, in turn, produces feelings of dehumanization and alienation, accompanied by the labeling of each group by the other as the "enemy." This state of affairs was the genesis of the labor movement. As workers felt increasingly dehumanized and alienated, they learned to band together in unions to beat the system. The same processes now seem to be going on in social institutions like education, politics, and social work.

In open systems persons are regarded as dynamic forces, and their participation is active rather than passive. Because they participate in decisions, commitment is far less a problem and responsibility, for personal action is more likely to be a consequence. Because persons are valued as individuals, personal effort is greater and creativity is a more frequent outcome. A sense of teamwork and identification is more likely in an open system with a greater degree of caring for fellow participants.

Control in Closed and Open Systems

In a closed system the directors, managers, or administrators are responsible for seeing that ends are achieved. The pattern of helping is similar to the medical model with which most of us are familiar. One goes to the doctor and states his problem. The doctor then diagnoses the situation, determines the goals to be achieved, and writes a prescription for the patient who is expected to carry out the doctor's orders. Responsibility for control and direction is almost exclusively that of the helper-manager, with the student, client, or patient in a passive or subservient role. To do this well, helpers must be expert diagnosticians, who know at any moment precisely what is going on and where events must be channelled next. In the medical profession this leads to the principle of "total responsibility" for the patient. The model is also familiar in the structure of modern industry, the military, and many other institutions.

Such "expert" roles place a heavy burden on closed system helpers. The necessity for being an expert diagnostician is a two-edged sword. On the one hand it endows the helper with a special aura of respect and admiration from others and personal feelings of power over people and events. This is a heady business. History has been replete with horrible examples of leaders blinded by such adoration who came to believe it was justly deserved and abused their power. Leadership in a closed system is a terrible responsibility; managers cannot be wrong.

Not many people can stand on top of a pedestal, so opportunities for intimate human contacts become increasingly difficult. Relationships with other people also become distorted by the superiority-inferiority role definition imposed by a closed system. It is a normal human reaction to fear those with authority over us and just as normal to find ways of defending one's self against such threats. In consequence, closed system helpers must spend much time and effort attempting to deal with other persons whose attitudes are likely to be apathetic, passive, or hostile.

Open systems have a different locus of responsibility. Since operations are problem-centered products are not known in advance. Responsibility for outcomes, therefore, cannot be centered in a leader or manager; it is shared by all who confront the problem. This jointly shared responsibility removes a great burden from the helper. Helpers do not *have* to be right. Mistakes need not be seen as disastrous calamities or evidence of personal failure. They can be taken in stride as normal, even acceptable, aspects of process.

The emphasis in open systems is on participation by all with shared power and decision making. The role of the helper is not director but facilitator. His skill is expressed in the advancement of processes, in creating conditions conducive to solving problems. His role is helper, aid, minister, assistant, or consultant to an ongoing process. Such an emphasis calls for skill in facilitating the processes of interaction.

The facilitating role of helpers in an open system has accompanying effects on the relationship between helpers and their clientele. When responsibility for outcomes is shared, the helping process can be more

Two Frames of Reference for Working with People   **105**

relaxed, open, and humane. Helpers, too, are participants, and such a role is likely to result in far more satisfactory interpersonal relationships between leaders and clients. Helpers are not so likely to be regarded as an enemy to be sabotaged or fawned upon. They have much more chance of relating to others in warm and human terms and of being regarded with respect and affection by those they work with.

Philosophical Implications of Closed and Open Systems

The choice of systems we make for dealing with human events also commits us to different philosophical positions. For example, closed system operations depend upon control of affairs by a management class. Since goals must be known in advance, someone must decide the outcomes to be sought. This leads directly to a "great man" philosophy, someone "who knows where the people should go" so others can set up the machinery to make certain they get there. Carried to its logical extreme, such a concept leads to dictatorship.

Open systems of thinking result in another type of philosophy and social organization. Open systems are egalitarian and essentially democratic. The basic concept of democracy holds that "when people are free, they can find their own best ways." The big "if" in the democratic philosophy, of course, is the phrase "when people are free." Providing that freedom is what the helping professions are all about.

THE PSYCHOLOGY OF CLOSED AND OPEN SYSTEMS

The purpose of theory in science is to order information in ways that make it useful for dealing with problems. It is not surprising then, that closed and open systems of thought have each produced a number of psychological theories.

Closed System Psychologies

Within the closed system of thought, two great movements have grown up in American psychology. The first and still most widely used is *stimulus-response psychology,* also known as S-R, behavioristic, or objective psychology by its various adherents. It is a point of view that seeks explanations of behavior in the stimuli to which the organism is subjected or in the observed consequences of behavior.

Looking at human behavior in this way has influenced every aspect of our lives. The S-R principle is as much a part of us as breathing.

We learn very early that subjecting people to the proper pressures or blandishments often makes it possible to control and direct their behavior. This is true whether we are speaking of individuals or of nations. S-R is the approach we use most often in dealing with friends and relatives. It is also widely used in advertising and in selling, in friendly persuasion, and in more or less disguised techniques of threat and power. Behavior-oriented psychologists base their investigations on the same basic principle. They approach their research, however, with a good deal more care and control than the man in the street, and explore the nature and conditions of the S-R relationship at great depth and with much sophistication. These studies have yielded understandings about human behavior of great significance to every aspect of modern society. Approaching human behavior in this way can also contribute much to the work of helping professionals. Within the objective frame of reference, the work of Sigmund Freud influenced a second great movement in psychological thought. Freud and his contemporaries, and later his students, developed a theory known as psychoanalysis. This second force in the closed system of thinking extended our understanding of the stimulus and its effects upon the individual in three important ways.

1. *Genetic Principle*

Freud and his followers pointed out the importance of the individual's history in determining his present behavior. To understand behavior, they said, it is necessary to understand not just the stimuli to which a person is currently being subjected, but all those stimuli that have acted upon him since the time of his conception.

2. *Effects of Internal Stimuli*

A second major contribution of the psychoanalytic movement was the attention it called to internal stimuli affecting behavior. Freud and his students pointed out that people do not behave only in terms of external stimuli. Some of our most important behaviors, they said, are a consequence of stimuli arising from within the person. These include such stimuli as human values, wants, desires, and appetites, and needs for food, water, warmth, affection, and sexual satisfaction.

3. *Unconscious Stimuli*

A third great contribution of the psychoanalytic movement was the attention it called to the importance of "unconscious" stimuli in the determination of behavior. They pointed out that not all of the stimuli to which the individual reacts can be clearly perceived either by outside observers or by the individual himself. Many of the stimuli that affect behavior exist at such low levels of awareness that persons may not be able to report them to other people when asked to do so.

Although we have been speaking of S-R psychology and psychoanalysis as two great expressions of closed system thinking, it should not be supposed that these schools of thought exist as "pure cases." There are really a great many points of view among psychologists working in the external frame of reference. Some of these tend toward the stimulus-response view, some to the psychoanalytic view, and others to various combinations of these positions. All psychologists using the external approach, however, interpret behavior as the result of the forces at work on the individual. Most of their study is designed to seek out these forces and to understand the nature of their impact. Their conclusions are based on careful objective observation and on the manipulation of the forces at work on their subjects. Over the years, psychologists have learned how to make these kinds of observations with great precision and have contrived ingenious devices for assuring that their observations are as accurate as can be. Out of their work has come a vast amount of literature, which has provided us with an understanding of the nature of people and their behavior.

Open System Psychologies

Open systems, too, require appropriate psychological theory. This need is currently expressed in a number of varieties of humanistic psychology. These new psychologies are expressly designed to understand the internal life of human beings and the qualities of human interactions. Since feelings, values, beliefs, and purposes lie inside people and are not available for direct observation by outsiders, psychologists dealing with these matters are forced to operate from the internal frame of reference, also called the phenomenological or perceptual frame of reference.

Psychologists in the humanist movement call themselves by a bewildering variety of names. This often occurs whenever scholars from widely different backgrounds and experience begin to explore a new subject and create their own vocabularies and concepts. So, psychologists working in the humanist movement sometimes call themselves transactionalists, personalists, phenomenologists, self-psychologists, humanists, existentialists, or perceptualists. By whatever name, all are trying to understand behavior as the person himself experiences it. The authors of this book are primarily associated with that branch of the humanist movement called *perceptual psychology*.

The humanist movement in psychology is much younger than behavior-oriented psychologies. It came into vigorous being only in the last thirty years largely in response to the great human problems of modern society. It is primarily the product of applied psychologists—persons engaged in one way or another with the practice of psychology. Most of its contributors have come from the ranks of social work, teaching, counseling, clinical or child psychology, and psychiatry. The influence of these kinds of workers on humanistic psychology has been so great that it has sometimes been called the "practitioner's" psychology. It has special relevance for the work of those engaged in the helping professions.

The Behaviorist-Humanist Argument

In recent years discussions of open and closed systems of thinking and their accompanying psychological positions have often resulted in heated controversy, with differences between these views rather than accomodations being stressed. One symposium on phenomenology and behaviorism, for example, was described by some reviews as aggressive, hostile, and emotional with little likelihood of a reconciliation between the two schools of thought. The most obvious applications of open and closed systems in the helping professions have been "humanism" and "behaviorism." They have also been most often characterized by the kind of hostilities mentioned above. The argument can be highly confusing to students of helping processes and a comment about this debate may be helpful.

Developments during the first half of this century made the humanist-behaviorist debate understandable as well as inevitable. Behaviorism was originally concerned, almost entirely, with the development of a science of living organisms. It was essentially amoral and asocial, having as its purpose the discovery of theories, principles, laws, and processes that would make the study of behavior a true science. Its thrust was not much concerned with the human condition, solutions to human problems, or the relief of pain and suffering. Leading behaviorists saw the goal of psychology as the attainment of a high level of quantification of behavior theory and the development of a science of living organisms, with the emphasis on science.

Humanists, on the other hand, while concerned with the development of a science, also had the social worker's burning desire to make things better, to apply research and theory in a way that would produce happier, more productive people and relieve suffering. Sometimes their enthusiasm to foster the cause of humanity and alleviate pain and suffering caused humanists to develop ideas and engage in practices that had very little, if any, scientific basis. This kind of willingness to go "beyond the data" was totally unacceptable to behaviorists, who regarded such behavior as a violation of the basic requirement for a true science. But the humanists believed that something of a therapeutic nature must be done. Their position is somewhat expressed by the following story that circulates around the authors' campus: It is said that one of the deans of the local medical school is always asked to address incoming students, and invariably makes the following admission. "Ladies and Gentlemen, as you advance through our program, you may find many occasions to question the validity of what you are being taught. This feeling is not without justification, for, by the time you graduate, half of what you have learned will have proven to be false information. Our only problem is, we don't know which half."

Humanists, dynamic psychologists, therapists, or professional helpers of every description are in much the same predicament. When one's major concern is to help develop more adequate people and minister to the desperate, disabled, and deprived, *something* must be done. One cannot wait for totally verifiable principles to develop a pure science. Helpers are forced to go beyond the data.

Thus, battle lines were drawn, and the humanist-behaviorist debate began. Humanists were labeled "soft-headed" and were accused of having "bleeding hearts" and generating untestable concepts. Behaviorists, on the other hand, were labeled "hard-headed" because of their amoral attitude and refusal to deal with anything but empirical data. To this day, we speak of hard and soft psychologies with these distinctions in mind. Humanists, to be sure, hypothesize about internal conditions that cannot be directly observed, and are hard to verify. But behaviorists often generalize from subhuman to human behavior, and behavioristic positions are as hard to verify with human populations as are humanistic ones because of the many legal, social, and moral restrictions placed on the manipulation of human behavior. In any event, developments in the second half of this century have made vituperative argument over humanist-behaviorist positions futile.

One such development is a major change in the attitudes of behaviorists themselves. Pioneered by such men as Joseph Wolpe and B. F. Skinner, many behaviorists have begun to move behaviorism from the laboratory to therapeutic and educational settings, even to preventive and remedial suggestions for society. Increasingly, they have become concerned with the human condition and how to improve it, developing in the process a number of techniques for making people more successful and healthier.

Another factor inflaming the humanist-behaviorist debate centers around the term *humanist*. Describing one's self as a humanist seems to imply that other people are *nonhumanists,* a category few persons find acceptable. As a matter of fact, persons calling themselves humanists are so diverse that there is often as much disagreement among them

110   **Psychological Bases for Helping**

as between humanists and behaviorists. For example, some humanists employ sensitivity groups extensively while others will have no part of them. Some consider nude encounters to be therapeutic, while others consider such events to be forms of self-indulgence. Understanding this diversity has gone far to discourage dichotomous labelling.

A third event that detracts from the validity of the humanist-behaviorist debate is the increasing amount and sophistication of humanistic research. Recent humanists are not satisfied with the exclusive philosophical approaches of earlier workers. Just as behaviorists are moving towards application, humanistic psychologists are devoting more time and attention to sophisticated research.

Finally, behaviorists and humanists alike increasingly see the futility of hostile exchanges and are coming to the conclusion that their positions are not mutually exclusive. Behaviorists, for example, are becoming concerned with the importance of internal conditions, while humanists now appreciate the usefulness of behavioristic techniques for the pursuit of humanistic goals. The present authors believe there are complementary aspects in open and closed systems, and seeking them is far more fruitful than open warfare.

SELECTING TOOLS FOR HELPING

There is always a temptation to simplify problems by forcing them into clear-cut categories or dichotomies of black or white, right or wrong, for me or against me, and so on. It is necessary to recognize, however, that a theory or frame of reference is only a convenient way of looking at a problem or organizing data. The question we need to raise when choosing is, "Which frame of reference is most appropriate for the purpose we have in mind?" Using an inappropriate system may be like trying to dig a canal with a soupspoon or trying to eat soup with a steam shovel. It is necessary to understand our tools and how they can best be employed. The problem is not choosing a frame of reference that is somehow right in itself, but choosing one that is appropriate to the problems we have to deal with.

Behaviorism and humanism are only tools for dealing with psychological problems. A professional worker who has two tools at his command is far more likely to find good solutions to problems than the worker with only one. When a student comes to the office of one of the authors to inquire what he must do to demonstrate his competence, he is told clearly, straightforwardly in stimulus-response terms. Goals and procedures to be met are clearly defined in behavioral terms. The same student on another occasion, who comes to the office in deep distress because he is not getting along with his wife finds the author behaving in humanist terms, employing the open system of effective counseling.

The behavior of professional workers, like everyone else, is determined by the perceptions they hold. The frame of reference chosen inevitably imposes directions and determines the nature of the tools and techniques employed in carrying out the helping role. Each frame of reference for understanding behavior has its advantages and disadvantages. Each also commits the user to its peculiar philosophy, goals, and programs of action. The truly effective helper will be clearly aware of the choices.

Selected Readings

Starred entries indicate appearance in whole or part in Donald L. Avila, Arthur W. Combs, and William W. Purkey, *The Helping Relationship Sourcebook,* Boston: Allyn and Bacon, 1977.

*Avila, D. L., and Purkey, W. W. "Self-Theory and Behaviorism: A Rapprochment." *Psychology in the Schools* 3, 1972, pp. 124–126.

Bonner, H. *On Being Mindful of Man.* Boston: Houghton Mifflin, 1965.

Bugental, J. F. T., ed. *Challenges of Humanistic Psychology.* New York: McGraw-Hill Book Co., 1967.

Child, I. L. *Humanistic Psychology and the Research Tradition: Their Several Virtues.* New York: John Wiley & Sons, 1973.

*Combs, A. W. "Why the Humanist Movement Needs a Perceptual Psychology." *Journal of the Association for the Study of Perception* 9, 1974, pp. 1–13.

Frick, W. B. *Humanistic Psychology: Interviews with Maslow, Murphy and Rogers.* Columbus, Ohio: Charles E. Merrill Publishing Co., 1971.

*Hitt, W. D. "Two Models of Man." *American Psychologist* 24, 1969, pp. 651–658.

Keen, E. *A Primer of Phenomenological Psychology.* New York: Holt, Rinehart and Winston, 1975.

Laszlo, E. *The Systems View of the World.* New York: Braziller, 1972.

Severin, F. T. *Humanistic Viewpoints in Psychology.* New York: McGraw-Hill Book Co., 1965.

Shaw, M. E., and Costanzo, P. R. *Theories of Social Psychology.* New York: McGraw-Hill Book Co., 1970.

Skinner, B. F. *Beyond Freedom and Dignity.* New York: Alfred A. Knopf, 1971.

Wann, T. W., ed. *Behaviorism and Phenomenology: Contrasting Bases for Modern Psychology.* Chicago: University of Chicago Press, 1964.

II
HELPING PROCESSES

The internally consistent belief systems characteristic of effective helpers may be obtained in part from psychological concepts like those we have been exploring in Section 1. How helpers approach their tasks will also be dependent upon the beliefs they hold about the goals and dynamics of the helping process. This is the subject of Section 2.

The section begins with an exploration of the goals of helping and some of the responsibilities of professional helpers in Chapter 8.

A prime ingredient for effective helping processes is sensitivity or empathy, the ability of helpers to see the world through another's eyes. Chapter 9 explores this vital requirement and suggests some ways in which helpers can increase their capacity for empathy.

Most helping processes provide, in one form or another, for three essential phases of helping relationships: (a) provision of an atmosphere that facilitates exploration of personal meanings, (b) encounter with new information or experience, and (c) active assistance in the personal discovery of meaning. These important phases are explored in Chapter 10, "The Helping-Learning Atmosphere"; Chapter 11, "Providing Experience and Information"; and Chapter 12, "Modes of Helping."

The section concludes with an examination of the helper as person and citizen, including suggestions for ways in which helper-learners can contribute to their own growth and development as effective helpers.

8

Goals and Responsibilities of Helping

The behavior of teachers will be quite different if they believe their purpose is to mold children in the "proper" directions or to help them grow toward maximum achievement of their potential. Similarly, counselors will behave differently toward a couple considering divorce, depending upon whether they believe their proper function is to keep the couple together or to help them find their own best solutions. Social workers who perceive their tasks as saving the taxpayers' money will behave differently from those who seek to help their clients make the best possible adjustment. Even the personal reasons for helpers joining a profession vary widely and inevitably affect the ways in which they operate. Helpers who join the profession because they like feeling powerful, need to find solutions to their own problems, enjoy having others dependent on them, or feel deep commitments to the human race will behave quite differently even in what seems to be the same situations.

Even if the purposes that motivate individuals are not very clear to themselves, they are often very clear to others. Here, for example, are three reactions to a speech given by one of the authors:

First person: "Don't you just love it when you're up there and the spotlight is on you and there you are!"

Second person, extending his clenched fist: "That was beautiful! You really had them! Right there in your hand!"

Third person: "Very adroit! Very adroit!"

To the author, who had actually wanted very much to make his point clear and at the same time felt great anxiety over whether his audience would accept him, none of these reactions seemed anywhere near appropriate. Each comment, however, revealed a great deal about the purposes of the commentator!

An important part of the perceptual organization of helpers has to do with goals and purposes; helpers' conceptions of what it is they are trying to do in the helping process. Research shows, for example, that the effective helper's goals in helping tend to be freeing rather than controlling, larger rather than smaller, and self-revealing rather than self-concealing. Some conception of goals and purposes of helping is an essential part of the helper's frame of reference. One step toward the internally consistent perceptual organization characteristic of effective helpers is a personal exploration of the goals of helping.

CHANGING GOALS OF THE HELPING PROFESSIONS

Most of the helping professions originally came into being for rehabilitative reasons. Guidance programs in the public schools, for instance, came into being to help those youngsters who were unable, for one reason or another, to fit into the usual molds. The task was to fix up and patch up, to deal with the misfits, the casualties of the system. Most of the helping professions began with this rehabilitative emphasis. Even the oldest professions, like teaching and the clergy, evolved out of a major desire to "save" their subjects—in one case from stupidity, in the other, from sin.

Later the helping professions became increasingly interested in the problems of prevention—keeping people from getting sick. After one has gotten into difficulties, rehabilitation is always more difficult and expensive than staying out of trouble in the first place. This phase in the development of the helping professions was stimulated by the development of such social sciences as anthropology, psychology, and sociology, which provided clues to how people got into difficulties and so opened the way to more effective diagnosis and prevention. The invention of psychological tests provided an additional tool by which workers might discover persons in need of help. The creation of the "guidance counselor" in our public schools was one of the products of the testing movement. Today, school counselors do much more than administer psychological tests. But in the early days of this profession, tests were both the guidance worker's major tools and his primary professional reason for being.

Expanding the purpose of the helping professions from rehabilitation to prevention also expanded the clientele. The sick are comparatively few; the potentially sick includes all of us. As a consequence, the helping professions have grown tremendously with the adoption of a preventive goal. Education, for example, is newly esteemed for what it can do to prevent cultural deprivation. Counseling and guidance are regarded as important services for all children. Psychotherapy is now so accepted that in some circles it has become quite fashionable to have been "in treatment." We are increasingly recognizing the social worker's value for social planning and the operation of a wide variety of agencies devoted to helping people individually or in groups at every level of need. We have even seen the development of new helping professions almost exclusively designed for preventive problems like public health nursing, some forms of group work, mental health clinics, and premarital counseling services.

Change in our conceptions of the purpose of the helping professions has not stopped with prevention. Our new understandings of human capacities and the nature of self-actualization have opened whole new vistas. Our new conceptions of human capacity make it clear that human potential is vast beyond belief, while research on self-actualization points to ways it may be achieved. The fundamental purpose for society, itself, is the fulfillment of human need. The ultimate goal of the helping professions must be freeing human potential. That is not simply a matter of patching up failures or even preventing distress. A forward press is called for, a reaching for the heights, and the fullest possible realization of self not for just a few, but for everyone!

It is precisely to meet those new needs that humanistic psychology has been invented, to aid persons of all walks of life to move toward greater personal fulfillment. The same goal has given rise to a wide variety of schools of thought concerned with human awareness, sensitivity, and the expansion of consciousness. Whether helping is rehabilitative, preventive, or fulfilling, the primary goal is the same—freeing human potential. The only change is the definition of the problem and the numbers of persons affected.

THE BASIC DYNAMICS OF HELPING

The Focus of Helping

The fundamental strategies of helping are always directed toward one or more of three targets represented diagrammatically in Figure 8.1: the person (A), the goal (B), or the barriers (C). At any moment we choose to look in on the state of a person's being, we will find him in some kind of goal-related behavior, striving for something, even if it is only to continue a nap. The ultimate goal toward which the person is striving is always self-fulfillment; but, of course, this goal is defined in many different terms, shifting and changing according to the requirements of need satisfaction. Human problems arise when the striving of the organism is blocked by barriers from the achievement of fulfillment. These barriers may exist in the world outside the individual, or they may exist in his own perceptual structure. In seeking to help their clients, stu-

Figure 8.1. Diagram of the Helping Problem.

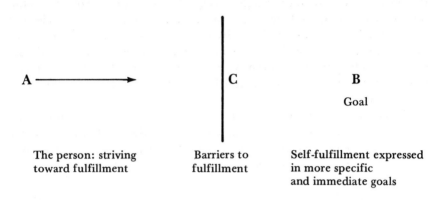

A ⟶	C	B
		Goal
The person: striving toward fulfillment	Barriers to fulfillment	Self-fulfillment expressed in more specific and immediate goals

dents, or patients, members of the helping professions may direct their energies toward any of these barriers, either singly or in combination.

The most common illustration of this paradigm may be found in the medical model familiar to almost everyone: for one reason or another the normal striving of the body toward health is impeded by a malfunctioning organ, a germ, malnutrition, or injury. The physician helps through removing such barriers by prescribing drugs, rest, nutrition, elimination of the offending organism, an operation, or the like. In the same way, social science workers may aid their students, clients, or patients by directing their helping efforts to the person, the barriers, or the goal.

The medical model is not completely appropriate for most helping professions. The doctor-patient relationship is essentially a closed system involving a person who knows (the doctor) and a person who does not (the patient). This is often appropriate for producing change in the physical body. Changing human feelings, attitudes, beliefs, and understanding calls for a different model. Perceptions lie inside people and are not open to direct manipulation. Helping persons change generally requires an open system relationship. The diagnosing and prescribing techniques used by the physician in helping his patient are only occasionally successful when problems are psychological. In most helping relationships, it is the helpee who knows and the helper who does not; the client has far more information than the helper. He or she lives with it twenty four hours a day.

Helper and helpee both want the same thing—increased fulfillment for the client or student. As we have seen in Chapter 3, the motive power toward self-fulfillment is inherent in the person. The helper's task is to contribute however he can to setting it free to operate. He does this by concentrating on any of the phases indicated in Figure 8.1.

Building Personal Resources

One way of helping is to build up the helpee's resources, the ability to mount the necessary effort. This is a matter of increasing human potential. The greater the strength the person can call upon, the better the chances of success in the dialogues of life. This is the condition the physician seeks when prescribing rest or a diet. It is the goal of the teacher who provides information and success experience, and what the counselor hopes to produce by expressing faith in his client.

Whatever increases a person's intelligence places him in a more favorable position for dealing effectively with events. This is, in fact, the major purpose of our educational system. Increases in human potential are also created by strengthening factors contributing to self-actualization. A positive view of self, for example, provides a firm foundation for interacting vigorously and assuredly with life. The same is true for feelings of identification. People who feel they "belong" are in far stronger positions to deal with life than those who do not feel so. Factors governing intelligence and self-actualization thus provide helpers with important clues to ways in which they can contribute to the growth resources of those they seek to assist.

Removing Barriers

The goals of helping can also be achieved by removing blocks which lie in the path of a person's striving. The helper, by removing the block himself or having it done by others, might do this *for* a person. If the blocks occur in the exterior world, it may be possible to remove them physically. Different approaches are necessary when blocks are conceptual or attitudinal and lie inside the person.

The principles governing the experience of challenge or threat are pertinent here. Obstructions perceived as challenging may be confronted as fascinating problems, whereas barriers perceived as threatening may be frustrating and destructive. Much effort in all of the helping professions is devoted to aiding clients to perceive the barriers they confront in less threatening terms. Sometimes a barrier can be surmounted, as for example, when a child learns to handle a mathematical function he previously could not. Sometimes barriers may be changed in such fashion that coping with them becomes possible, or sometimes they may simply have to be accepted and lived with.

A case in point involves one of the authors' clients who, in middle age, married a bachelor who had lived all his life with his mother. The couple moved in with the old lady who immediately began a campaign to make life miserable for her daughter-in-law; but she was so clever about it that her son was never aware of what was going on between the two women when he was not around. The poor bride was trapped in a situation that her husband could never be expected to understand, and she had no way to deal with her mother-in-law. After struggling with her problem for months, she became quite ill and sought help in therapy. During the course of counseling she carefully considered the possibilities of doing away with the old lady, but decided that was no solution because it would mean the end for her too. At long last she decided, "I'm thirty years younger than she is. I'll wait her out!" Having accepted the necessity to live with the barrier and having found a way to cope with it, her neurotic symptoms disappeared and she found herself able to tolerate her problem. Sure enough, a few years later the old woman died and left her daughter-in-law triumphantly in charge of the scene.

Changing Goals

Encouraging growth may also be fostered through a change in goals. A person who is blocked in one direction may find it possible to solve his problems by turning to another field of endeavor. The world we live in is characterized by an ever increasing need for change. To cope successfully requires more and more flexible citizens able to adapt to new demands and new conditions with ease and grace and a minimum of distress. New inventions may throw thousands of people out of work or require thousands to learn new skills, even change their accustomed ways of life. A major cause of the so-called "generation gap" is the inability of parents to understand or accept the goals of youth, because they are too divergent from those the parents learned from their experience. Adjusting our goals to new conditions of life is not just a way of solving problems; it is a necessary step for achieving more satisfying levels of fulfillment.

Seeking new goals is not simply a device for solving existing problems; it is also a way of *creating* problems and so leads the way to further growth and development. The genius of good teaching, for example, lies, not in simply helping children satisfy their needs, as necessary to learning as that may be. Good education requires much more; it requires helping students discover needs they never knew they had. In this fashion, lives may be greatly enriched and possibilities for fulfillment enormously expanded.

Conflicting Goals in Helping

Understanding the fundamental goal of helping relationships or their specific formulation in clients and students is only one facet of the helper's concern about goals and purposes. Though everyone involved in helping processes may agree that the primary goal is helping students or clients, the methods used to accomplish this may be a matter of far less agreement. So counselor and client may have very different conceptions of what ought to be going on in the counseling hour, and students, teachers, parents, administrators, and professors of education may all have different conceptions about what should be happening in a schoolroom. Sometimes arguments about these differences in the perception of desirable goals can become very heated, and helpers may find themselves confronted with conflicting demands and expectations. Here are a few examples surrounding a hospital patient:

A nurse wants a patient to walk, the approval of the other nurses, and the personal gratification of solving the problem.

The patient wants to avoid pain, stay in bed, be loved and cared for, and avoid embarrassment or humiliation.

The hospital wants the patient out as soon as possible. So do the patient's relatives. The physician wants the patient to walk, and the nurse wants to get the job done. Everyone wants the patient well. Everyone also has differing conceptions of how it is to be brought about, to say nothing of personal goals that are unrelated to the welfare of the patient. All these purposes must somehow be resolved in the process of helping the patient get well.

The resolution of goals and purposes can be much more complex and difficult when the helper must deal with directly contrary goals. For example, the teacher under attack from parents for teaching a topic they disapprove of; the counselor who learns that his client intends to act illegally; the social worker whose supervisor demands information obtained in confidence. Confrontation with such diverse demands can be a painful experience for helpers. It may also contribute much to the helper's growth by clarifying and refining personal systems of belief.

HOW HELPERS ARE ALIKE

The goal of the helping professions is self-actualization. This goal is the same for every helping profession whether it be counseling, social work, pastoral care, nursing, teaching, group work, or any of the dozens of other specialties currently recognized in the field. While practitioners may behave in many different ways to assist people in achieving self-fulfillment, the primary goal remains the same for all.

In a study of the beliefs of psychotherapists, F. E. Fiedler found that experienced psychotherapists—no matter what school of thought they were working in—were closer together in what they believed constituted a good helping relationship than were beginning therapists and expert therapists in the same school of thought. Apparently, as they became more expert in their professions, they grew closer together. This seems to suggest that there is probably a "good" helping relationship toward which people move as they become more expert. Even more intriguing, Fiedler found that the "man in the street" could describe the good helping relationship about as well as the experts! Apparently there is a "good" helping condition, which all of us are vaguely aware of even if that is not our primary business.

In a similar experiment, R. W. Heine came to the conclusion that there is probably only one basic psychotherapy, and all therapists approach that common principle to some degree. Other studies show that the belief systems of good counselers, teachers, resident advisers, school psychologists, even good politicians and Episcopal priests are basically alike.[1] Such findings should not really surprise us. After all, if the basic nature of persons and the laws of behavior are stable, one would expect applications of these basic principles to show in common practice. Since they arise from common bases, the principles governing the operation of effective helping relationships *ought* to be similar.

Helping as Learning and Teaching

The process of helping is a process in problem-solving governed by our knowledge about learning dynamics. Helping people discover more effective and satisfying relationships between themselves and the world is an exercise in learning. In that sense all helpers of whatever schools are fundamentally teachers. Some helpers will no doubt recoil from the thought of helpers as teachers. What they do seems so different from the kinds of teaching they have observed or experienced. This is probably because they are accustomed to thinking of teaching as "telling." The techniques used by helpers in the one-to-one relationships of counseling, for example, seems a far cry from such procedures as lecturing, assigning, evaluating, rewarding, and punishing. Teaching seems to them synonymous with controlling, directing, and even coercing people. Such practices are employed by some teachers. Many modern teachers, however, regard them just as distastefully as their colleagues in other helping professions.

There is little reason to suppose that classroom learning is basically different from that occuring in the varied relationships of any of the other helping professions. All are concerned with learning, and all must devise ways of operating from the same basic concepts about the nature

1. See, for example, studies by the following, listed in the bibliography: R. G. Brown, C. Choy, C. V. Dedrick, D. A. Dellow, E. J. Doyle, G. D. Jennings, R. G. Koffman, A. O'Roark, J. Parker, P. W. Pendergrass, R. H. Usher, J. L. Swanson, and H. G. Vonk.

of learning and how it is brought about. Each hopes to assist the student or client to learn new and better ways of dealing with himself and the world about him. The best teachers today are a far cry from the forbidding, authoritarian stereotypes characteristic of a generation ago. Helping people learn is the basic problem of the helping professions, and helping people learn is precisely what we mean by teaching. In a very real sense, then, every therapist is a teacher, and every teacher is to some degree a therapist.

In the early days of the development of the helping professions, various branches sometimes sought to establish exclusive domain over the right to practice in one aspect or another. For example, at one time some persons hoped to define the practice of psychotherapy so as to make it the exclusive prerogative of the medical profession. After years of effort, it became apparent that counseling and psychotherapy cannot be defined in ways that do not involve what thousands of others in the helping professions do or, even, what some people generally do in daily life. If warm, friendly talk or the giving of advice were made the exclusive property of a particular profession, few of us, whether professional or not, could long remain out of jail!

SOME ETHICAL CONSIDERATIONS

Keeping Perspective

It may appear to some readers that our emphasis upon the common character of the various helping professions is like making a mountain out of a molehill. The point, however, is important. It will often be necessary for two or more helpers to work together with a particular student or client. Without a clear understanding of commonalities, effectiveness can easily be destroyed. It is a disaster for a student or client to find himself caught in a cross fire of helpers at war with one another. In a team or institutional setting, it is important that helpers recognize and appreciate their common goals and purposes. Unhappily, this is often not the case. Teachers and counselors, for example, sometimes deal with each other as antagonists rather than coworkers. Some counselors may delight in gossiping about the terrible things that parents and teachers have done to the children they are working with. And there are teachers who regard the work of counselors as unwarranted invasions of their prerogatives and speak with disdain of "head-shrinkers." Such attitudes are not only bad for the persons in need of help, they also seriously undermine the *esprit de corps* of the institution itself. Helpers who treat each other with disdain are unlikely to work together in effective ways. They are themselves in need of help.

Persons in the helping professions need to be keenly aware of the distorting effects of their own self-concepts. Helping people is a "heady" business and can sometimes result in exaggerated views of one's personal power or indispensability. One's own activities naturally seem to be right and important. What others do may then seem less important or valuable because it is less understood. Carried to extremes this can result in a kind of cult with firm beliefs that its practitioners are "the chosen ones." These attitudes may be further institutionalized with elaborate entrance ceremonies designed to maintain the "purity" of the profession. Persons in the helping professions must understand the basic commonality of their tasks and appreciate the work of other professions with sympathy and understanding. The goals of helping are so great that no branch of the profession can hope to make the helping process its exclusive prerogative. The professions must work in concert.

The task of helpers is to provide the conditions that will free the client's own need for self-fulfillment. This is a process of problem-solving and learning in which the helper serves as catalyst (to set events in motion) and teacher or guide (to assure the process has maximum opportunities for producing positive growth). The specific ways in which this process is brought about will differ from one branch of the helping professions to another, but, whatever the branch, the moral responsibility of the helper is the same—to assist his clients in the quickest, most effective ways possible. It is cruel and inhuman to permit people to suffer a lack of fulfillment any longer than absolutely necessary. Persons in the helping professions must always, therefore, employ the most efficient ways possible to help their clients achieve maximum growth and health. It is not enough for helpers "to do their own thing" because it is their thing to do; they must be keenly aware of their personal assets and limitations and those of the peculiar branch of the helping professions with which they are identified. This is essential for all helpers, especially for those working with clients in trouble or suffering deprivation.

The responsibility of helpers goes further. It is not enough to understand one's self and one's branch of the profession. Helpers must see themselves and their professional efforts in the broad perspective of the whole helping process, including a proper appreciation of the contributions of other branches. Clinical files bulge with unfortunate cases of persons who did not get the help they needed because the helper they chose was either too enamored of his own special competencies or too ignorant of the possibilities inherent in other aspects of the professions to use them. It is clearly impossible for each person in the helping professions to be competent in all others. The truly effective practitioner is aware of community resources and is free to use them. Among those resources are the other helping professions. In addition to their own specialties, it is therefore necessary that helpers have an understanding of the potentialities of others and the will to make maximum use of them.

PROFESSIONAL ACCOUNTABILITY[2]

Who Is Responsible for What?

Helpers surely must be accountable, but what can they truly be held accountable for? Can helpers be held accountable for the behavior of their clients? To answer that question we need to answer a prior one, namely, to what extent can *any* person, helper or not, be held accountable for another person's behavior?

Since complex behavior is never the exclusive product of any one stimulus or set of stimuli provided by another person, it follows that no human being can ever be held responsible for the behavior of another except under three possible conditions:

1. *If the other person is too weak or too sick to be responsible for himself.* Adults have to be responsible for some aspects of children's behavior, especially acts that might prove harmful to the child or to others. The same rule applies to persons who are too sick to be able to care for themselves and who need the help of others. Acceptance of the responsibility to aid them has long been a basic tenet of Judeo-Christian philosophy. Such conditions of responsibility are comparatively short-lived, however, existing only until the individual can care for himself. Generally speaking, the older a child becomes, the more necessary it is for him to assume responsibility for himself. The principle is clearly recognized in our courts. It is also the goal of human development as the organism strives for freedom, autonomy, and self-actualization. It ought to be the goal of helpers as well.

2. *If one person makes another person dependent upon him.* Whoever assumes the responsibility of making decisions for another person also assumes responsibility for his behavior. A person who, for whatever reason, induces or seduces another to surrender his autonomy at the same time assumes responsibility for his actions. This may occur in the case of physicians who accept the principle of "total responsibility for the patient." It may also occur in the case of the psychotherapist who permits his client to develop a deep transference, or in the case of a teacher who seeks to assume the role of a child's mother. Such dependent relationships may sometimes be desirable

2. This section is adapted from a more extensive discussion in A. W. Combs, *Educational Accountability: Beyond Behavioral Objectives* (Washington, D.C.: Association for Supervision and Curriculum Development, 1972).

Goals and Responsibilities of Helping **125**

in the doctor-patient relationship. In most of the other helping professions, which are not dependent on the helper *doing* something to his client, the development of such dependency is generally regarded as unfortunate and undesirable. Most modern approaches to psychotherapy, for example, carefully eschew the development of dependent relationships, because they believe strong client dependence on the therapist saps the client's problem-solving capacities and unduly prolongs the therapeutic relationship. The development of dependency runs counter to the basic objective of helping professions, which is the production of intelligent persons, capable of acting autonomously and freely with full responsibility for themselves.

3. *If responsibility is demanded by role definition.* Sometimes responsibility for another may be imposed on persons by virtue of peculiarly assigned roles. An example might be the responsibility of the prison guard to make certain that prisoners do not escape. Such role-defined responsibilities for the behavior of others, however, are ordinarily extremely limited and generally restricted to preventive kinds of activities. So a teacher, by reason of his role, might be held responsible for keeping two children from fighting with each other. Holding him responsible for whether or not a child does his homework is quite another question. One cannot, after all, be held responsible for events not truly within his control, and few of us have much direct control over even the simplest behaviors of others.

The basic democratic philosophy on which our society rests holds that "when persons are free they can find their own best ways." Citizens are regarded as free and responsible agents. Each is held accountable for his own behavior, very rarely for the behavior of others.

But what of professional responsibility? For what can helpers be held accountable simply because they are helpers? Surely not for the behavior of students, clients, or patients five years from now; too many others have had or will have their fingers in that pie. A teacher's influence, for example, cannot be clearly established even on the simplest forms of student behavior in the classroom. As children get older, even these simple behaviors can less frequently be attributed to the teacher. The attempt to hold helpers responsible for what clients do is impossible for all practical purposes.

Even if this were not so, modern conceptions of the helper's role would make such an attempt futile. Helping is not a matter of control and direction, but of help and facilitation. Helpers are asked to be facilitators rather than controllers, aids rather than directors. They are asked to be assisters, encouragers, enrichers, inspirers. The concept of helpers as makers, forcers, molders, or coercers is no longer considered the ideal role for helpers, a position firmly buttressed by evidence from research. Helping is a process of ministering to personal growth rather than a process of manipulating client behavior.

Helpers can and should be held accountable for behaving professionally. A profession is a vocation requiring some special knowledge or skill; but the factor that distinguishes it from more mechanical occupations is its dependence upon the professional worker as a thinking, problem-solving human being, who has learned how to use self, knowledge, and skills effectively and efficiently to carry out personal, professional, and social purposes. Professional helpers can properly be held accountable for at least five things:

1. They can be held accountable for being informed in their field of expertise. This is so self-evident as to need no further discussion.

2. Professional responsibility requires concern for the persons involved in the process, and such concern can and should be demanded of helpers.

3. Helpers can also be held professionally responsible for their understanding of human beings and how they behave. Since people behave in terms of their beliefs, the beliefs helpers hold about what clients are like and how and why they behave as they do play a crucial role in their performance. Professional helpers need the most accurate, sensitive, effective understandings about people and their behavior that it is possible to acquire in our generation. This also seems self-evident but is all too often violated in practice.

4. Helpers may be held professionally responsible for the purposes they seek to carry out. Human behavior is purposive. Each helper behaves in terms of what he believes is the purpose of society, of its institutions, of his branch of the helping professions, and, most especially, in terms of his own personal needs and goals. The purposes held by helpers play a vital role in determining what happens to clients. They provide the basic dynamics from which practices are evolved. They determine the nature of what goes on in the helping relationship. Yet purposes can also be explored, evaluated, and, when necessary, changed. As a consequence, any system of accountability must give the exploration, assessment, and continuous review of helper's purposes an important place in the attempt to help these professions achieve their fundamental objectives.

5. Professional helpers can be held responsible for the methods they use in carrying out their own and society's purposes. This does not mean they must be required to use some previously determined "right" kinds of methods. Methods, in themselves, are neither good nor bad. They can only be judged in terms of the purposes they were used

to advance and the impact they had on the persons subject to them. The methods helpers use must fit the helper, the students, or clients, and the circumstances in which they are employed. The essence of good professional work calls for thinking practitioners able to confront problems and find effective solutions. These solutions may be highly unique and personal.

Professional responsibility does not demand a prescribed way of behaving, but it does demand that whatever methods are used have reasonable expectations of being good for the client. The emphasis is not upon guaranteed outcomes but on the defensible character of what is done. Doctors, for example, are not held responsible for the death of the patient. What they are held responsible for is being able to defend in the eyes of their peers that whatever they did had the presumption of being helpful when applied. Helpers, too, must be prepared to stand this kind of professional scrutiny of their information, beliefs, purposes, and the adequacy of the techniques they use. Their actions should be based on good and sufficient reasons, defensible in terms of rational thought or as a consequence of informal or empirical research.

The professional helper is not "just another person." He or she must be a significant other, informed, disciplined, experienced, and skillful in carrying out the helper's special role. The manifest objective is increased adequacy of client, student, or patient. The professional's success will be dependent upon his skill in mobilizing events to this end. This process must be predictable and controllable. Helpers cannot operate on faith nor do what "might help" without some reason to believe that outcomes will be positive rather than negative. We are not suggesting that helpers must at all times and in all places be clearly able to predict the full consequences of their actions. At this stage of our knowledge no man or woman can be expected to meet that requirement. Responsible professional service, however, is not fortuitous. It must be predicated upon reasonable presumptions of positive effect. To be significant, a helper's self must have well-ordered direction.

Whether we like it or not, all of us are at the mercy of the belief systems of those we trust. Mixed-up thinking is very likely to produce mixed-up behavior. But the sensitive helper whose thinking is clear and consistent, whose motives are positive and humane, and whose experience has provided effective ways of working with others need not frighten anyone. All human interaction is built upon beliefs. A set of well thought out beliefs, which have been thoroughly tested in experience deserves to be trusted.

Selected Readings

Combs, A. W. *Educational Accountability: Beyond Behavioral Objectives.* Washington, D. C.: Association for Supervision and Curriculum Development, 1972.

Fiedler, F. E. *A Theory of Leadership Effectiveness.* New York: McGraw-Hill Series in Management, 1967.

Lakin, M. "Some Ethical Issues in Sensitivity Training." *American Psychologist* 24, 1969, pp. 923–928.

Raimy, V. *Misunderstandings of the Self.* San Francisco: Jossey-Bass Publishers, 1975.

Rokeach, M. *The Nature of Human Values.* New York: Free Press, 1973.

Soar, R. S. "Teacher-pupil Interaction." In *A New Look at Progressive Education,* 1972 Yearbook, pp. 166–204. Washington, D.C.: Association for Supervision and Curriculum Development, 1972.

Truax, C. B., and Carkhuff, R. R. *Toward Effective Counseling and Psychotherapy: Training and Practice.* Chicago: Aldine, 1967.

9
Empathy: Essential Skill of Helping

The goal of helping is to aid clients in discovering new and more adequate ways of perceiving themselves and the world in which they live. How successfully helpers are able to use themselves as instruments for achieving that goal will be dependent upon how well they are able to place themselves in a client's shoes and perceive the world through their client's eyes.

Helper sensitivity is so important for the helping process that Carl Rogers named the quality of empathy first among his three "necessary and sufficient conditions" for effective helping relationships: empathy, congruence, and positive regard. The crucial character of sensitivity in the helping process has also been demonstrated in a whole series of research studies with helpers like counselors, teachers, and pastors. Such studies show that effective helpers are characteristically sensitive to the ways their helpees are seeing themselves and the world in the moment-to-moment encounters of helping. Ineffective helpers are more concerned with how things look to themselves than to their clients or students.

In an earlier chapter we observed that the dynamics of helping can only be understood in terms of the helper's goals and the helpee's perceptions. These perceptions are the primary data for understanding the helpee's world. Such data is equally important for the helper's own behavior. It provides feedback by which to judge the effects of the things helpers do or say in the process of helping. What a helper intended, after all, is irrelevant and immaterial if the client did not perceive it so. To monitor their own activities and provide the data for further decisions, helpers need accurate conceptions of the ways their clients are thinking, feeling, and perceiving themselves and their worlds.

DEVELOPING SENSITIVITY

Everyone, of course, has some measure of sensitivity to other people. Without this, no one could exist for very long in modern interdependent society. Some people develop high degrees of empathy as a normal part of their growing up. Others have to sharpen their capacities, either by accident or design, in the course of training or experience in the professions. Either way, the development of sensitivity is essential for effective use of the helper's self.

The development of sensitivity does not require learning a new skill. Most of us are already sensitive to those people important to us. Even little children are keenly aware of the feelings and attitudes of the adults who surround them and may be heard warning one another: "Watch out for Daddy! He's angry!" For little children sensitivity is a matter of survival. On the way from childhood to maturity, however, most of us discover that it is not necessary to be sensitive to everyone, only to those who have important roles with respect to us. So we continue to be sensitive to our sweethearts, bosses, supervisors, or those in positions to help us or harm us. Conversely, we may lose sensitivity for the feelings of those less important or subservient to us. Learning to be more sensitive is not a question of learning something new; it is a matter of learning to do explicitly and frequently what we naturally do implicitly and occasionally. It would seem that ought to be easy enough. All that is necessary is to decide what is really important and then go ahead and do it. Unfortunately, it is not that simple.

Believing Sensitivity Is Important

Obvious things are often the most difficult to perceive. We do not lack for data about people and their behavior. We live immersed in such data every hour of our experience. We need but open our eyes to see and our ears to hear, and other people will be willing and eager to impress upon us their personal interpretations of people and the world. We are surrounded by people clamoring to be heard, often desperately seeking to be understood. But what we see and what we hear is largely dependent upon what we believe is important.

It is possible to live in the midst of events and never know they exist until they are brought into figure by a change in need. One can drive past a house a hundred times and never really see it until it is necessary to call on someone who lives there. The teacher preoccupied with "getting the lesson across" may miss completely what her students are really comprehending. For many years one of the authors had passed through the Grand Concourse of Grand Central Station in New York City several times a day. Then, one evening at Christmas time, while standing in line for tickets he became aware of an English gentleman just in front of him, apparently newly arrived in the United States, who stood entranced, looking up at the ceiling and murmuring, "Incredible, simply incredible! Magnificent!" At this the author looked up, too, and discovered to his astonishment that indeed it was incredible. He had seen the beautiful ceiling for the very first time! Perception is a selective process. What is perceived depends upon the need of the observer. Unless it seems important to understand someone, it is practically certain he will not be understood. To develop sensitivity it is necessary to want to.

The way things seem to each individual has such a complete feeling of reality that one seldom questions it. Because our own experience seems so right and so real, it is difficult to understand the world of another without making an effort. It is even more difficult when another person's reality seems contrary to our own. Then we are faced with the distasteful possibility that we may be wrong. The development of sensitivity requires an understanding of this characteristic of our perceptions and a willingness to accept the reality of another's perceptions as real *for him.* For example, while visiting a ward in a mental hospital one day a patient tore open his shirt and rushed up to one of the authors. In obvious pain he exclaimed, "Doctor, there are fourteen devils on my chest! They are stabbing me with spears! See them?" Of course, the author did not see them, but it was clear the patient felt them. So, he replied, "No, Joe, I don't, but I can see that you feel them. I am sorry about that." Had the author scoffed at the devils the patient saw and felt, he would simply have demonstrated how little he understood. By being willing to accept the patient's reality as real for him the doors of communication were kept open and it was possible to maintain the rapport necessary for long hours of further discussion. It is not necessary to give up one's own reality to understand that of another. What is required is a willingness to recognize that someone else's ways of perceiving are equally real to him.

Reading Behavior Backward

Basically, developing sensitivity is a matter of learning to read behavior backwards. When we see a child drink, we can infer that he felt thirsty. When we see a player duck the ball thrown at him, we can infer he was afraid it was going to hit him. If a person's behavior is a function of perceptions, it follows that if we observe behavior carefully, it should be possible to reconstruct the feelings, attitudes, purposes, in the perceptual field of the behaver that produced the acts we observed.

"Getting the feel" of other people in this fashion is something that everyone does quite automatically in dealing with other people. The teacher, for example, observes a child who is not reading very well. As she watches him, she asks: "Now what is his trouble? How is he seeing what he is doing?" She formulates inferences as she makes her observations. "Does he understand the sound?" she wonders, and then tests this hypothesis by further observation of the child's behavior in reading various materials selected to test that hypothesis. As a result she may decide that he does hear the sound and makes a new hypothesis: "Perhaps he is not distinguishing between A and O, T and TH." Then she tests this hypothesis, perhaps through the use of diagnostic tests. By such a process of observation, inference, and test she arrives at an understanding of how things are with the child, and she may then be in a position to help him perceive more adequately in the future. Developing sensitivity for the professional worker is not a matter of learning to do something new, but of learning to do more effectively and efficiently what he now does accidentally, crudely, and occasionally.

Can Inference Be Scientific?

Some objective psychologists take exception to the use of inference as a technique for understanding behavior. They feel it is too subjective, too open to possibilities of error and distortion introduced by the person doing the observing. Their concern is certainly a valid one. The use of self as an instrument for making observations does, indeed, add a possible source of distortion not present in more mechanical ways of observing and recording behavior. This does not warrant rejection of the method, however, if the sources of error can be controlled.

All sciences are dependent upon the making and testing of hypotheses. To control the accuracy of this process, scientists have invented tests of validity to be applied to the testing of hypotheses as follows:

1. Feelings of subjective certainty. Does the hypothesis seem reasonable and accurate to the possessor?
2. Is the hypothesis consistent with all the known facts? Does it fit? Does it provide an adequate explanation of all the data?
3. Will it stand the test of mental juggling? Will it still ring true when confronted intellectually and subjected to the impact of other concepts, explanations, or suppositions?
4. Can it be used to predict? Using the hypothesis to make predictions, will these predictions be borne out in fact?
5. Is the hypothesis acceptable to other workers, especially recognized experts? Have other persons independently reached the same conclusions?
6. Is the hypothesis internally consistent? Does the hypothesis stand up when various interpretations are made to confront one another?

The products of all the sciences (including the physical ones that we customarily regard as the essence of accuracy and precision) are, in the final analysis, dependent upon one or more of these tests in establishing what is "fact." The tests listed above may be used to determine the acceptability of inferences about human behavior in the same fashion as the astronomer tests his inferences about a new galaxy or the physicist tests his inference about quantum theory. The making of inferences, in itself, is not unscientific. Every science, including the science of persons, depends upon inference to extend its horizons beyond the immediate and the palpable. To reject the use of inference would seriously hamper our attempts to understand people. Our problem is not to reject this valuable tool, but to learn to use it properly.

Learning to Listen

For most people real listening is a seldom used art. The purpose of much conversation is not to hear what the other person has to say, but to enjoy the opportunity to express one's self. Listening in on the conversation at a tea, cocktail party, or casual conversation on the street, quickly reveals that no one is really listening. The speakers are amusing themselves while the audience patiently, or not so patiently, waits to get the floor to tell about their operations or trips to San Francisco.

The kind of listening required for effective helping is much more than mere attention to words. It is an active search for meaning and calls for sharply focused attention and interest. Such "listening with the third ear" involves attending to all that the client, student, or patient is expressing, not just verbally but nonverbally as well, in gestures, movements, inflections, even to what is not specifically said. Carl Rogers has called the disciplined listening of helpers "non-evaluative listening." By this he means a reading of the whole person, an attempt to understand the nature of the helpee without the distortion of the helper's own judgments, preconceptions, or values.

People are always telling us how things are with them through the ways in which they behave. Psychologists have learned to use play, for example, both as a diagnostic device to explore how children are thinking and feeling, and for treatment in helping them change their perceptions of themselves and the world. One need not be a mind reader to get the message about how a child feels as one watches him lambast the "baby brother" doll or flush a drawing of the teacher down the toilet! The behavior of adults is especially revealing. Most of us soon know what to expect from friends, neighbors, bosses, or enemies as we have opportunities to observe them in action.

Philip Jackson, in an interview study with teachers, reports how teachers use fleeting behavioral cues to tell how well they are doing on their jobs. Here are a few excerpts from those interviews:

Interviewer: How can you tell when you are doing a good job:

Teacher: Oh, look at their faces.

Interviewer: Will you tell me more about that?

Teacher: Why, sure, they look alert; they look interested; they look questioning—like they're ready to question something. They look like they're anxious to learn more about it. . . At other times, you know you haven't done a good job when they look blah or look disinterested or I-don't-care attitude, well, then I feel bad, you know, I've done a bad job.

Another teacher says:

"The reaction, I think, of the children, and what they seem to have gained from it. Their interest; their expression; the way they look."

Still another says:

I can tell by the way they sound. There is a sound that you can tell and you can tell when they are really working.

Interviewer: You mean the sound of the room in general?

Teacher: The sound of the room in general. Now it doesn't always have to be a quiet sound—it can be a noisy, buzzing sound and you're still doing a good job and everybody is working.

Interviewer: But can you tell?

Teacher: I can tell. You can feel it.

And still another says:

It's the easiest thing in the world. You know you're missing at the first yawn. Teaching and learning, if they're not enjoyable and fun, are both very difficult to accomplish. When the kids aren't having a good time, if they're not paying attention and sitting up, that's it—a theatrical sense is something you can't learn, but a good actor can sense his audience. He knows when a performance is going well or not going well, simply by the feeling in the air. And it's that way in the classroom. You can feel when the kids are resistant.[1]

The Listening Game

One technique devised by counselors for teaching beginners to listen is called the Listening Game, which some readers might like to try. In a group session, all the participants agree that no one may speak until he or she has first stated the gist of what the previous speaker had to say, in a fashion satisfactory to the previous speaker. It is fascinating how the application of this rule slows down the conversation! Most people playing this game quickly discover that listening is, indeed, a difficult art,

---

1. From P. W. Jackson, *Life in Classrooms* (New York: Holt, Rinehart and Winston, 1968). Reprinted with permission of the author and publisher.

and they are chagrined to discover how little they normally hear of what is being expressed by those around them. The discipline of paying close attention and seeing through another's eyes can greatly improve the helper's capacity for empathy.

Attending to Meanings

Developing sensitivity is a matter of listening to *meanings* as well as observing behavior. Every behavior is in some measure expressive of perceptions, but behaviors resulting from very strong feelings are almost impossible to dissemble. The very attempts that others make to hide their feelings only serve to reveal them more. Like the comment by Hamlet's mother, "The lady doth protest too much, methinks," our suspicions are aroused by overdone behavior. A counseling client of one of the authors once said it this way: "Sometimes when I am talking to you I try to keep you from really knowing. I act like a mother bird defending her nest by pretending she has a broken wing to lead you away from what I don't want you to see. But you know; you always know."

Concentration of attention upon the person's meaning is characteristic of effective helpers in all branches of the helping professions. It is a widely used technique in counseling and psychotherapy, in social work, in pastoral counseling, and in the interactions of group leaders with members in a wide variety of group experiences. One can hear it used by the teacher who says, "Jimmy, I can see you are very angry at Paul. I can understand that, but you must not hit him with the shovel"; or the nurse who says to her patient, "I realize you are not sure you can do it, Mrs. Smith. I know it will not be easy for you." Some authors have also tried to make this kind of listening, so valuable to counselors and therapists, available to wider audiences of teachers, parents, and persons in various administrative or leadership roles in business and industry.[2] Some of these have also been accompanied by specialized training programs designed to teach parents, teachers, and others the techniques of listening to personal meanings.

Listening Is Therapeutic

The importance of listening extends far beyond its value for understanding other people. The act of listening, itself, conveys important messages to others. The careful listener is paying others the highest form of compliment. He is saying in effect, "You are a truly significant person to me and what you are saying is important." So, also, the teacher listening to a student may be conveying, "I really care about you and

2. See, for example, works by H. Ginot and T. Gordon listed in the bibliography.

what you think and believe." Such a message is an active, living demonstration, which may speak loudly and clearly to students, clients, and patients. In the case of unhappy or maladjusted persons with deep feelings of deprivation and alienation, being really listened to is much more than communication; it is a therapeutic experience in itself.

Growth may be facilitated by a sympathetic listener even if he does little else. In this sense every human being who ever listened patiently to the problems of another is as much a helper at that moment as those who claim impressive titles by reason of position or academic degrees. One of the authors knew a woman whose life experience clearly demonstrated the significant role of the sympathetic listener. Most people who interacted with her came away from the experience feeling much better and looking much brighter. And, almost without exception, they would say something like, "Oh, what a fine person she is! She's one of the most interesting people I have ever talked wtih. I could talk to her all day!" From these comments, one would think she must have been a very dynamic person. As a matter of fact, she was never responsible for more than 5 or 10 percent of the conversations she engaged in. She was actually very shy and retiring, albeit most sensitive and empathic.

Reading Programs

A reading program can be one valuable source for developing sensitivity. Anything that provides insight into the nature of people and their problems, hopes, and desires may contribute greatly to the development of sensitivity, either as general background for interpretation or, more directly, as participation in human experience. In this connection, one naturally thinks of professional and scientific literature about the social sciences; these materials are invaluable for persons working in the helping professions. Out of such reading helpers may acquire the setting or backdrop against which the understanding of a particular individual may be seen with greater clarity. A program of reading in the social sciences, however, is by no means enough for persons in the helping professions. Scientific material is usually objective and descriptive. It presents human beings as they are perceived by outside observers. Much of it is also couched in statistical or normative terms descriptive of populations rather than individuals. People engaged in the helping professions, therefore, must usually acquire subjective understanding from other sources or from their own experiences.

A fruitful source of subjective understanding of other people is to be found in nonscientific literature. It has often been said that our best psychologists are poets and novelists, and, in a very real sense, this is true. While scientists are highly skilled in providing understanding of people in normative terms, poets and novelists are far superior in helping us grasp the essential humanity of people. Drama, poetry, autobiography, and novels can expand our experience vicariously. We can enter the world of seeing and feeling, believing, hoping, trusting, caring, loving, and hating as these are experienced by other people. As we give ourselves up to the spell woven by these kinds of writers, we can be for a time what we are not, never have been, or perhaps never could be. With James Agee we can experience "A Death in the Family," even if we have never had one. With Malcolm X we can feel something of what it is like to be black and to grow up in the slums of a city. Through literature we can experience the frustrations and power of being a president, the growth of intelligence with Helen Keller, or the pitiful searching of Marilyn Monroe. The understanding, empathy, and capacity for a deep sympathetic identification with others, which the poet, dramatist, and novelist put down on paper are the very same qualities that persons in the helping professions must actively put to work in carrying out their respective functions.

Observing

A good deal of sensitivity can also be acquired by looking receptively. The choices people make are not haphazard. They have meaning. So, the kind of cars people drive, the sort of houses they build, the care they give their yards, the clothes they wear, or the pictures they paint all have something to say about them. What is observed when watching others also depends on the intent of the observer. What is seen is likely to be what one expects or is prepared to see. Idly watching, one may see almost nothing. If observation is to be used for increased sensitivity, it must be directed beyond surface manifestations to the nature of personal meaning behind the behavior observed.

Every science must begin its work from disciplined observation, and most training programs for the helping professions include extensive practice in observing. The approach to making observations advocated by these programs will depend upon the general frame of reference stressed by the trainers. Those operating from an objective orientation emphasize careful reporting of precisely what was done by the subject. Here, for example, is part of a report made by a young social worker:

Time: 3:30 P.M., January 4, 1968
Place: Third Avenue Playground.
When I arrived, Mr. Albert pointed out Jimmy Christianson to me. He is ten years old but seems small for his age. He was dressed in blue jeans, sneakers and an old brown zipper jacket with a big tear under the left arm. He was sitting on the bench along the first base line with four other boys waiting his turn to go to bat. Jimmy kept swinging his feet back and forth and gripping the bench with his two hands as he did so. He seemed pretty excited about the game and kept yelling, "Sock it to 'em, Eddie!

Attaboy!" to the boy up at the bat. Every once in a while he would turn and say something to one of his bench mates but I could not hear what it was he said. Once, when Eddie swung and missed, Jimmy groaned and hid his face in the back of the boy next to him. Then he picked up his first baseman's glove, pounded his fist in it and yelled, "That's O.K., Eddie! Let 'em have it!"

The purpose of such detailed reporting is to teach the beginner to make careful observations and to see precisely what is going on with a minimum of distortion. Observations made with such care and detail are usually more valuable for the discipline they demand of the learner than for improving the capacity for empathy, because they concentrate the observer's attention on behavior rather than the internal conditions producing behavior.

More often the helper will need to make observations from a subjective frame of reference. By operating in this way, helpers are less concerned about recording precise details and devote attention to those aspects of special significance in understanding the behavior of the subject from his or her own point of view. It involves steeping himself in the experience and making and remaking hyoptheses consistent with the behavior observed. In this fashion the helper seeks to understand the ways in which the subject sees self and the peculiar searching and strivings which motivate him. Here is a sample from the report of a beginning teacher:

When I arrived at Miss Anthony's class on Tuesday, the children were in the middle of a project running a store. Leslie was in a group of three who were supposed to be making a big sign for the store front. They had a large sheet of paper on the floor and were drawing on it with crayons. Like his behavior on the playground yesterday, Leslie was very bossy, continually telling the other two children what to do, how to do it and constantly criticizing them. He seems to need to be always the center of attention. It's as though, for him, imposing his will on the other children is far more important than the production they are working on. When the teacher came close at one point he ran to her and pulled her by the hand to come see their sign, but even as he did so, he managed to stand directly in front of the other two kids so they were pretty effectively blocked off from the teacher. From the look on his face you could see he was eating up every word of praise the teacher said like it was "manna from heaven." He seems to have a terrible need for attention at all times. Even the way he poises his body seems to be saying, "Please, please, please look at me! Give me! Pay attention to me!"

THE USE OF SELF IN EMPATHY

Properly used, one's own experience may be very helpful in understanding others; improperly used it may lead one badly astray. Scientists in all fields must calibrate their instruments to assure the most accurate possible measurements. They adjust their voltmeters to zero before reading the strength of the current, and carefully balance their scales before using them to weigh things. In similar fashion the human instrument can be calibrated to provide increasingly accurate inferences about what goes on in people. It is a matter of choosing a reliable instrument to start with and using it thereafter with care and discipline to assure trustworthy and reliable readings.

Using Experience as Data

The most obvious source of information for the making of inferences is our own experience. Each of us has been intimately involved in the growth and development of at least one person. This is important data and its proper use can add immeasurably to our understanding of others. Even the suffering we have endured can help us understand and sympathize with others who suffer. This effect, however, is not automatic. One can observe in the lives of friends and acquaintances how hardship, isolation, or tragedy have made some persons angry, hostile, and closed-off from other people while others seem to have become increasingly warm, gentle, and understanding as a consequence of what they have been through. What seems to make the difference is the individual's ability to accept or be open to his experience. Persons who have been deeply hurt often build walls around themselves for self-protection. Such walls serve to protect individuals from interaction with others but, unfortunately, also prevent getting through to them.

Intimate experiences, wherein one has an opportunity to communicate with others deeply and meaningfully, add much to the capacity of individuals to act sympathetically with others. These experiences provide the raw material from which understanding is built. Research evidence shows that persons who have not been loved are incapable of loving and acceptance of others is related to acceptance of self. Apparently one needs to have experienced a feeling to be able to truly grasp its meaning for another. This does not mean that it is necessary to have experienced the same event that another person did. That, of course, is impossible. What *can* be experienced are the meanings of events, feelings, attitudes, beliefs, or understandings. Since the authors of this book are males, they cannot experience childbirth. They can and have, however, experienced with their wives the joys, anxieties, fears, and fulfillment of childbirth, to say nothing of their common experience of the problems of parenthood.

It is probable that any peak experience in which an individual is living and participating "to the hilt" contributes something significant to his capacity to interact with life and with others. Having felt the glory of a sunset, one can know much better what it means to another. Having won, lost, loved, hated, and suffered disillusionment or triumphed over adversity; these qualities of living can make one more alive. Intimate experiences wherein one is able to communicate heart to heart with another, for no matter how short a period, extend and increase one's capacity for understanding.

Postponing Personal Need

Developing sensitivity requires willingness to postpone immediate need satisfactions in the interests of another. This is often difficult. Our own ways of perceiving and thinking have such a feeling of "goodness" or "rightness" and the tendency to impose our own structure on events is so strong that a conscious effort is required to set them aside even for a little while. An outstanding teacher of our acquaintance once illustrated this. The evening before class, she spent many hours working out a new project. The next day she waited for an appropriate moment to tell the class about the exciting project she had worked out for them. Everyone in the class was busy and interested in what they were doing, and for a long time she had no opportunity to break in. Finally, she started to tell them about the new project but no one paid any heed! After several attempts to capture their attention she said to them with some irritation, "I guess you just don't want to hear what I have arranged for you!" This brought no response from anyone. Everyone continued with the projects they were already engaged in except for one lad, who could always be counted on for some kind of comment. He replied, "Not today, Mrs. Smith." She told us some time later, "You know, I was really kind of hurt. I thought it was a wonderful idea and I had worked so hard getting it ready! Somehow, though, my good sense managed to prevail and I set my own idea aside for a later occasion." It often takes a real wrench to break loose from our own predilections to follow the thinking and needs of others.

Freud once observed that we seldom recognize a problem in others that we have not wrestled with ourselves. Psychiatrists and clinical psychologists, presumably well trained in making careful diagnoses, have been known to describe their clients as having the psychiatrist's or psychologist's own problems. The personal discipline required for the development of sensitivity is greatly facilitated by the possession of a deep conviction that "I, too, could be wrong." Nothing gets in the way of empathy more than the bland assumption of infallibility. It is helpful to understand that there is literally nothing a person (including one's self) might not do if exposed to the right combination of unhappy circumstances. Uncomfortable as it may be, belief in one's own fallibility makes the development of empathy with others much easier.

Sensitivity to others is a difficult skill to display in the absence of positive personal satisfactions. The capacity to set one's own needs aside in the interest of someone else is a quality of persons achieving some measure of self-actualization. Inadequate and threatened persons must be so continuously on guard against the world that there is little time or inclination remaining to be concerned about others. Only a free self can give of itself. An important prerequisite for the development of sensitivity, therefore, is the opportunity for fulfilling experiences in the life of the helper.

Selected Readings

Starred entries indicate appearance in whole or in part in Donald L. Avila, Arthur W. Combs, and William W. Purkey, *The Helping Relationship Sourcebook*, Boston: Allyn and Bacon, 1977.

*Aspy, D. N. "How Did He Get There?" *Peabody Journal of Education* 47, 1969, pp. 152–153.

Glasser, W. *Schools Without Failure*. New York: Harper & Row Publishers, 1968.

Jackson, P. W. *Life in Classrooms*. New York: Holt, Rinehart and Winston, 1968.

Moustakas, C. E. *The Authentic Teacher: Sensitivity Awareness in the Classroom*. Cambridge, Massachusetts: Howard A. Doyle Publishing Co., 1966.

McNeil, E. B. *Being Human: The Psychological Experience*. New York: Harper & Row Publishers, 1973.

O'Banion, T., and O'Connell, A. *The Shared Journey: An Introduction to Encounter*. Englewood Cliffs, New Jersey: Prentice-Hall, 1970.

*Richards, F. "Counselor Training: Educating for the Beautiful and Noble Person." *Colorado Journal of Educational Research* 12, 1972, pp. 11–16.

Rogers, C. *Carl Rogers on Encounter Groups*. New York: Harper & Row Publishers, 1970.

Stevens, J. O. *Awareness: Exploring, Experimenting, Experiencing*. Lafayette, California: Real People Press, 1971.

10

The Helping-Learning Atmosphere

To bring about change in personal meanings, workers in the helping professions need to be skilled in creating the kinds of atmospheres that will make self-involvement likely. Generally speaking, this calls for conditions in which a person feels: (a) it is safe to try, (b) assured that he can deal with events, (c) encouraged to make the attempt, and (d) more fulfilled for having done so. The relationship helpers create must be seen by clients as promising fulfillment on one hand and safe enough to risk encounter on the other.

THE SPECIAL NATURE OF THE
HELPING ATMOSPHERE

Helping relationships are special ones. Most ordinary life experiences are dialogues in which all parties seek personal enhancement. In the helping relationship, one party resolves to set aside personal needs temporarily to help another. For many persons seeking help, the helping relationship is an entirely new experience and often begins with students or clients spending considerable time exploring the atmosphere of the helping-learning encounter. The techniques helpers use to help clients and students discover what the encounter is like and how to use it most effectively is sometimes called "structuring the relationship."

Establishing atmospheres to aid clients and students work out new and more satisfying relationships often requires temporarily protecting people or sheltering them from the accustomed pressures of the world they live in. Social expectancies may be short-circuited and the usual consequences of a person's acts may be temporarily set aside. So children may be able to express hatred of a teacher without being told they "mustn't feel that way" or that they are "naughty." The anger of a worker toward a foreman can be safely expressed without fear of reprisal. The helping relationship thus provides a safe haven in which the helpee is temporarily excused for errors. Hindrances to communication may also be systematically eliminated or reduced so that free expression becomes possible in a manner rarely experienced in daily life.

TWO GENERAL APPROACHES TO THE HELPING ATMOSPHERE

A great many models for effective leadership have been explored by psychologists, educators, sociologists, and persons interested in management and personnel over the past forty years.

One of the earliest, a study by Lewin, Lippitt, and White in 1939, examined the behavior of boys in clubs, under authoritarian, laissez-faire and democratic leadership. They found that boys in democratic groups carried on their organization and sustained their levels of productivity when leaders were absent, but boys in the other groups did not. From this and other observations the authors concluded that democratic approaches to leadership were generally superior. Many additional studies have been carried on since then comparing leadership styles described as autocratic-democratic, authoritarian-nonauthoritarian, task-oriented–human relations-oriented, supervisory-participatory, directive-nondirective, freeing-controlling, and status-emergent to name but a few. Results of these studies are by no means clear. Apparently, any of these approaches to leadership produces positive results, depending upon the outcomes desired and the circumstances in which they are used.

The leadership styles listed above are, in general, expressions of the closed and open systems of thinking already discussed in Chapter 7. Helpers may consciously or unconciously choose an objective, structured, authoritarian frame of reference or a client-centered, existential, democratic one. Of course, these choices rarely appear in practice as pure cases. Helpers are hardly ever entirely authoritarian or entirely democratic; rather these categories represent ends of a continuum along which practices can be observed to lean more or less one way or another. Nevertheless, the atmospheres helpers create will surely be affected by helpers' leadership choices and helpers' need to be aware of the full implications of the frames of reference they select.

THE HELPER'S IMPACT ON THE ATMOSPHERE FOR HELPING

The helper is not a passive object in helping relationships. There can be no relationship with a nonentity. Helpers have to *be* somebody. The helper's actions give direction to the helping process. The choices they make in responding to students or clients communicate messages about the relationship. The teacher who ignores a child's behavior is not inert. She is teaching the child something about himself and his place in the class. From being ignored, he may learn patience, the "right" way to behave, that his teacher doesn't like him, or a hundred other lessons. The message communicated by a teacher's behavior is real to the child and helps establish the nature of the dialogue whether the teacher wishes it so or not.

Whatever helpers do or do not do inevitably affects the relationships they establish. Some of the effects are direct, straightforward outcomes and are exactly what the helper intended. Others are concomitant effects occurring in more or less subtle ways and are the consequences of the student-client's personal interpretation of what is going on. Such side effects cannot be ignored. They must be clearly perceived and taken into account. Since side effects can never be eliminated, they should be understood and can be used to advantage if helpers are keenly enough aware of their existence.

To develop awareness of potential side effects helpers may find it useful to ask themselves three basic questions.

1. *Are the objectives in this relationship the important ones?* Not all objectives are equally important. It is easy to be seduced by quick, easy, or dramatic results, which provide illusions of growth without making a significant impact upon the helpee. An example of this may be seen in the teacher's acceptance of easily measured achievements in basic skills as evidence of learning while overlooking important educational objectives like creativity, responsibility, concern for other people, problem-solving ability, and intelligent behavior.

2. *What is the effect of the helper's choices on the helper?* Whatever the helper's purposes, their expression in practice inevitably affects the ways helpers are perceived by those they are seeking to assist. Even when the helper's purposes are simple and clear in his own eyes, they may be perceived quite differently by students and clients. For example, while working with a deeply rejected client, one of the authors was annoyed by someone repeatedly knocking on his office door despite the "Do Not Disturb" sign hanging there. When the knocking continued, he excused himself for a moment, went to the door, and angrily asked the person there to observe and honor the sign on the door. Returning to his chair he found his client halfway to the door. "What's the trouble?" he asked. "I guess you are too busy to see me today," said the client. "Not at all, not at all," said the author, and he found it necessary to spend the next five minutes reassuring his client that this was her time and hers alone. Helpers cannot escape creating expectancies in the eyes of those they seek to help. They can,

The Helping-Learning Atmosphere 145

however, be aware of their impact, and so be in better position to correct inhibiting impressions and reinforce more positive ones.

3. *What is the effect of the helper's purpose on the helpee?* Nowhere is sensitivity more important than in providing continuous clues for helpers about the dynamics of the relationships they are engaged in. Checking the outcomes of helping from the point of view of students or clients is not simply a device for measuring final outcomes. It is a process continuously employed by effective helpers in every phase of the relationship.

The Helper as Model

Persons in the helping professions expect to exert their influence as significant others in the lives of those they work with. The more significant they become, the greater the degree to which they will be regarded as models by their students and clients. This will occur whether the helper wants to be placed in that position or not.

Helpers cannot escape being models. Since their actions indicate who they are and what they believe more clearly than speech, what they say will often not be heard. The helper who advocates doing something he is unwilling to do himself will not be very convincing. This is not to suggest that helpers must be paragons of virtue—only that one of the best ways to convince other people that a certain behavior is worthwhile is to see it manifest in the helper's own behavior.

Helper Authenticity

A good deal of discussion goes on among persons in the helping professions concerning the proper role of the counselor, teacher, administrator, social worker, or nurse. Examining the functions of the professional helper in that light, however, is not likely to be very helpful. The term *role* ordinarily refers to some form of acting, so we speak of "playing a role." This focuses attention on the wrong question. It is possible, of course, for teachers, counselors, or social workers to act a part in the relationship they have with their clients and students. But such relationships can seldom be maintained for very long, for people behave according to their perceptions—and the moment a person's guard is down, fundamental beliefs become apparent to others in spite of one's self.

A person with a position is always likely to reveal a stronger posture than a person without. Even a negative conviction, if it is clear and unambiguous, may be easier for a student or client to relate to than a vacillating stance. This is one of the reasons for rejecting eclecticism as a workable philosophy for helpers. Choosing methods or techniques from widely divergent sources may be highly effective, providing they are tied together by an internally consistent theoretical or philosophical position. An eclectic approach in which a helper is trying things simply "because they might work" will likely be a disaster.

The helper with a consistent system of beliefs can disclose himself and maintain the client's confidence; the helper without such a system dares not disclose himself lest the client discover the disordered state of the helper's thinking. Authentic helpers are more visible, and the impressions they convey are likely to be those of confidence, assurance, and strength. Without authenticity the helper is likely to create an impression of doubt, hesitation, dishonesty, and a sneaking suspicion in the minds of clients that he really is a fraud. With authenticity, many things become easy; without it, helpers create unnecessary barriers for themselves and those they seek to help. Helpers willing to be open and honest about themselves have a tremendous advantage. They can forget themselves and so give themselves much more freely to the task at hand. Interactions tend to be straightforward, uncomplicated, and hence, more appropriate.

Making Self Visible

The kind of communication required for most helping relationships calls for openness in the helper, a willingness to level with students or clients. Carl Rogers includes the quality of genuineness in the counselor as one of the basic requirements for successful counseling, along with congruence, empathy, and unconditional positive regard. Aspy, Carkhuff, Truax, and others have tested these hypotheses with counselors and teachers and they find these are, indeed, qualities of effective helpers. Sidney Jourard, in a series of researches, demonstrated the importance of self-disclosure for helping relationships in several professional groups. Further confirmation is found in studies reporting good helpers to be "self-revealing" while poor ones were "self-concealing."

There is good reason why this quality of sharing self is important for effective helping relationships. To interact effectively with a helper, the helpee needs to know what to expect in order to select his own behavior safely. This requires feedback that has the feel of solidity. Psychologists sometimes call this "making one's self visible." Without this quality, the atmosphere for helping becomes confused and frustrating.

This can be observed in the "control panic" unhappily experienced by some beginning teachers. When assigned to an unusually lively or difficult class, first efforts at capturing attention meet with little success. To meet this problem the teacher searches for "methods to handle them." If these methods are authentic, the class may quiet down. If they are not, the class senses this and begins to explore the teacher's limits. This launches a spiral of trying and testing, which rises higher and higher as the teacher desperately tries to control the class using methods in which he really has no confidence or skill; the students, made more and more uncertain by lack of consistent structure, search ever more wildly to discover the limits. If long continued, this state of confusion may end with the students in control and the teacher reduced to a state of utter helplessness. Many a beginning teacher suffers through this nightmare, brought on by a "gimmick approach," and some become so demoralized that they leave the profession forever.

The methods helpers use must fit them so that they use them smoothly and naturally. Preoccupation with techniques is certain to make them seem contrived. When learning to dance, one watches his feet and falls all over them. When he learns to relax and follow the music, dancing improves and becomes a pleasurable experience for both dancer and partner. So it is with methods. Authenticity frees the helper to devote full attention to the problems at hand. His behavior can be smoothly congruent, *en rapport* with students, clients, and the world.

HELPING BEGINS WITH ACCEPTANCE

A major requirement for the creation of atmospheres for change is acceptance. Growth cannot proceed from where people are not; it can only begin from where people are. Accordingly, the atmosphere for helping must start from a base that accepts the person as he is. Acceptance, as we are using the term here, does not mean approval or disapproval. Acceptance has to do with confrontation, one's willingness to face the world the way it is. Students, clients, or patients are accepted just as they are in the helping relationship.

The experience of being accepted reduces the feeling of threat and so makes possible more open approaches to examining self and the world. The counselor, for example, accepts unjudgmentally his client's expression of hatred for his brother, and thus makes it possible for his client to look at his feelings. A teacher may accept the error of the student without judgment as simply a matter of fact. This makes it possible for student and teacher to find a better solution. The pastor, too, accepts the sin of his parishioner as understandable and so makes it possible to talk about and find more effective ways of behaving. In the following report a nurse describes the value of acceptance for one of her patients.

> While making the rounds of my floor, I saw a woman patient start to cry. Her face just crumpled in spite of what seemed to be great efforts to maintain composure. I went into her room and stood by the bed; her eyes were closed with tears running from under the lids. She seemed to sense my presence for she took my hand and held on to it with a very tight grip. I waited, for I didn't wish to pry, yet felt that this was not a casual thing

148   **Helping Processes**

which was occurring. For several minutes I stood there while she cried silently. After a time, she told me why she was crying. She had had surgery three days previously; her physician had just told her that she had inoperable carcinoma. She had been given the hope that a relatively new antimetabolite might offer relief, longer life, and, she hoped, a cure. Her choice was to accept the risks inherent in the treatment or to refuse. She was also trying to decide what to tell her husband and son. There was nothing I could offer her except myself as a person to listen; her decision had to be hers. I stood and listened while she cried and talked.

The knowledge I had about the course of her illness, the new treatment, the support she would need from her family, physician, other people, none of this was what she needed. The need at this moment was for a fellow human to listen to her. I felt that I was such a person, one who could listen. Her world had turned inside out and upside down. She was the very attractive wife of a successful businessman, the mother of a handsome son, an interesting, vital, well-educated woman who was having to accept the fact that she was facing invalidism, prolonged illness, and death. She said that she was not a woman who cried easily, yet she seemed to accept a nurse as a person with whom she could cry; by some very great effort she regained her composure before her son and husband came to visit her.

For many persons the very experience of being accepted is, in itself, a most important release from the negative effects of threat.

Since the way things seem to each of us has such a feeling of reality, it is easy to reject the reality of others and demonstrate a lack of acceptance in relationships. Helpers have been known, for example, to reject the surly, unmannerly delinquent upon first contact. He has grown up in a world that largely rejects him and comes in with a chip on his shoulder. In his world toughness and defiance are the means to prestige and status, so he slouches in his chair and snarls his replies to questions. Such behavior can be infuriating to the helper who does not understand his business, and it seems "only natural" to lash out and demand that the subject "Behave yourself! Be polite! Sit up and pay attention!" From the point of view of the delinquent, such behaviors are not only undesirable, but being polite in the world he lives in could ruin him! Even from the helper's own point of view such demands do not make much sense. We hope for courteous and respectful behavior from the subject *when he gets better*. To demand such behavior of him now is like a doctor saying to the patient; "Go away and get better. Then come back and I'll help you!"

To begin the helping process with a denial of the facts of the situation is hardly likely to create an atmosphere for facilitating change and growth. Nevertheless, with the best of intentions many helpers fail to be effective by closing the doors to consideration of events at the beginning of a conference. A child who expresses a shocking or naughty attitude may be told, "Why, Jimmy, you mustn't feel that way!" Thus his feelings, the very things he must explore to get over his difficulty, are barred from examination. Before one can examine feelings one must be allowed to have them. The experience of being accepted provides the atmosphere in which exploration of self and the world can take place.

CHALLENGE AND THREAT IN THE
ATMOSPHERE FOR CHANGE

To a large extent, creating the proper atmosphere for learning involves dealing with challenge and threat. As we have observed in an earlier chapter, people feel challenged when confronted with problems that interest them and seem to lie within their capacities. People feel threatened when confronted with problems they do not feel able to deal with. Producing the kind of atmosphere usually needed for the helping process requires the creation of challenge and the avoidance of threat.

Behavior can of course be changed by threat. People do learn from such experiences. As we have seen, however, the effect of threat is to narrow perceptions to the threatening object. What is learned, therefore, is likely to be both of highly specific and negative character—one learns what *not* to do. Thus, a spanking may teach a child not to cross a street, and a fine may teach a grownup not to speed (at least, not when there are police officers in sight). When the goal is simple and clearly defined, threat can result in learning. It is a technique used to control others by persons in authority for thousands of years. Because a device sometimes works, however, is no good reason to adopt it as a general principle for continuing action. Helpers' tools must be used with precision and must be applied to the problems for which they are uniquely appropriate. This is especially true in the use of threat, for its side effects extend far beyond what is directly observable. To operate without awareness of these side effects may destroy with one hand what is so carefully built with the other.

Most clients achieve health from the attainment of positive goals rather than negative ones, from seeking or obtaining rather than avoiding. The specificity of goals required for the use of threat is seldom appropriate for the helping professions. The learning of subject matter, solving of personal problems, or achievement of maximum self-actualization can rarely be defined in precise terms. Goals like these require openness to experience and freedom to depart from specifics. The purpose of the helping professions is to expand, to open up, to encourage exploration and discovery. These ends can rarely be achieved by experiences of threat. To get a mouse out of a mousehole one does not poke at it with a broomstick. One must entice it out by making things more desirable outside the hole than in. Just so, a person's self must be encouraged towards expression. It cannot be heedlessly placed in jeopardy. The self can only be committed when there is some likelihood that "coming out of the hole" will result in a measure of fulfillment and the self will not be damaged in the process.

Even where the specific and negative aspects of threat can be overcome, its use in the helping professions would still be limited for another reason: the destructive effect of the use of threat on the helping relationship itself. Most of us do not take kindly to people who threaten us. Threatening people are regarded with suspicion, and what they have to say is generally heard with reservations if, indeed, it is heard at all. Most people respond to threat by resistance, suppression, negativism, or rationalization—responses unlikely to enhance the relationships between helper and helpee. Helping relationships are dependent upon establishing rapport between helper and client. Whatever destroys this capacity for dialogue interferes with the process.

In Chapter 3 we described two effects of the experience of threat; narrowing of perception and defense of self. Both of these are directly contrary to the primary goals of helping—to produce some change in personal meaning. For this reason, workers in the helping professions generally seek to create nonthreatening atmospheres for helping-learning processes and advocate such conditions as warmth, understanding, acceptance, congruence, support, and freedom.

REMOVING BARRIERS TO
INVOLVEMENT

The creation of a freeing atmosphere is partly a matter of the client's finding promise of satisfaction. It is also a matter of eliminating as nearly as possible the blocks that lie in the path of the client's innate move toward health. This is accomplished by awareness of the nature of such barriers and a systematic attempt to find ways of removing them. The following anecdote illustrates how this was first learned by one of the authors.

During the Great Depression of the thirties, one of the authors was employed as school psychologist in a large high school in a northern city. He was also faculty adviser for the Hi-Y, a service club for boys. The school had a regulation that any money obtained from students by a service club during the year had to be returned to the students in some form before the end of the year. One year the club came to the end of the year with thirty-five dollars in the treasury. What to do with it? The club held a meeting to decide.

Somebody suggested giving a party for the school. Another said, "Well, it ought to be for everybody." The adviser said, "Let's see if we can figure out a way of getting everybody into the act." Someone else suggested, "Well, we could have a dance. But if we do have a dance, the people who can't dance won't come. Then another person said, "Well, maybe we could have a dance that everybody will come to." That was a novel idea and the question immediately arose as to what kind of dance it could be. Somebody came up with the idea, "Let's have a square dance, and we'll teach them when they get there." Since this was a large city high school and nobody knew how to square dance, so far as anyone knew, this met the criterion.

Then somebody said, "Even if we have a square dance, some people won't come because they don't have the right clothes." The reply: "Well, this is a country dance; we won't let anyone in who looks too sharp!" And that was adopted as policy. Somebody else pointed out, "Well, they won't come if they aren't able to get a date," and somebody else countered, "We could make it stag. We could let the boys in one door and let the girls in the other on opposite sides of the gym, and nobody would know who had a date."

Then somebody suggested, "Some people won't come because they won't have enough money and after the dance was over they would want to buy something to eat for the girl they were with." So it was decided, "Let's feed them at the dance." A committee was set up to enlist the aid of mothers in baking cakes and another to make a deal with a soft drink distributor. After all this, someone said, "We've still got a problem: Some won't come because they can't afford it." After much figuring on the cost of the band and an estimate of how many people would come, the price of the dance was finally set at eight cents.

Many people had doubts whether such a program would succeed and said, "It will never work!" When the night of the dance finally came, the largest crowd turned out that had ever been in the gymnasium. In fact, so many came that nobody could dance!

A similar technique can be applied to any helping relationship by systematically searching for the barriers to commitment and eliminating them. They may be attitudinal, physical, inherent in the structure of the relationship, and in rules, regulations, or administrative machinery. They may even be found in the helper himself. The authors have successfully applied the method to the practice of counseling, psychotherapy, teacher education, group process, and consulting relationships of many varieties. Not all blocks are easily removed, of course, and some may have to be lived with. The device has value, however, for focusing on the critical blocks to the helping process and helping create more effective atmospheres. A search for barriers in any of our helping institutions will, almost certainly, reveal an extraordinary number of hindering concepts or practices. Some of these are expressions of myths, generally held ideas about people or events that are not really true.[1] Others are practices established to solve problems that have changed or no longer exist. Still others seem to exist for no very clear reasons at all. The following are a few common barriers, which often impede the helping atmosphere.

The Dependence Barrier

The goal of helping is the production of free and intelligent persons able to operate by themselves as free and autonomous agents. Whatever increases dependence and interferes with independent self-direction, therefore, obstructs the helping encounter. Instead of strengthening the self, dependence requires surrender. Too great a dependence on the helper gets in the way of the free atmosphere desired for effective helping.

Persons who need help are often willing, even anxious, to let someone else solve their dilemmas, and helpers with the best of intentions can easily be seduced into developing dependent relationships. Our own perceptions feel so right, and our perceptions of situations often seem so uncomplicated, that we come to believe that, surely, they must be similarly appropriate for others. It seems much quicker to tell others the obvious answers, and we may feel we are being cruel and heartless to permit them to flounder about in search of solutions. So, without malice, but rather with generosity and good-will, the helper may tell those he would like to help the answers to their problems, and in so doing, create dependence and destroy self-direction in the people he seeks to help. Persons skilled in the helping professions have generally learned to avoid "telling" and "advising," not only because their advice may be wrong, but because the advising itself may create dependence and interfere with the processes of self-propulsion.

Preoccupation with the Past

A further interference with the free atmosphere required for effective helping is often found in the preoccupation of helpers with the past. If learning is conceived as the acquisition of right answers, then persons in need of help should be provided with these as quickly as possible. Furthermore, where better to find the right answers than in the past experience of other people? Thinking this way about learning inevitably leads the helper to a preoccupation with the information aspects of

1. For a more extensive discussion of myths as they apply to education, see A. W. Combs, *Myths in Education: Beliefs that Hinder Progress and Their Alternatives* (Boston: Allyn and Bacon, in press).

learning and to heavy reliance upon history or the solutions others have found for their problems. This procedure usually fails for at least three reasons: First, one's own problems always seem unique; secondly, the answers others have found rarely fit our own problems because the circumstances we confront are different or times have changed; thirdly, even if the answers others have found are appropriate, they are likely to seem so only after completion of one's own explorations. The "fit" of answers is discovered in the process of exploring problems. Too much preoccupation with past information or the experience of others may have the effect of turning off the helping process.

Restricting Effects of Evaluative Processes

Many barriers to exploration masquerade as aids to learning. Devices established ostensibly to motivate people turn out, instead, to get in the way of learning. Perhaps the worst offender is overemphasis on evaluation. Educators, for example, begin with the assumption that people need to know where they stand. Surely, no one could take much issue with that! They also believe that people need to be motivated to do their very best. Accordingly, a grading system is introduced to perform two excellent functions: to let people know where they stand and provide a system of rewards and punishments to spur them on. The theory sounds unassailable, but all too often it fails in practice. In the first place, it frequently evaluates people who neither want nor need it—at least, not in the terms provided. For some, grades become the goal of learning; worse still, students sometimes give up their own goals for the meaningless symbols of grades. For others, grades appear irrelevant, a waste of time, to be met with a minimum of involvement. Thus, the grading system, which sets out to bring about involvement in exploration, often ends by diverting, restricting, narrowing, or even shutting off completely the very events it was designed to encourage.[2]

Evaluation is more a convenience for the helper than a procedure of value to the helpee. This is especially true of evaluative techniques that compare the helpee's performance with the performance of others. Generally speaking, informal evaluations, which help the student or client assess where he is and what he needs to do next are likely to be far superior to formalized, standardized assessment devices. The procedures finally used must be adopted with full understanding of the probable

2. An analysis of grades and grading practices in our public schools may be found in H. Kirschenbaum, R. W. Napier, and S. B. Simon, *Wad Ja Get? The Grading Game in American Education* (New York: Hart Publishing Co., 1971) and S. B. Simon, and J. A. Bellanca, *Degrading the Grading Myths: A Primer of Alternatives and Marks* (Washington, D.C.: Association for Supervision and Curriculum Development, 1976).

meanings they convey to the helpee. It is no accident that psychotherapists generally avoid making evaluations and judgments in counseling practice. This is because they have discovered from long experience that evaluating tends to destroy rapport, creates resistance, and generally interferes with the free atmosphere so essential for encouraging discovery of personal meaning.

Fear of Making Mistakes

One of the most certain destroyers of the atmosphere for exploration and discovery is the fear of making mistakes. This fear is often held both by helpers and those they seek to assist. Many helpers, acting out of kindness, try to keep their students, clients, or patients from making mistakes. With the best of intentions, they point out the horrible pitfalls along the way, or seek to protect the client from them. Sometimes they may even punish helpees to make certain they do not fall into error. Unfortunately, a rejection of mistake-making can often destroy the very things that both helper and helpee are seeking. The atmosphere for helping must encourage looking. A fear of mistakes has the opposite effect; it discourages searching and exploration, no matter what the intentions of the helper. People who are afraid to make mistakes are afraid to try. And, when people are afraid to try, the sources of creativity and innovation are dried up.

Protecting people from error can often cut them off from important learning experiences. For example, a consultant arrived at a school shortly after the election of a new student body president. He found the administrators and teachers in a high state of indignation, because the students had just elected a youngster who vigorously campaigned for office on a platform he obviously could not deliver. He promised his constituents such things as no detention halls, every Friday afternoon off, free dances every week, and a dozen other equally unlikely benefits. The faculty was so incensed by the young man's election that they were seriously considering invalidating the election. They asked the consultant if he did not feel that this action should be taken. He disagreed and pointed out to the faculty that, with the best of intentions, they were about to rob the students of a valuable lesson in practical democracy. How else can one learn the value of a vote? What better way to learn the importance of a careful choice of leadership than having to live for a while with a bad one you elected yourself? Counselors and social workers call this "confrontation with reality." They recognize its value. Instead of overly protecting their clients from making mistakes, they seek instead to help them explore and discover the meanings to be gained from such experiences.

LIMITS IN HELPING RELATIONSHIPS

Every life situation has limits. This holds for helping relationships as well. People need limits; few of us could live without them. Knowing the boundaries of a situation provides a feeling of security and so has the effect of creating freedom. The traffic light on the corner limits freedom in one sense, but its existence makes it possible for people to go where they desire in safety. The amount of freedom we have is often determined by our willingness to give up some degree of autonomy in one area for the greater good of increased freedom in another.

We live surrounded by limits of many kinds and become so used to them that the first thing most people do on entering a new situation is to begin testing the limits. Students do this the first day of class when they ask the teacher: "How many books shall I read?" "Do you want the papers in on Tuesday?" "How long do I have to get ready for my presentation?" They also ask each other: "Do you think she means it?" "What kind of guy is he?" People cannot deal constructively with events until they establish boundaries.

The establishment of clear limits is particularly important for children, because a large part of their growth is accomplished by pushing against them. In this way they find out what they can and cannot do. Substitute teachers know how avidly children pursue the search to discover what this new person is like, what he will stand for and what he will not, whether he means what he says, knows whereof he speaks, and the like.

Freedom and License

Laymen often mistakenly believe that "experts" in human behavior advocate that helping relationships should be completely free of limits. Many parents and educators labor under this misconception, probably because of confusion over the term *permissive* and the advice of child-care specialists to involve children in self-directed activity. The helper's concern to create freeing atmospheres has often been translated by parents and citizens as "letting people do as they please." In part, such concern arises from age-old beliefs in the untrustworthy nature of the human organism and the personal experience of most people with authoritarian ways of dealing with others, which is so characteristic of much of our culture.

Freedom, for the professional helper, is not license to "do whatever one pleases." To helpers freedom means creating conditions designed to free clientele to confront significant problems effectively and efficiently. That is no laissez-faire abrogation of responsibility. It is a purposeful, meaningful design for helping, supported by fundamental theory and successful practice. Likewise, "permissive" for the professional helper does not mean "no control," as laymen often fear; it means permitting clients and students to explore what is personally relevant, to play a major role in the process of their own growth. So far as we are aware, no professional person has ever advocated rearing children, or conducting helping relationships without limits. No human being could exist very long without them. The important question is not *whether* limits but *what* limits, and the answer must be decided in terms of their effects on the persons they are applied to.

Effective helping relationships need limits, and the sooner they are understood the sooner both helper and helpees can proceed toward more creative and fruitful endeavors. Sometimes this may be accomplished by stating limits outright at the beginning of a relationship. Most helpers, however, have learned by sad experience that this seldom works very well. In the opening sessions of a helping relationship statements about limits will frequently not be heard. People are often confused and a little suspicious and therefore often fail to hear what is said. Furthermore, they are likely to be trying to see if what the helper says matches what he does, and so may miss many of the words being spoken.

Generally speaking, the establishment of limits is best governed by the behavior of the helper. Most persons learn, beginning in early childhood, the superiority of action over words for understanding what people are really about, so they learn most effectively about the structure of helping relationships primarily from their own experience of them. Even so, they may need to re-explore limits now and then, if only to assure themselves they have not changed. Where young children are concerned, it may even be necessary to provide continuous reminders of what the limits are as long as the relationship exists.

Stability of Limits

It is important that the limits of helping relationships be stable. If limits keep shifting, people do not know how to respond. They become upset and begin to mistrust the helper. One of the authors recalls overhearing three little boys discussing their next year's teacher at the end of the term. One of them asked another, "Who you got next year?" "I got Miss Johnson," he replied. "Oh, I feel sorry for you. She's terrible!" Then he went on in great detail about how bad Miss Johnson was. The third child finally ended the conversation saying, "Yeah, she's bad. So okay! You'll get used to her!" This is true. People can adjust to almost anything if it stands still. It's the ambiguity and the contradictions that drive people wild and keep them constantly re-examining the limits.

Helpers are often admonished to be consistent and this is often interpreted as a demand to behave in the same fashion. Helpers should, indeed, be consistent, but the consistency required is of the helper's belief system, not his behavior. Behavior, as we have seen, is only the external expression of personal meanings or beliefs. A given belief may produce many kinds of behavior, or different beliefs may result in similar behavior depending upon the persons and circumstances involved. The limits established by the clinician for the sick child and the healthy one, for example, will necessarily be quite different though the basic intent of the clinician may be the same with both children.

The helper who seeks consistency by concentrating on behavior will only succeed in becoming rigid and inflexible. Truly consistent helpers are those who have acquired internally consistent understanding about themselves, other people, the goals and purposes of helping, and the techniques or methods appropriate for the particular tasks they confront. The development of such congruent frames of reference takes time, experience, and continuous exploration of the helper's own personal meanings.

Selected Readings

Brophy, J. E., and Good, T. L. *Teacher-Student Relationships: Causes and Consequences.* New York: Holt, Rinehart and Winston, 1974.

Combs, A. W. "The Personal Approach to Good Teaching." *Educational Leadership* 21, 1964, pp. 369–378.

Glasser, W. *Reality Therapy: A New Approach to Psychiatry.* New York: Harper & Row Publishers, 1965.

Makarenko, A. S. *The Collective Family: A Handbook for Russian Parents.* Garden City, N.Y.: Doubleday, 1967.

Rogers, C. R. *On Becoming a Person: A Therapist's View of Psychotherapy.* Boston: Houghton-Mifflin, 1961.

Schmuck, R. A., and Schmuck, P. A. *Group Processes in the Classroom.* Dubuque, Iowa: Wm. C. Brown, 1971.

Schutz, W. C. *Joy: Expanding Human Awareness.* New York: Grove Press, 1967.

Webster, S. W. *Discipline in the Classroom.* San Francisco: Chandler, 1968.

11
Providing Experience and Information

Learning always has two aspects: exposure to new experience and the discovery of its meaning. The new experience may occur as a consequence of the interaction of a person with some aspect of the physical world. Of far more importance to most of us, however, are those experiences that occur as a result of trying to communicate with other people. While everyone engages in these attempts with varying degrees of success, the processes of communication are especially important for the helping professions. They are the primary tools of the trade. What happens in the interactions of teacher and pupil, counselor and client, priest and parishioner, supervisor and worker will largely depend on the communication skills of the helper.

COMMUNICATION: A FUNCTION OF COMMON MEANINGS

Communication is much more than a matter of words. The development of language is a great human accomplishment and facilitates more effective communication of meanings. But even as we admire this accomplishment, we must keep in mind that words are no more than symbols. In themselves, without their underlying meanings, they lack the impact to produce the changes in meanings necessary for modifications in behavior. We are all familiar with the fact that the behavior of many of our friends and acquaintances is often vastly different from the words they speak. Many a teacher has been dismayed at the glibness with which students are able to say the "right" things even while they behave as though they had never heard of them.

Communication is a function of common meanings, the overlapping of the perceptual fields of the communicator and the person who receives the communication. It is a matter of acquiring common "maps," so that the meaning existing for one person may exist for others as well. Successful communication depends only in part on what is said or happening outside the individual. More importantly, comprehension is determined by what goes on inside persons, in the peculiar world of meaning that makes up their perceptual fields.

When meanings overlap we have the feeling of understanding or of being understood. When meanings fail to overlap, communication breaks down and misunderstandings occur. A teachers' college dropped the name "probationer" for students getting practical field experience when they discovered that some people in the communities they served thought the students were just out of jail! Breakdowns are also amusingly illustrated in the faux pas that children make on test papers in school or the reports they make to adults about their experiences. We are amused when the child tells us "God's name is Harold," because in Sunday School he prayed, "Harold be Thy name." Or when he tells us he sang in church about "the consecrated cross-eyed bear!" Failures of common meanings that leave us standing on a freezing street corner for a half-hour because the friend we were supposed to meet thought we said 2:45 instead of 2:15 are much less amusing. They can even be disastrous for the world when nations misunderstand each other so badly that they go to war.

What Is Communicated?

What is communicated is not what is intended but what is comprehended. Here, for example, is what one child comprehended from the "Pledge of Allegiance." When asked to explain the pledge word by word, it came out something like this:

"I give a lot of money to the old soldiers for the flag of the United States and the flag holder on which it stands, one country under God, that you can't take apart, where you do as you please—just you and me and for everybody else!"

The fact that words do not mean the same things to all people is a common observation. The fact is so important in human affairs as to have resulted in the science of semantics, which was developed to provide us with a better understanding of the importance and use of words. A well-known semanticist, S. I. Hayakawa, points out that words do not only differ in the *content* of their meaning, they also differ greatly in their accompanying *emotional impact*. Such words as pretty or ugly do not describe only an objective quality of appearance; they also carry connotations of goodness or badness, of attraction or repulsion. Descriptive words like democrat or republican are always associated with shades of feeling, which are likely to be far more important than the factual circumstances they describe. Even the simplest of words we use in daily life have emotional attachments, especially when the words are concerned with belief, values, attitudes, or feelings. The meanings attached to words do not remain static. They shift with changing times and places. The connotations of words like sex, pill, moon, black, and pot are notorious examples of how word meanings have changed in recent times.

To be unaware of changes in meanings can create important misunderstandings. One of the authors recently witnessed a heated argument between two young lovers because of the failure of one to recognize that a common word had taken on a new meaning. The word was commitment. Traditionally this word often meant something one had to do against one's will. Recently the word has come to mean that one is dedicated to a cause, has devoted himself body and soul to some idea or person. The quarrel began because the young man had assimilated this new connotation while the young lady still interpreted the word as meaning an obligation, a task one was forced to do. Consequently, when the young man said he was committed to his love, she flew at him indignantly, asking, "What do you mean you're committed? I'm not going to force you into anything!" And a serious argument began.

The concomitant meanings attached to words have sometimes been known as "incidental" learnings. They often create annoying problems for research workers because they introduce factors into experiments that cannot be easily controlled by the experimenter. For the professional helper the "incidental" aspects of words will often be far more significant than the words themselves. In some helping situations the words used between helper and helpee may even be of no consequence whatever. The act of engaging in a human interaction with another person may, itself, be the important facet of the helping relationship. Humans are intensely social animals and often very lonely ones, even when surrounded by thousands of other people. Accordingly, the very fact of being able to get through to someone else may fill an important need. This is especially true for those afflicted with deep feelings of alienation. Almost everyone has had the experience of sitting next to a stranger on a train or plane and being surprised at the depths and extent of feelings communicated by his seatmate. In such instances, the stranger is not interested in any advice you have for him. He has chosen to talk precisely because he will not have to listen to advice. What the stranger seeks is the experience of release in telling his story to someone—anyone! All he needs is a willing listener.

Nonverbal Communication

Because of the importance of language in daily life, most of us are keenly aware of our verbal exchanges. But communication also occurs without words. While growing up, people learn to interpret various types of behavior that act as clues to help them understand the motives and actions of others. Some nonverbal behaviors, like certain facial expressions and attitudes of fright, anger, or hostility, are common enough to be easily read by everyone. Some are restricted to members of the same culture, subculture, occupation, or locality. Others are highly individual, so characteristic of a particular personality that friends and acquaintances know at once what the person is thinking and feeling. Even from a great distance we can spot our friends by the way they walk or the gestures they make. Who has not spoken to a friend by a look? Shrugged his shoulders in resignation? Made a face at an enemy? Conveyed concern by a touch of the hand? These nonverbal communications are often far more powerful means of conveying meanings than a book full of words.

While traveling to Washington with a friend, one of the authors experienced a nonverbal, deeply meaningful communication with a total stranger that occurred in the twinkling of an eye. While walking down the aisle after the plane had landed, the author glanced at a young woman seated next to the window holding her baby. She was slowly moving her nose back and forth through her baby's hair. As the author passed, she glanced up, met his eye, and instantly they shared an eloquent experience. As they descended the steps from the plane, the author's friend asked, "Do you know that girl?"

"Never saw her in my life before," the author replied.

"Well! She certainly talked to you!" exclaimed the friend.

"Yes, and I talked to her, too!" said the author.

The young woman was caught in the act of smelling her baby's head, a meaningless gesture to most of the passengers debarking. But, she was thoroughly enjoying the experience, for there is something very special about the smell of a baby's head. It is a sensuous, loving experience that the author, too, had known with babies of his own. So, in an instant two strangers shared a deeply meaningful experience and never a word was spoken.

Helpers need to be aware of the nonverbal messages they convey, for they play an important part in the kinds of relationships helpers establish and affect success or failure of those interactions. Nonverbal statements may even disclose to others purposes not clearly perceived by the behaver. This fact was clearly brought home to one of the authors during the following incident: During the course of a workshop the author spent some time sitting with various groups. Coming to one group, he picked up a chair, carried it to the circle, turned it backwards, and sat down straddling the chair with his arms across the back. After a minute or two the leader of the group said to the author, "Why don't you join our group?" To this the author replied, "I thought I was."

"Look at the way you are sitting," said the group leader. "How come you have that fence between you and us?" The author was taken aback. He thought to himself, "I am really sitting this way because I wanted to be kind of informal." Thinking about the matter still further, however, he had to admit to himself that he really did not want to join the group; he really wanted to hold himself aloof. His nonverbal behavior betrayed his true feelings to others even when they were not clear to the author himself.

The importance of nonverbal aspects of relationships has been repeatedly demonstrated in research on the helping professions. It has also led educators responsible for the training of workers in the helping professions to concentrate greater attention on the beliefs students hold, the sensitivity they develop, and the messages they convey to those they seek to help. Nonverbal communication is too large a topic to cover in this volume. It is a fascinating subject, however, and helpers wishing to become better acquainted with that topic will find helpful references in the footnote below and in the selected readings at the end of this chapter.[1]

Responsibility for Communication

When understanding fails to come about in human interaction, it is common to blame the other person. If he does not understand, it is easy to point out, "We told him what to do!" This neatly places the responsibility for communication on the receiver. In a helping relationship, it also absolves the helper of blame. He can wash his hands of the affair and continue to feel successful no matter how great a disaster he has produced for his client. Communication, to be sure, is always an interaction, but in a helping relationship the responsibility for its breakdown must lie with the person assuming the helping role. Persons assuming the role of helpers have an obligation to deliver, and responsibility for communication lies with the communicator, not the receiver.

If we are acting as helpers and others do not understand us, that is our fault, not theirs. If the reader of this book does not understand what the authors are saying, then we haven't said it well enough for the reader. If the person in the receiving role accepts some responsibility for listening carefully or trying to understand what is being conveyed, that, of course, facilitates a meaningful exchange. It cannot, however, be demanded, or even expected by the helper. A major goal of helping is freeing people so that they will be able to enter into effective dialogue. It is unfair to expect the student or client to already have achieved the very goals the helping process is designed to produce! If helpers use

1. Interested readers may find a useful introduction to the topic of nonverbal communication in the work of Hinde, Larson, and Tessar, listed in the bibliography.

language, they need to understand and employ the basic principles of communication.

COMMUNICATION MUST BE
RELATED TO NEED

How well helpers are understood is ordinarily a function of three major factors:

1. The relationship of information to need.
2. The relationship to existing information already in the field.
3. The openness of the field at the moment of communication.

In Chapter 3 we observed the effects of need on perception. Other things being equal, we perceive those events we need to perceive. Although we may pass a street innumerable times, we do not perceive its location until it becomes necessary to find the home of a new friend there. Ads for new cars are bypassed until we begin to feel that the old car is getting a bit shabby. Despite daily familiarity with the principle in practice it is easy to overlook its role in communication.

People take in the information they need. The rest, if they perceive it at all, is likely to leave them unmoved. This fact creates a great problem for educators, who must provide information and experience for students who may not need that information for years to come. Teaching people what they currently want to know is comparatively easy, but it takes real genius to communicate when need is not patently evident. A major portion of the time and efforts of good teachers is devoted to creating needs even before information is provided. This is what the first grade teacher does when she sets up a store in her classroom. In the course of running the store the children need to know about money and arithmetic, because they have to make change. Spelling is important, because they have to make a sign. They must know how to read to understand the label on a bottle. They need to know how to get along with others, for running a store and selling its goods require cooperation. Some people, who do not know any better, regard such teaching activities with suspicion, because they're too much fun. Though it may look like play to outsiders, what is really going on is an ingenious way of creating problems for children, the crucial first step in learning. In higher grade levels the creation of need may be accomplished through involving students in planning their own educational experiences, operating their own student governments, or designing procedures to enable the student to use his own resources with ever increasing opportunities for self-direction.

The importance of the relevance principle for communication can also be observed in other helping professions. People who are given psychological tests that they have not asked for, for example, are likely to have little or no interest in the valuable information or advice the counselor would like to give. Social workers know that giving a client information he sees no need for will cause the worker to be regarded by clients as ignorant or annoying. Dieticians are often frustrated because, despite the vast quantities of information they have about proper nutrition, the people they want to help frequently ignore the information and continue eating what they like. A common complaint of clergymen everywhere is that the people who need sermons most are the ones who never come to church. Donald Snygg once pointed out that "there is nothing in this world so useless as answers we do not have problems for!" It is the attempt to provide such answers that frequently results in failures of communication in all aspects of the helping professions.

Information and Censorship

People need information in order to deal with life. If they cannot get it when they need it, they may be plunged even deeper into the problems they face. Without access to accurate information, adjustments to life must be made on the basis of distorted or inaccurate data. Thus, there is no place for censorship in effective helping processes. Rather, the process requires helping clients to obtain whatever information is needed with the greatest possible dispatch.

Sometimes information may be withheld by well-meaning persons "for fear of hurting" those they work with, or for fear their clients may not be able to adequately deal with the problems the information creates for them. Nurses and doctors, for example, have been known to lie to patients with terminal cancer who asked them if they would get well. Well-meaning attempts to shield the patient often rob him of the opportunity to do something he might wish to do before it is too late. Proper planning only occurs in the light of accurate information.

Teachers and counselors also may have to decide what information to provide a student or client. Should a child be told her intelligence test scores, for example? Applying the principle that "there is no information about himself that a person ought not have," the answer would seem to be unequivocably "yes." The problem of communication, however, involves more than simply providing information. It is a question of meaning. To provide people with test scores they do not understand may actually have the effect of providing them with false information. The helper who supplies information, therefore, has an additional responsibility to insure it is understood. This may be such a difficult, time-consuming task that a helper may prefer not to give the information in the first place. The time required to assure adequate understanding (granting the competence of the helper to do so) may be so large a

Providing Experience and Information 165

factor as to warrant withholding information—not on the grounds of whether it is good for the student, but whether the helper has the time and energy available for the necessary clarification or the wish to engage in the discussion.

The methods helpers use to relate information to need are extraordinarily varied. Many counselors, for example, have learned to wait for their clients to express a need to know. They do this because they know that information given prior to need is often fruitless and may even be destructive to the helping relationship. Consequently they rely upon the client's own drives for health, recognizing that if they successfully help the client to search for meaning, sooner or later, the client will realize he lacks important information. At this point the counselor can help him to get it in whatever way is most appropriate at the time. For example, the mother who has finally reached the conclusion that her child needs special help can then be helped to find the appropriate agency. If the same information had been given to her when she first came for aid, she might have received the impression that the helper was not interested in the case and was trying to pass the problem on to another helper. Or, she might have felt guilty and frustrated at being unable to care for the child herself. It is not an easy matter to admit that one has failed with her own child. Information about where and how to send one's child to an agency or institution must be preceded by the question of whether to send the child at all. Even that can only be dealt with when one has come to terms with one's own inadequacies. Giving people information they cannot use is an exercise in futility.

Teachers have discovered by experience that self-direction is an effective way of helping students relate information to need. Students will search out information they need with ingenuity and vigor. What is more, knowledge acquired through such research is far more likely to be permanent and pertinent to future needs. Accordingly, modern educators devote much time and attention to getting students involved in the learning process and creating needs they never knew they had. This makes the learning process more efficient and the presentation of information more meaningful for the student.

Social workers have learned in practice the value of "confrontation with reality"—that is, the importance of permitting a client to come face to face with his problems, to accept the consequences of his own behavior. A potent source of information for everyone is the feedback people get from their own behavior. Protecting a person from such information may constitute a kind of censorship wherein the individual is robbed of experience that could be significant in his return to health. The delinquent, continuously excused for his misbehavior, for example, may thus be led to *expect* to escape responsibility for his actions and so may not perceive the necessity for better kinds of adjustment.

Information Must Be Relevant
to Immediate Need

It is not enough that information should seem important to the receiver; if it is to be effective, it must also be related to current problems or interests. Immediate needs are always more pressing and pertinent than those at a distance. Telling a woman who has just broken up with her lover, "Never mind, there will be many others," is unlikely even to be comprehended. People are rarely helped by information they will not need for years to come. Failure to understand this fact produces much of the teenager's disenchantment when adults, with the best of intentions, attempt to provide "good advice." Many failures in school are direct consequences of the effort to provide students information they will need "some day."

The Self-Ideal Fallacy

Another application of this principle is to be found in the lack of relationship between an individual's stated self-ideal and behavior. Many people have assumed that a person's stated goals of what he would like to be were important dynamics of behavior. Logically, the way to help people change would be to have them examine what they would like to be, what they are, and then make themselves behave in the new ways. Unfortunately, this rarely turns out to be helpful. For most of us, the self-ideal (if we think about it at all) is something we dig up to tell people when they ask us what we would like to become. Even if this report is a fairly true aspiration, it seldom affects our behavior, because it is too remote to have much motive power. It is an academic exercise with little or no dynamic effect on moment to moment behavior. Immediate goals are the ones that affect behavior.

Long-term goals initiate and direct behavior, but they do not sustain it. If one's behavior is to be maintained along a path toward the attainment of a major goal, the process must be enhancing and reinforcing along the way, or a person will not continue. People go to college to get a degree, but that goal alone will not keep them there. The nature of day to day experiences will determine whether or not they will continue. If the process of becoming "educated" proves to be satisfying, people will remain until they take a degree and perhaps continue to do further work toward higher degrees. If the process is not satisfying, they will drop out to pursue some other more satisfying course. Long-term goals are significant only as they can be translated into more immediate steps for action. Almost anyone can observe in other people how far-off goals, no matter how explicitly stated, are frequently belied by short-term actions. The student who loudly protests that he wants to be a doctor more than anything in the world, even while failing required courses for entrance into medical school, is a common example.

INFORMATION MUST BE RELATED
TO EXISTING MEANINGS

The Importance of Fit

Whether information can be truly communicated will be dependent on the readiness of the receiver to absorb it. We have already seen that the meaning of events is a question of the relationship of an experience to the existing organization of the perceptual field. It is only as a person discovers the relationship of new experience to that which is already in existence that it can be comprehended. We have also observed that meanings often exist in a kind of hierarchy, in which complex ones are dependent upon the prior existence of simpler concepts.

A great many frustrations in communication come about because communicators have not successfully helped their clientele perceive the place of new information in their existing fields of awareness. This failure to relate the new to the old results in what Festinger has called cognitive dissonance. He points out how difficult it is to absorb new ideas when they cannot be brought into harmony with those already present. Piaget also emphasized this fact in his descriptions of growth in children's reasoning. He called it the "problem of the match." Prescott Lecky talked of the individual's need for self-consistency and pointed out that the acquisition of meaning was a consequence of a person's attempts to achieve order in his experience. The principle also operates when we find ourselves in a social situation where our usual expectancies do not fit, as, for example, when we go to an unfamiliar church with a friend and find ourselves confused about how to behave in this new setting.

Speed and Pacing

Communication takes time. While information can be transmitted from one person to another with great speed, comprehension is another matter. This requires a searching of the field, matching and adjustment of new understandings into the total gestalt. One of the most common destroyers of communication is the impatience of the communicator. Experienced lecturers know that it is a rare audience that can be expected to carry away more than one or two new ideas.

Every experienced teacher or counselor is familiar with and every inexperienced teacher or counselor frightened of what is sometimes called the "pregnant pause." Many times during a teaching or counseling session a helper will make a statement hoping to evoke a response from a student or client—but nothing happens; there is absolute silence. To an inexperienced helper this can be terrifying. Like the stand-up comic telling a favorite joke who receives little or no response from his audience, the helper feels like he or she has just bombed out, laid an egg, feels the proverbial lump in the throat and knot in the stomach.

The experienced helper, however, comes to learn that this may be a "moment of truth," a pause full of significance. During such pauses many helpees are actually thinking deeply, experiencing perceptual reorganization, or collecting their thoughts. Such pauses are difficult, to be sure. If one feels responsible for making things happen, a moment can seem like forever. But if one lets the moment run its course, one often finds it leads to important communicative breakthroughs.

Time spent in making certain that meanings are conveyed is not time wasted. People in the helping professions often destroy their own effectiveness for failure to recognize the time required for communication. They become so preoccupied with "covering the subject," "getting on with the discussion," or "coming to a decision" that clients or students are lost in the race. People do not put up with this for long. They have more important things to do so they "turn the speaker off," fall asleep, or amuse themselves in the best ways they can. One's own behavior when listening to a boring speaker provides a similar example. Many speakers are lucky that people are mostly well-mannered. On the other hand, it might improve the quality of speaking if audiences expressed their displeasure, and speakers had to accept the full consequences of their behavior.

Effective communication calls for pacing material to the comprehension of hearers. The principle is well known to educators, and many efforts of curriculum planners are devoted to finding ways to adjust subject matter to the readiness of children to deal with a specific curriculum at a particular time. The importance of pacing is equally evident in other helping professions, and may be observed in the practice of counseling, social work, pastoral care, and nursing.

While communication may often fail because the receiver is not yet ready to comprehend it, it can also be rendered ineffective or useless when receivers are long past the readiness point. Who has not passed a very dull hour listening to a speaker tell him interminably what he already knew? Many a helper has made himself unproductive by providing information his student, client, or patient already has or has long since passed beyond.

The Value of Simplicity

Other things being equal, simpler material is more likely to be comprehended. What is simple, however, is a highly individual matter. What is easy for the student of calculus will seem quite difficult to the person struggling with basic multiplication. The importance of simplicity seems obvious but is frequently violated in practice. There are even some people in the helping professions who honestly believe it is good for persons to be confronted with terribly difficult and complex tasks. They operate on the principle, "the harder the better." To be sure, people need to confront problems, but information that is complex beyond the subject's readiness to grasp it can only result in discouragement.

Some communicators make themselves ineffective because they are really more interested in the impression they are making than in communicating. So, graduate students and learned scholars are often dreadful writers. They really don't care what they communicate so long as they display their own erudition. They write to impress their colleagues or their bosses. Whether anyone else comprehends is a minor concern. Indeed, if others don't understand them, they may take this as further proof of their own intellectual superiority.

One of the authors had this point made by a professor when he was an undergraduate student. Like many college students the author was in awe of anything in print. Reading an article his instructor had given him, he was dismayed to find he couldn't understand a word. He became overwhelmed with a sense of inadequacy, and began to doubt that he had the capacity to fulfill his dream of going to graduate school. He went privately to his professor by way of making a confession. "Sir, I'm sorry, but I can't analyze this thing in class. I have read and re-read that article, and it just doesn't make any sense to me. I can't understand a word he is saying!"

"You feel pretty bad about it," the professor said.

"Yes."

About that time the professor broke out laughing, then said, "Don't feel bad, young man. It doesn't make any sense to me either, because the writer didn't say anything. It's included in the articles I asked you to read as an example of the worst kind of writing, reporting, and research I could find. If that guy said anything in that article, we are both pretty dumb."

People who really want to communicate do not regard simplicity as unscholarly. They recognize simplicity as a factor that affects comprehension and use it to make communication more successful. A goal of science is to make things comprehensible by reducing events to the simplest possible terms. This is known as the *law of parsimony*.

Principles and Details in Communication

A variation of the need for simplicity in communication can be observed in the general or specific character of information. There is almost no end to the number of details one can find in a given body of information. Helpers are more likely to facilitate changes in meaning by emphasizing general principles than by concentrating upon details. This fact led Bruner and others to emphasize the importance of the "structure" of knowledge rather than the facts of knowledge. They point out that general principles are much more likely to find translation into the existing field of information than details, and advocate that education orient teaching to emphasize principles rather than details. Unfortunately, many information providers often emphasize the opposite. They focus attention upon details rather than structure. Professors, for example, frequently fill their lectures with details, test their students on details in objective examinations, and concentrate so exclusively on the students' handling of details that students soon "get the message": it is the details that are important. These they try to memorize. Since unrelated facts are difficult to fit into already existing information without the unifying principles that give them meaning, they are quickly lost. Effective communication is dependent upon the sensitivity of the communicator to what is going on in the listener. Good communicators are continuously searching the feedback they get from their audiences and adjusting their own behavior accordingly to assure maximum impact.

Many of the principles discussed in the preceding pages can be observed in operation in the behavior of effective public speakers. An interesting example of this is the famous speech made years ago by Russell Conwell who traveled the Chautauqua circuit giving a speech entitled, "Acres of Diamonds." This single speech was so immensely successful that Mr. Conwell amassed a fortune, which he later used to found Temple University. The structure of this speech is a very simple one. Throughout, a basic thought is stated in the simplest possible terms, then illustrated in ways that make it possible for the hearer to fit the principle to his own need and daily experience. The pattern is repeated over and over throughout the address.

OPENNESS AND COMMUNICATION

A major factor in determining the success of communication is the condition of the receiver. In an earlier chapter we saw how the experience of threat interferes with the individual's perceptions by creating tunnel vision and self-defense mechanisms. Both of these phenomena interfere with communication. Every human being has an insatiable drive towards enhancing himself. To do this, he must also defend himself against humiliation and degradation. No organism can deal with everything simultaneously. Selection is necessary. People take in what they need and defend themselves against what seems disruptive or destructive.

Figure 11.1. Threat and Counter-Threat in Communication.

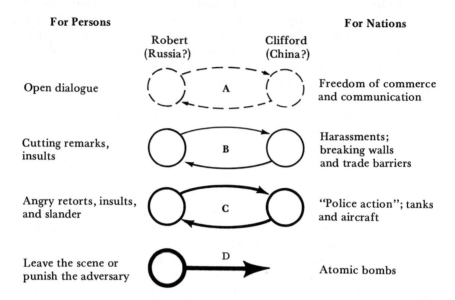

For Persons		For Nations
Open dialogue	Robert (Russia?) — A — Clifford (China?)	Freedom of commerce and communication
Cutting remarks, insults	B	Harassments; breaking walls and trade barriers
Angry retorts, insults, and slander	C	"Police action"; tanks and aircraft
Leave the scene or punish the adversary	D	Atomic bombs

Highly self-actualized persons, as we have seen, are maximally open to the world. Deeply threatened ones are surrounded by walls that isolate them from human intercourse.

Barriers established in response to the experience of threat are even more important for communication because of the threat counter-threat spiral. These cyclic effects have the potential to destroy communication, and even, in their extremes, to result in destruction of the communicators themselves. Once begun, the experience of threat may bounce back and forth from one communicator to the other, spiraling upward to increased intensity and increased interference with communication. Barriers to communication are brought about both by attempts at self-defense and by retaliatory attacks (also a kind of defense) of one against the other. Imagine, for example, a pleasant conversation going on between Robert and Clifford represented by A in Figure 11.1. In this conversation Robert and Clifford are fairly open to each other, and their conversation moves back and forth with little resistance and a maximum of comprehension. In the course of conversation B, Clifford says something to Robert that, intentionally or not, seems to Robert quite uncomplimentary. Robert is hurt by this comment and feels threatened. Accordingly, his defenses rise to protect himself from Clifford, which, of course, begins to interfere with his abilities to grasp what Clifford is saying. As a further defense he lets loose a mildly cutting remark at Clifford. Now, at C, Clifford, feeling himself under attack, raises his own defenses and retaliates in kind. This proves what Robert thought in the first place—that Clifford was trying to insult him. Therefore, he raises his defenses still higher and looses a tougher retort, which forces Clifford to do the same. So the spiral is well on its way. The greater the threat the less the ability to hear, and the greater the necessity to respond with greater threat. If something does not stop this interaction, the pressure may eventually build up such a head of steam that it can only be resolved by some kind of drastic action D.

This spiraling effect of threat and counter-threat, of course, is not limited to individuals. It also happens to nations, as illustrated on the right-hand side of Figure 11.1. Between nations the spiral can escalate to such heights that threat eventually becomes intolerable, and war breaks out to eliminate the threat posed by the "enemy." This can be done by physically destroying him or by reducing his capacity to threaten to a point where it can be coped with successfully. Once embarked on a threat counter-threat spiral, it is difficult to stop, and communication is likely to get worse unless the experience of threat can somehow be reduced and the channels of communication reopened.

Breaking the deadly threat counter-threat cycle will call for some combination of the following:

1. *Attention to the feelings involved in the process of dialogue.* Preoccupation of the participants with action (who did what to whom and what is to be done in retaliation) inflames the threat counter-threat cycle. It obscures the causes of difficulty and turns the attention of the dialogue from the sources of cure. To resolve a threat, one or both parties must become concerned with the feeling aspect. In the helping professions this is a major task of helpers, and finds expression in almost everything they do.

2. *Absorbing or draining off feelings of threat.* If one or both parties can find a way to respond with less threat than they receive, the vicious circle can be interrupted and hostility can be given opportunity to decrease. The helper can do this by absorbing the threat, as the teacher does when he lets a child work off his anger in some harmless fashion, or as the counselor does by staying calm and not expressing shock at what his client has to tell him.

3. *Contributing to the personal feelings of security in participants.* Positive feelings about self make possible greater toleration of threat and less need for self-defense. Helpers accomplish this goal by helping clients to achieve greater feelings of self-actualization, either through their own interactions with their clients or through the manipulation of external events to this end.

4. *Adjusting the interchange to the tolerance levels of the reactors.* Matters are consciously arranged to assure that communications have as little inflammability as possible. The helper cannot do this for the

Providing Experience and Information **173**

client. He can, however, control his own responses or set an example by his own behavior. To do this requires a great deal of sensitivity and a high degree of self-discipline.

5. *Recognition of difference.* Appreciation of difference and its value in human affairs will, of itself, help to lower the temperature of interactions. It contributes to the feeling that "it is all right to be me" and acceptance of a similar right in others. For this reason much of the work of helpers revolves around the recognition and acceptance of difference expressed in innumerable ways in the various branches of these professions.

6. *Resolving the attack-appease dilemma.* To deal with threatening situations, many persons behave as though there were but two possible solutions: to attack or appease. Such a dichotomy, however, presents a person with two completely unpalatable choices. Appeasement requires giving in, surrendering one's own interests, or worse still yielding to blackmail. Attack, on the other hand, has equally inacceptable connotations. Though we are willing to defend ourselves with vigor and determination, to attack others without provocation is as repugnant in one direction as appeasement is in the other. We are essentially a peace-loving people. Attack seems the method of the bully or the despot, and its use seems morally indefensible.

There is an alternative to appeasement and attack, which is an approach that social scientists have discovered is basic to good human relationships everywhere. It is not so much an alternative to attack or appeasement, since it approaches the problems of threat and counter-threat on a different axis altogether. It is a position that says: "I am a person of dignity and integrity. I stand four square in the security of my fundamental convictions. I have no need to attack you, nor will I permit you to attack me. I do not fear you, and I will give you no cause to fear me." This position is neither attack nor appeasement. It is not concerned with winning or losing. It is solely concerned with the maintenance of the dignity and integrity of persons and the preservation of freedom for people to grow and develop.

Appeasement destroys the dignity of the appeaser. Attack violates the integrity of others. The position above maintains the dignity and integrity of the helper without violating the rights of others or relinquishing one's own in the process. It is a position of strength and security, which stands *for* something as well as against something. It is equally applicable to relationships, in the various helping professions, the internal operations of schools, classrooms, and institutions, or to international affairs.

A further difficulty with threat in communication is the fact that symbols of hostility and the reasons for people's anger generally outlast the conditions that created them. Therefore, the effects of threat carry on far beyond the original confrontation, and failures of communication may continue for long periods even after the reasons for hostility may have disappeared. Notable examples of this can be seen in feuds that sometimes occur in the mountains of Appalachia or in family quarrels between husband and wife who go about not speaking to one another long after they have forgotten the original source of their anger.

Just as threat interferes with communication, challenge tends to improve it. Each human being is a neatly balanced system continuously in the process of seeking fulfillment. This drive continually pushes the person forward, but each individual also contains his own checks and balances—his accelerators, brakes, and safety valves. How far and how fast he will go depends upon how he sees himself and the situations in which he is involved. Because his drive is insatiable, he must move if the way seems open to him and within his capacities. But the drive for fulfillment will also not permit him to behave in ways that seem likely to destroy his self-realization.

Effective helpers learn to work with people's checks and balances rather than against them. They learn to follow the lead of their students, clients, and parishioners. They know their clients will confront what they need to when they can, so helpers devote their attention to creating the conditions that will make this possible.

Authority and Communication

An interesting illustration of the effects of challenge and threat on communication may be observed in people's responses to unearned authority. Unearned authority is that prestige and status that a helper or leader has when he first confronts the people he seeks to help. The group leader, for example, comes to the meeting with built-in status and authority because he is the "leader," perhaps also because he has a doctor's degree, wrote a book, or has a reputation in the community. This authority is unearned because it was not given to him by the people he now seeks to communicate with. He may have earned it elsewhere, but not with these people. Over a period of time he may earn authority with them, as group members discover for themselves what the leader has to offer. Each member invests the leader with more or less authority, dependent upon the individual's experience of the leader as a person, as a knower, speaker, demonstrator, and as a sensitive or insensitive human being.

Unearned authority, for most people, is likely to be threatening. Accordingly, all of the effects of threat discussed in this book are likely to accompany the interaction and get in the way of effective communication. It is a common observation that students and clients simply do not hear teachers and group leaders in the very first sessions. Instructions given, advice proffered, information outlined—all have a very low incidence of comprehension and must almost always be repeated in more or less detail on later occasions.

With increased experience on the part of clients, students, parishioners, or group members the leader is given more or less positive or negative authority. If the earned authority is positive, the leader's words are likely to be received as challenging and enhancing. These effects may be so pervasive as to cancel out such ordinary drawbacks as lack of experience and the like. Herman Wessels wrote of a young first-year teacher he had known:

> When he left last June for further study there was an astounding outpouring of affection on the part of his students, and this surprised him. For he had come to us shy and not too sure of himself, and he had found his steadfast purpose through these bright, seeking youngsters whom he taught. He emerged as a person who carried the authority not of age and life experience, but the authority of commitment and true caring.[2]

Communication is immensely increased by positive earned authority, so much so that some of the usual crutches to aid communication may no longer be necessary. When unearned authority is high, for example, college students take notes. As earned authority increases, less notes are likely to be taken. In the case of negative earned authority, this happens because the student has discovered that what the teacher has to say is not important. Where there is a high degree of positive earned authority, however, there may also be a slackening off of note-taking for a different reason, because people are less likely to forget what important people say.

Selected Readings

Carr, D. E. *The Forgotten Senses.* Garden City, New York: Doubleday & Co., 1972.

Hall, E. T. *The Silent Language.* New York: Fawcett World Library, 1959.

Hayakawa, S. I. *Language in Thought and Action.* New York: Harcourt, Brace & World, 1964.

Hinde, R. A., ed. *Non-Verbal Communication.* New York: Cambridge University Press, 1972.

Larson, C. V. *Communication: Everyday Encounters.* Belmont, California: Wadsworth Publishing Co., 1976.

MacDonald, J. B. "Gamesmanship in the Classroom." *National Association of Secondary School Principals Bulletin* 50, 1966, pp. 51–68.

Mehrabian, A. *Nonverbal Communication.* Chicago: Aldine-Atherton, 1972.

2. H. M. Wessels, "Four Teachers I Have Known" (*Saturday Review of Literature,* June 7, 1961).

12

Modes of Helping

To aid in the search for new meanings, helpers must do more than create freeing atmospheres; they must actively assist students and clients in the process of discovering meanings more likely to lead to self-fulfillment than those they had before. In part, this may be accomplished by the provision of new experience or information discussed in Chapter 11. Much more important for most helping professions are the experiences professional helpers provide through the ways they choose to work with students and clients. Some of these choices have to do with management or facilitation of processes; whether to work with clients directly or through control of environment; individually or in groups; in this frame of reference or that. These will be discussed in this chapter. Other choices have to do more specifically with the helper's self, as a person and professional practitioner, and with the helper's own being and becoming. These are the topics of the chapter to follow.

SOME POSSIBLE MODES OF WORKING

In Chapter 1 we listed six factors that determine how helpers use themselves. These included:

1. The helper's knowledge of the subject.
2. The helper's frame of reference in approaching the helping task.
3. The helper's beliefs about what people are like.
4. The helper's own self-concept.
5. The goals and purposes helpers seek.
6. The methods or techniques helpers choose.

To these we need to add a seventh factor, namely, the peculiar circumstances within which helpers must carry out their tasks. These include such factors as the limits of time and place in which helpers work, the numbers they must deal with, and the particular definitions of role and function demanded by the positions they hold. From the helper's personal "mix" of all these factors will come decisions of how best to use themselves as effective instruments for helping.

The following are a few of the more general functions they might serve:

As authority figures, directing the processes of helping toward the achievement of clear-cut goals. This may include a vast array of control techniques ranging from gentle persuasion to open force focused on the processes of helping or on helpees themselves.

As mentors, teaching students and clients things they ought or need to know. The need may arise from outside the helpee in the requirements of others or may be formulated out of the helpee's own interests or aspirations. Helpers in the teaching role may vary from highly authoritarian task masters or "fountainheads of knowledge," to friendly representatives of society, to those who practice modern conceptions of teaching, whose functions are practically indistinguishable from the functions of counselors and psychotherapists.

As facilitators, aids, assistants, or counselors, helping students and clients discover new meanings about themselves and the world. Helpers in these roles operate from an open system orientation, concentrating on creating conditions that facilitate self-discovery for those they work with. The group includes a number of "schools" in counseling, psychotherapy, social work, and humanistic education.

As consultants, working with and through other people. In these roles helpers exert their influence as third parties, contributing to the work of other helping persons rather than directly to helpees themselves. Examples of such roles might be the school psychologist helping a teacher find more effective ways to help a difficult child, or human relations consultants aiding persons in schools, industry, or public office to carry out their functions more effectively.

As private individuals or citizens. Helpers are not always professional persons. They live and work and play like everyone else in families, institutions, and society, and the ways they function in these settings determine their personal happiness and fulfillment on one hand, and the kind of contributions they make to the welfare of other citizens and to the communities in which they live on the other.

Changing the Environment

All helpers at one time or another will be called upon to influence the environment of those they seek to help. Sometimes this influence will be quite direct. At other times it may be occasional or fortuitous. For some helpers it will represent the primary way in which they work with other people; for others it will be a device used only on occasion. In the broadest sense, all forms of helping are accomplished through effecting some kind of change in the helpee's environment. Changing parents' attitudes changes the environment for their child. Even the changes produced in psychotherapy by the most nondirective counselor are brought about by the relationship created by the therapist's presence and behavior, which is a form of modifying the client's environment.

The physical world is the place where we live, and it provides us with the physical needs for growth and survival. Whatever can be done to make it more productive, healthful, and beautiful must be a primary goal to everyone interested in the welfare of humanity. It is also a major social problem of our times, and no matter what a helper does in a professional role, exerting his influence as a private citizen to create a better environment for all must remain a major responsibility. When students and clients can be helped by environmental means, these may be the best and most efficient ways of helping. If a child's school difficulties can be solved by simply changing his teacher, for example, it is probably better to take that action, if it can be arranged. Helping, after all, ought to be done in the quickest possible ways.

Controlling the environment is not always feasible for professional helpers. What, for example, can the school nurse do about the family of a child who feels unloved or unwanted, with his parents on the edge of divorce? What can a teacher do about a brutal or alcoholic father, or an immature, overanxious mother? A physician may know that smoking is dangerous for a patient but be totally unable to prevent him from smoking cigarettes.

Generally speaking, the older an individual gets, the more difficult it becomes to affect behavior by controlling the person's environment. The world of a helpless infant is very small, composed for the most part of parents and the home. But as the child grows older, the world to which it responds grows ever larger and infinitely more complex. By the time the child has reached adulthood, the possibilities of controlling behavior by attempting to control his world have become very slim, if not altogether impossible. Parents can easily remove dangerous objects beyond the reach of the toddler, but imagine the problems involved in preventing a grownup from finding the means to commit suicide if he really wants to do it. Relatives of alcoholics know only too well the impossibility of keeping liquor from their loved ones who have become addicted to the drug. Attempting to affect behavior through control of the environment rapidly loses its value as an effective tool for the helping professions by the time most people have reached adolescence. After that, some other means to help must be found. If the environment surrounding clients is to be changed, more often than not it will have to be changed by clients themselves, and helpers will need to exert their primary efforts toward helping clients change their perceptions about themselves and the world.

One-to-One Relationships

Some helpers, like counselors or nurses, work almost exclusively with individuals. But all helpers must, at one time or another, whether superficially or in depth, carry out some part of their functions in a face-to-face relationship with one other person. Helping people in one-to-one relationships might be thought of as a continuum of purpose—from interviews (*getting* information from the client) through advising (*giving* information or guidance) to counseling and psychotherapy (*facilitating* personal discovery of meaning at deeper and deeper levels).

Many of the needs people have for help can be satisfied by simply providing information. More difficult and personal problems, however, are likely to be moral ones; matters of decision, desire, hope, frustration, or deprivation. Persons who come for such assistance already have most of the information they need. Certainly withholding information that could help a person get better more quickly is cruel and inhuman. On the other hand, giving people information that they do not need or cannot use only sidetracks the helping process. Modern practices in counseling and psychotherapy, therefore, are much less concerned with giving people information, and much more concerned with developing relationships designed to help persons explore and discover new and more effective ways of perceiving.

Early in the history of counseling, it was assumed that the advice given by counselors made the difference. Later on, improvements in the client's health were thought to be a function of the *methods* that counselors used, and practitioners argued at great length about whether directive or nondirective methods were most efficient. More recently, the *relationship* between counselor and client has come to be regarded as the most significant aspect. At first, this came about because counselors focused on the facilitating effect of the relationship on the exploration of meaning. Now, we are beginning to understand that the relationship does much more than simply facilitate; it teaches as well. As we have seen in Chapter 6, the criteria for self-actualization offer important clues for the construction of effective helping relationships.

Helping Through Groups

Through the use of group sessions, the number of persons who can be helped is enormously increased. As a consequence, people in the helping professions are experimenting in a variety of ways with the use of groups for human growth and fulfillment. Major considerations in education, for example, are how to group children for most effective learning, and how to use group discussion as a tool of teaching. Social workers are experimenting with family therapy groups and community action programs. Counselors and psychologists are much concerned with sensitivity groups, basic encounter groups, group play therapy, and the use of groups for the advancement of mental health. Occupational and recreational therapy have become most important branches of the healing arts, and human relations experts are concerned with the problems and resolution of group conflict. The kinds of group experiences constructed by helpers to achieve these ends may vary widely from groups that are little more than pleasant pastimes to intensely therapeutic groups. They can generally be classified in four major categories: conversation, instruction, decision, or discovery groups.

Conversation Groups

These groups are characterized by the social dialogue engaged in by everyone interacting with others on a casual basis. The prototype may be found in the college student's "bull session," a pleasant pastime in which one seeks to regale others by descriptions or stories. Ordinarily, conversation groups proceed at considerable speed as one person after another tells a story, an anecdote, or makes a comment. Verbal participation is likely to be high, and the group tends to maintain a size such that everyone can get a chance to speak. If waiting gets too long, the session is likely to break up into smaller groups where more people have a chance to comment. Most of the talk is descriptive—"I saw . . . ," "Did you read where . . . ?" "Once I . . . ," "My uncle has . . . ," and so on. Learning and growth in such a group are likely to be minimal, and such groups are used only occasionally by most professional helpers as a means of establishing rapport.

Instruction Groups

These kinds of groups exist exclusively to show or tell participants something. Members may range from a very few to the millions reached by television. The group leader is responsible for most of the activity in such groups. The task of group members is to listen, watch, and absorb. Attention is focused on subject matter. Interactions are likely to be confined to those between teacher and student. Interactions of students with students are limited, if they exist at all. Much teaching, especially at the college level, is still carried on in this time-honored lecture-demonstration tradition. Modern concepts of teaching and learning, however, no longer accept so narrow a view of the task. "Telling" is no longer regarded as the primary function of teachers.

Decision Groups

Some groups are formed to arrive at a consensus or decision on some matter. A group of people come together to study a question and arrive at a solution or program of action, perhaps to nominate a slate of officers, decide where to go on a picnic, formulate a set of rules for a school system, negotiate a contract, or settle a dispute among members. The group proceeds by sharing information on the problem, listening to proposals and counter-proposals for solution, and sooner or later taking a vote to record its decision. Such groups can often prove highly useful in bringing about agreement on some plan of action, but have limited applicability for the helping process, which seeks more fundamental changes in personal meanings.

Prior experience of persons in decision groups, in fact, raises problems for helpers, for decision groups have the unhappy effect of coercing members to arrive at approved solutions once the group has reached a point of decision. Even the democratic procedure of taking a vote is often no more than a way of stopping a discussion. When the vote is taken, discussion halts and the minority is coerced into whatever decision the majority has arrived at. So, the behavior of a minority member of a decision group is often quite unaffected by his participation. Worse still, he may later approach group encounters with suspicion and fear. This creates problems for helpers, because people who have experienced such groups develop an expectancy that this is the way in which a group "ought" to operate. As a consequence they often delay or destroy the effectiveness of helping groups set up for other purposes, until group leaders have been able to help them perceive that the new situation is quite different from their previous experience.

Discovery Groups

In the past thirty or forty years, special types of groups have been developed by various branches of the helping professions to aid students, clients, and patients explore new and more adequate understandings of themselves and their relationships to the world. Leaders of such groups generally concentrate much more upon the group process than upon specific outcomes. Emphasis is on the experience of participating in the group and what the individual can make of it. Such groups are now in wide use in many aspects of the helping professions and are generally used for three kinds of purposes:

1. *Sensitivity training.* Group experiences are used to help participants develop increased sensitivity to themselves and to other people. Some forms of these groups are also called encounter groups or confrontation sessions. Sensitivity groups have been particularly popular in the

182 Helping Processes

training of workers in the helping professions, the training of executives in industry, and in public relations.

2. *Group therapy.* Groups are used for their therapeutic value, especially in assisting patients or clients with personality problems. Such techniques have been widely used, for example, with prison inmates, potential juvenile delinquents, marital partners, and parent education.

3. *Learning Groups.* Group techniques are used to assist students in the exploration and discovery of the meaning of ideas in many content fields. In recent years, learning groups have been especially employed in humanistically-oriented school programs like open classrooms, values clarification, role playing, class discussions, and a wide variety of techniques for involving students in decision making and responsibility for their own learning.

Keeping Perspective

Whenever people hit upon a new technique or idea for dealing with human problems, a period of testing will likely follow in which the idea is tried in a variety of ways. In this process the idea may be pushed to the limit and applied as a "pure case," or it may be interpreted in the most bizarre fashion. Such a period in the exploration of new ideas is also likely to be characterized by persons who develop great enthusiasm for their particular innovations. Since there are no "right" answers for dealing with human beings, even the wildest techniques may work for some people—especially if they believe they will. This evidence of success may corroborate the particular prejudices of the innovator, resulting for a time in numbers of people staunchly advocating the merits of a particular approach. This seems to be a necessary part of the evolution of almost any new idea and has value in providing a wide variety of test situations. In time, as the froth beaten up by all this activity settles down, the true dimensions of the new concept begin to emerge and are fitted into the fabric of our understanding with a clearer grasp of their limitations and possibilities.

Examples of this sort of experimentation can be observed in all aspects of the helping professions. They show up in education, for instance, as new concepts in curriculum organization, new methods of teaching reading, driver education, mental health, even new concepts of building construction. Similar waves of interest may appear in social work, psychotherapy, counseling, and pastoral care. Some innovations eventually turn out to be little more than passing fads, which run their course and soon disappear. Others stand the test of time and efficacy and become permanent fixtures in philosophy and practice.

Experimentation of this kind is currently going on extensively in such group activities as basic encounter. The variations being tried by proponents of these groups cover a vast range. There are groups that emphasize loving and caring and groups that encourage brutal confrontation. Groups may have single leaders, multiple leaders, or no leaders at all. There are large groups, small ones, groups that meet only once, and groups that meet for long periods. Some "marathon" groups meet for forty-eight hours and permit group members to leave the room only to use the lavatory. Some far out groups even meet in the nude or scramble sex partners. We will eventually discover more precisely what such groups can and cannot do and how to use them with maximum efficiency. In the meantime, we must be aware that such terms as counseling, basic encounter, group therapy, and the like cannot be understood as universal entities. One cannot simply be for or against them, because their names tell nothing about what goes on within. One cannot know, for example, what to think about basic encounter without knowing who is involved, the purpose of the group, how it proposes to operate, and especially, the philosophy, goals, and beliefs of the group leader.[1]

The Helper as Consultant

Helping is often conceived almost exclusively as dialogue or encounter between a helper and one or more helpees. But helpers in any branch of the professions find it necessary from time to time to work with and through other people. So, teachers seek to help children through parents; school psychologists by conferring with teachers; social workers may meet with judges or city councils to help the persons they serve in their home communities.

People who are good at their jobs are notorious for getting promoted to administrative or supervisory roles. So, expert counselors or teachers often find themselves in positions where they no longer work directly with clients or children. Instead, they must use their expertise through influence upon counselors and teachers. Helping effects must be produced at second or third hand. The specific techniques required for operating in such fashion will frequently differ from those employed when working more directly, but the basic dynamics do not change. The fundamental principles guiding the supervisor's or consultant's relationships are the same as those which guide the teacher, social worker, or counselor.

Among the special problems of helping indirectly is the frustration of having to rely on others to get things done. This is especially true if plans must be formulated at some distance from the scene of action. When one is away from the pressures of immediate events, appropriate paths for action can often be seen with great clarity. For helpers at the

1. An excellent evaluation of group processes can be found in C. R. Rogers, *Carl Rogers on Encounter Groups* (New York: Harper & Row, Publishers, 1970).

front line who are inescapably immersed in the problems, matters may be perceived very differently. Patience and understanding is even more essential when it is necessary to work with and through other persons. Effective helping from more remote levels of operation depends upon open communication. Many otherwise good programs have disintegrated because of failure to recognize and deal with the importance of this question. The farther away the helper must work from the scene of direct involvement, the more difficult to keep the lines of communication open both ways.

Who Is the Client?

Many a helper, forced to work in consulting roles, makes himself ineffective because of confusion about who the client is. The client is always the person with whom the helper is immediately in touch. For example, a teacher asks the school psychologist for help in working with a difficult child. If the psychologist sees her role primarily as one of working face-to-face with a child, at the time of the teacher's complaint she is likely to reply: "Very well, Mr. Atwood, send him down to my office and I'll see what I can do with him." In making this response the psychologist has lost a valuable opportunity to be of assistance. The proper client for a consultant is *whoever the consultant is confronting.* The school psychologist who sees herself in this broader role does not make the mistake of sending her primary client away. Instead, she tells Mr. Atwood, "I can see how difficult it must be for you to work with him. Sit down and let's talk about it." She begins her work by trying to help the teacher. She recognizes that helping the child involves helping the teacher to be able to deal with the child more effectively. Since the teacher is the person in daily intimate contact with the child, success will most likely be reached with and through the teacher. As the psychologist helps the teacher deal with his frustrations, she contributes directly to his strength and capacity to carry out his job, and he is better able to deal with the child who is his current problem.

When school psychologists work this way, they frequently do not have to work with the child at all. Sometimes the opportunity to discuss the problem works therapeutically and is enough to give the teacher new courage to try again and insight to try new approaches. Even if this does not occur, at the end of the session with a teacher the psychologist can still arrange to see the child and talk some more with the teacher on another occasion.

An additional complication for helpers working in consultant, administrative, or supervisory roles is created by the authority attached to such positions. Generally speaking, the greater the authority of the administrator or supervisor, the greater the anxiety and fear of encounter with him. This is likely to hinder creativity, create resistance, and impede communication between first and second level helpers. In earlier chapters we spoke of the importance of "visibility" in fostering helping relationships. It is especially important for helpers working at more remote levels, therefore, to give high priority to keeping open lines of communication with those they must work through.

SOME MANAGEMENT ASPECTS OF HELPING

Management and Manipulation

Methods of helping through control and direction of students, clients, and patients are often impatiently rejected by some workers in the helping professions, and the words "manipulation" and "management" have sometimes been regarded as though they were synonymous with "evil." It is, of course, true that behavioristic approaches to helping may become mechanistic and dehumanizing. But this must be so only if they are employed without a guiding philosophy. When used in a humane context, behavioristic principles, techniques, and methods can help people be more successful, lead to self-enhancement, and change self-concepts. Having stated a set of goals, there are many procedures one may select for achieving those ends. The only time helpers are forced to reject a particular way of achieving goals is when it violates their primary frame of reference.

We have stated the perceptual principle, that behavior changes when persons change their perceptions of themselves and the world. However, a change in environment can also result in changed perceptions and behavior. If persons are moved to new, more positive environments, where they begin to have reinforcing experiences, receive more rewards, and are treated better by those around them, their perceptions will almost certainly change. As we have seen there is no such thing as a good or right method of helping. The principle applies to manipulation. Of itself, it is neither good nor bad. It has acquired a bad name because it seems undemocratic to some helpers, a kind of violation of the dignity and integrity of the individual; or perhaps because it is not appropriate or effective for the kinds of problems some helpers deal with. But there is nothing inherently wrong with manipulation per se. All helpers manipulate something—the environment, the client, or themselves—to create a helping relationship. Like any other method, it may be used appropriately or inappropriately, positively or negatively, depending upon the skill and understanding of the helper, the goals being sought, and the helper's own frame of reference for approaching the helping task.

Reinforcement

The kinds of relationships established by helpers will largely determine what they reinforce. One of the oldest psychological principles is that people tend to learn those things that result in some kind of reward. Everyone has a need for self-enhancement, and what is experienced as enhancing will likely be sought on other occasions. The professional helper, whether teacher, counselor, social worker, or supervisor is important by virtue of his position. What he rewards, consequently, has special significance for those with whom he works.

The helper may employ reinforcement quite openly so that both he and his client are aware of what is happening—for example, a teacher might say: "That's right, Jimmy," or "That's the way! You're doing well." On the other hand, what a helper reinforces may be so subtle that it is not apparent to the helper himself. Many a counselor has had the unhappy experience of reassuring a client, with the intent of strengthening his confidence, only to find he has produced a transference and made his client dependent upon him. To avoid this kind of error, helpers need to be deeply sensitive to the meaning of their own behavior as seen through the eyes of clients. Otherwise, they may find themselves structuring the encounter in ways they had not bargained for.

Positive and Negative Reinforcement

The principle of positive reinforcement maintains that most learning depends on the presence or absence of reinforcement at the time behavior occurs. If a person's behavior is reinforced at the time of behaving, the probability of that behavior recurring is increased. When an infant utters a sound, a mother will often give the child something pleasing, like a drink of milk, a bit of food, or a kiss. Thus, that particular bit of behavior, the utterance, is positively reinforced, and will most likely occur again. The same thing is true for helping relationships. Authority figures, such as teachers, nurses, and lawyers, are powerful reinforcers. Behavior manifested in helping relationships will greatly depend on what helpers do and do not reinforce by their own words and nonverbal behavior.

The principle of negative reinforcement holds that a person's desired behavior will increase when noxious or irritating stimuli are removed. In other words, with positive reinforcement desired behavior is increased by adding something to the situation. With negative reinforcement, desired behavior is increased by taking something away from the situation. Both are intended to have positive results.

Modes of Helping   187

Reinforcement and Feedback

One of the greatest assets of reinforcement is the opportunity it presents for feedback. Learners need continuous opportunities to observe the consequences of their acts, to see the results of perceptions, and to correct faulty assumptions. Perhaps even more important, feedback frequently has the effect of raising new problems to be solved. An act that does not produce the expected results immediately confronts the learner with a new problem. Without feedback the learner will not know if his thinking needs further modification or not.

Effective learning, whether it be in connection with shooting on a rifle range, selling a product, raising a child, solving arithmetic problems, or making love, requires knowledge of results. Because this is so, much of the time and energy of helpers will be devoted to helping students and clients discover and deal with the consequences of their decisions. Sometimes they may do this by providing real opportunities to test out new meanings—as when a coach provides an opponent for a young boxer to test his new stance. Sometimes helpers can only wait while the client makes his own tests in the world he lives in. On occasion this may mean that counselors or teachers sit quietly while a helpee tries a solution that the helper knows in advance will probably not work.

Reinforcement Schedules

Whether in teaching, counseling, or some other helping relationship, varying the time, amount, or number of reinforcements is more effective than continuous reinforcement. In most helping relationships, reinforcement will happen on a variable schedule naturally, because most helpers do not deliberately or systematically pay attention to when they are or are not reinforcing a helper's behavior. However, by systematically and intentionally varying the reinforcement, results can often be achieved much more quickly than if the variability is occurring simply by chance.

Those responses that helpers seek to reinforce will depend upon the frame of reference from which the helper approaches the task. Operating from a closed system, the helper attempts to reinforce the student or client's behavior or those intermediate steps the client takes toward the achievement of objectives. Operating from an open system, the helper's reinforcements will be directed toward the conditions or processes of helping. That is to say, reinforcement is used to teach the student or client where to look for the most efficient discovery of new meaning.

Reinforcement in Counseling

One way counselors assist clients to explore personal meaning is to hold significant factors up for examination. Out of the mass of facts, feelings, description, comment, and explanation, the counselor responds to the feelings expressed by his client. This technique is sometimes called "recognition and acceptance of feeling." It could equally well be called recognition and acceptance of personal meaning. The technique focuses the client's attention upon personal meanings rather than upon factual material expressed. By continual response to personal meaning, the counselor reinforces the client's behavior, and before long the client begins to turn his attention increasingly to personal meanings, often without need for further reinforcement from the counselor.

Reading the protocols of almost any counseling session will reveal this process of reinforcement in action. In the following excerpt from a counseling case, note how the counselor bypasses the factual content of what his client is saying to respond to the personal meaning she is expressing. The young woman in the case came for help because of her deep distress over a shriveled hand, which was a birth defect.

Y. W.: I thought that—well, what I am trying to say is that I would try to push it off and I found that I couldn't.

C.: You found that that was impossible.

Y. W.: I thought that they were just being sorry and were trying to make up by giving me things.

C.: They were sorry—

Y. W.: (cutting in) That was no good. It did no one any good.

C.: You don't want people to feel sorry for you.

Y. W.: Never! I never want that!

C.: I see. Although you didn't want people to feel sorry for you, you felt you got it anyhow.

Y. W.: Yes, people didn't say anything but I could feel it. I used to wonder what would happen in a group if someone actually said something about it. It frightened me so. I think that I wouldn't know what to do. I am afraid of what they might do. I would rather not have my parents know what happens sometimes. Better that I know it just myself than all three of us.

C.: You prefer that they not know about it.

Y. W.: They must have known when I was little. In those days it didn't matter to me. I remember one instance when I went home from school—the only instance that I ever told them how I really felt. That was the time when I packed up here at school and took a train home. I just couldn't stand it any longer and called them up and told them I was coming home. I should never have done it. Some of the girls said something, and it got worse and worse until I couldn't stand it any more. So I went, and I was sorry I did.

C.: You feel that that was a mistake.

Y. W.: I don't know what happened. When I was on the train—I remember I called them and told them I was coming home and then on the train

I decided that I would not tell them anything. I'd make up some other story about something else. I was riding home from the train in the car when Mother said, "Is it about your hand?" And then I told her about it. I just broke down and told her. That was the only time.

C.: M-hm.

Y. W.: Afterwards I told them that I wanted something done. Something just had to be done! I had an appliance made, but it didn't work. I gave it up after a while and never mentioned it again. They didn't either. They didn't know the other times. I don't think there is anything to be gained now by telling them.

C.: So this has been a kind of secret that everybody knew, but nobody talked about?[2]

Pointing the Way in Adult-Child Relationships

Haim Ginott in a delightful book for parents has recommended a similar technique to improve communication between parents and children. Here, for example, are some sample conversations he reports between children and parents:

When a child comes home with a host of complaints about a friend or a teacher or about his life, it is best to respond to his feeling tone, instead of trying to ascertain facts to verify incidents.

Ten-year old Harold came home cranky and complaining.

Harold: What a miserable life! The teacher called me a liar, just because I told her that I forgot the homework. And she yelled; my goodness, did she yell! She said she'll write you a note.

Mother: You had a very rough day.

Harold: You can say that again.

Mother: It must have been terribly embarrassing to be called a liar in front of the whole class.

Harold: It sure was.

Mother: I bet inside yourself you wished her a few things!

Harold: Oh, yes! But how did you know?

Mother: That's what we usually do when someone hurts us.

Harold: That's a relief.[3]

Pointing the Way in School

Teachers accomplish a similar kind of focus with reinforcing comments like the following:

2. From the "Case of Edith Moore" by Arthur W. Combs. Reprinted by permission of the publisher from William U. Snyder, *Casebook of Non-Directive Counseling* (Boston: Houghton Mifflin Co., 1947).
3. From H. Ginott, *Between Parent and Child* (New York: Macmillan, 1965). Reprinted by permission.

"I can see that you feel very angry at Jimmy, Billy. I can understand how you might feel that way but you're not allowed to hit him."

"How do you feel about the poem, Helen?"

"Do you think the court was justified in the ruling?"

"What do you think is the purpose of the procedure?"

Extinction

Extinction is another behavioral principle useful for the professional helper. It is based on the old adage that if you ignore someone or something it will go away. Stated in behavioristic terms, if reinforcement is not present or is removed, behavior will extinguish, ie., disappear. Behavior that does not result in some form of feedback is very soon discarded, as many parents and teachers have discovered. Expert teachers, for example, handle many behavior problems by simply ignoring them. They know that without some reinforcement the behavior is likely to quickly spend itself. Similarly, many problems between parents and children could easily be avoided if the child's misbehavior were calmly ignored.

As a significant other, whatever the helper does or does not do conveys some sort of message to the student or client. The choices helpers make in reacting to clients or students are important. Helper's communicate meanings whether they want to or not. They are the data from which the helpee learns about self and subtly express the approved or disapproved uses of the relationship. If helpers are unaware of interactions and their meanings, they run the risk of behaving irresponsibly and of making helping processes fortuitous. To meet the obligations they have assumed as helpers and to raise techniques above the level of mere accident, helpers must be keenly aware of the impact they have upon their clients. This is even true when, as in the case of extinction, they do nothing at all.

Token Economies

Token economies are "little societies" based on the principles of operant conditioning. A group, say a public school class, earns tokens for performing specified tasks. In an elementary school class children might be given tokens for being neat, doing their school work, or cooperating. The tokens can be accumulated and exchanged later for something the student desires, such as free time, candy, and trinkets. The purpose is not to bribe children for learning or working. Hopefully, the behavior they are learning will become intrinsically rewarding, and the tokens will eventually be replaced by more abstract reinforcements. When tokens are given, they are usually associated with social rewards like praise. The goal is to replace the tokens with the intrinsic pleasure of learning and social reinforcers.

Precision Teaching and Charting Behavior

Precision teaching is also an outgrowth of operant conditioning. It has been so fully developed and refined, however, that it may be considered as a procedure on its own. Although it has been mainly developed for use in educational settings, some of the techniques growing out of its development are applicable in other helping relationships. For example, charting may be used to record the progress of any behavior change program. So, in precision teaching students are sometimes asked to carry out a self-improvement program designed to change almost any kind of behavior, including such things as decreasing smoking, losing weight, increasing sexual activity, and extinguishing tics. Charting begins by establishing what is called the base rate of on-going behavior (for example, the number of cigarettes smoked in a given length of time) when the program begins. Sometimes behavior like smoking will decrease simply from learning what the actual frequency is. Generally, however, some type of consequence has to be added to bring about a change. In the case of smoking, a person could be charged a dime for every cigarette he smoked or have to decrease the amount of time he can engage in another desired behavior. One could also increase the amount of desired behavior for every decrease in the amount of undesirable behavior, which would be more humanistic. In any case, behavior continues to be charted, and a graphic measure of the effects of intervention is established. Observers, whether observing their own or someone else's behavior, know precisely how their efforts are affecting behavior. Once one has learned the basic technique, it can be used by any layman or professional helper to change his own or another's behavior.[4]

SOME MANAGEMENT TECHNIQUES OF LIMITED VALUE FOR HELPING

Punishment

It is commonly assumed that punishment is a highly valued technique in behavioral approaches to helping. As a matter of fact, most proponents of operant conditioning stress the importance of positive consequences for facilitating change in behavior. B. F. Skinner has repeatedly expressed his reasons for the rejection of the use of punishment as a

---

4. Interested readers may find more detailed descriptions of charting and its uses in M. A. Koorland, and M. Mitchell. *Elementary Principles and Procedures of the Standard Behavior Chart* (Gainesville, Florida: Learning Environments, Inc., 1975).

device for producing significant change in human beings. One of his papers on punishment, for example, is subtitled, "A Questionable Technique."[5] There is really little place for punishment in helping relationships, and helpers of many persuasions, humanists and behaviorists alike, have expressed grave doubts about its appropriateness as a technique for at least two major reasons. First, there is reason to doubt that punishment works in anything more than temporary and superficial fashion; and second, the technique often causes side effects whose negative consequences far outweigh positive results.

In examining the question of punishment, it is necessary to differentiate between punishment in a physical context (a child burnt by a hot stove) and punishment in a social one (punishment by an angry parent). In the physical context, when a child touches a hot stove the consequences are usually no more than some slightly burnt little fingers. This is an objective, unemotional encounter with life, with causes and consequences clear even to a small child. A person, unless he is very ill, cannot remain angry or hold a grudge for long against a stove, and he certainly can't gain revenge on the punisher with much satisfaction.

Punishment inflicted upon one human by another is something else. That involves much subjectivity and emotion. Furthermore, the reasons for the punishment are seldom clearly understood, the justification is usually questioned, and retribution is a likely possibility. Punishment in a social context is a questionable technique indeed.

Punishment usually teaches people what *not* to do. Because it deals directly with behavior, punishment only treats symptoms. One of the authors is acquainted with a little girl in his neighborhood who presently knows two words. The first is "Jo Jo," the name of her dog, and the second is "No!" which needs no explanation. This child is typical of many who are glutted with no's and don'ts, but starved for do's and yeses. When punishment is used, only a part of the job has been done. There remains the more important task of teaching a person the good thing to do.

The effect of punishment, more often than not, is only temporary; in most instances it has only short-term effects. At the time punishment is administered, the culprit may stop what he is doing, especially if he is a small child being physically restrained by an adult. But there is every reason to believe, both in terms of scientific research and common observation, that the behavior will manifest itself again. This can be illustrated by an incident occurring in the neighborhood of one of the authors.

He lives in a typical housing development, with rows of houses back to back, small yards between, and each house with double sliding glass

5. B. F. Skinner, *Science and Human Behavior* (New York: The Macmillan Company, 1953).

doors facing his neighbor's double sliding glass doors. The children who live directly behind the author's house had a habit that infuriated their mother. When they wanted to play with the author's child, they would come to the double glass doors, yell and bang on the doors, and stare into the house. The irritated mother would often scold the children for this, telling them that it wasn't nice to stare into people's houses or to make a commotion around their doors and windows. But the scoldings had little effect and the children continued to make their presence known to the author's child in the same delicate manner.

One day the irritated mother waited until her children were engaged in the familiar act of attracting the attention of the author's child. Then she came flying across the yard, stick in hand, and proceeded to whale the daylights out of her offspring! What a scene—children crying, stick cracking, and mother screaming. The mother made it clear that this was only a sample of what would happen if she ever caught them bothering their neighbors in that manner again. Furthermore, in the future they were to wait for the author's child to come out to play, and not go after him again. That was that. The children had been punished, and that act, that particular bit of behavior had been stopped. The children have never since come to the back door, stared into the house, or called for the child. Now, they come around to bang on, stare into, and scream through the *front* sliding glass doors! At least the children's mother is happy, because "What you can't see or don't know won't hurt you."

The most significant arguments against the use of punishment, the authors believe, are not in regard to whether it works, but in connection with the side effects that accompany its use. There are many such side effects, of which the following are samples.

1. *Punishment of any kind generates negative responses.* Persons who are punished become fearful, anxious, and hostile, and because of these feelings often engage in "displacement"—that is, striking out at others in retaliation for the pain and embarrassment they have suffered. The results are seldom any better for the administrator of the punishment. Punishment is a vengeful human response and often has a snowballing effect. The more a person is punished the more frustrated and hostile he becomes. This causes him to strike back even more forcefully, thereby causing the punisher to become more frustrated and angry and to punish harder and with greater furor—hardly a pleasant or fruitful human experience.

2. *Punishment is often difficult, especially for young children, to associate with the undesirable behavior rather than with the self.* It is easy for a child to mistake badness in the self rather than in the act for which he is being punished. It is a simple thing to believe that it is "me," and not my behavior that is bad. This is likely to happen

particularly when the punishment for a single act is prolonged over a period of time, as when someone is given the "silent treatment" for long periods after committing an undesirable act, or when a child is told, "Wait till your father gets home. You'll get it then!"

3. *Punished behavior can generalize to desirable behavior.* Without realizing the consequences, behavior that is inappropriate at a certain age or time is often punished, even though the same behavior will be desirable at another age or time. The result is that individuals inadvertently are made incapable of performing highly desirable, and in many cases, absolutely necessary human acts. The following is a specific example familiar to one of the authors. One Christmas some parents decided that a nice gift for their three children would be a set of illustrated Bible stories. The set was beautiful, elaborate, expensive, and contained twenty-four volumes. It was accompanied by a wooden bookcase. The thought behind the gift was commendable, and the gift was a fine one indeed—but not for these children, at the time the set was given. All three children were much too young to appreciate it and were unable to care for it and use it appropriately. Nevertheless, on Christmas Day the children were shown the set, told it was theirs, and then were told they were not to handle it! If they wanted to use it or see some of the pictures they would have to call on one of the parents who could handle the books.

One can guess what happened. It was too much to expect that a child could understand how he could own something and yet not be allowed to touch it. So, time and again, one child or the other attempted to take a book from the case, and each time they did so, the mother or father would punish the child.

Thus, for a period of from one to three years, depending on which child was involved, his major encounter with books and religious material occurred under the stress and emotional turmoil of a situation in which he was yelled at, smacked, and generally dominated by an angry, reprimanding parent.

This kind of association may be the direct result of punishment for behavior that is bad at one time, but good at another. Sex-training, for example, is one area in which this frequently occurs. For years we punish, condemn, or manifest embarrassment at every response children make that has the slightest sexual connotation. Then, when they reach some magical age, or join in marriage, they are expected spontaneously to be accomplished lovers.

The use of punishment for controlling misbehavior is inevitable at times. Sometimes the consequences of the act that a person is about to perform are so dire that there may be no time for another alternative. Sometimes certain behavior must be stopped in the quickest way possible. As a tool for the helping professions, however, punishment generally leaves much to be desired. While it may, on occasion, be necessary to employ it, helpers need to be fully aware of the dynamics involved in its use and especially of the meanings it creates in the experience of the subject, lest helpers destroy with the left hand what the right hand is trying to build.

Competition

Many people in our society assume that competition is an excellent device for motivating persons to extend themselves in athletic events, business affairs, or getting an education. People do, indeed, appear to be highly motivated by competitive effort, if one examines the behavior of successful competitors. Examining the matter in larger perspective, especially when viewed from the point of view of the behaver, the value of competition looks quite different. We are very impressed by the competitive features of our society and like to think of ourselves as essentially a competitive people. Yet, we are thoroughly and completely dependent upon the goodwill and cooperation of our fellow citizens at every moment of our lives. In turn, other people are dependent on us. We are indeed "our brothers' keepers" as never before in history. Although we occasionally compete with others, competition is not the rule of life, but the exception. One needs but reflect on the past twenty-four hours to discover how overwhelmingly one's behavior has been cooperative and how seldom competitive. When understood in terms of the effects of challenge and threat, competition turns out to be a motivating force of limited value for some and downright destructive for others.[6]

Examined in the light of our understanding of challenge and threat, three things become apparent about the effects of competition:

1. *Competition has motivating force only for those persons who believe they have a chance of winning.* That is to say, it motivates those for whom competition is perceived as challenge. People do not work for things they feel they cannot achieve. They work only for things that seem within their grasp.

2. *Persons who are forced to compete, and who do not believe they have a chance of success are not motivated by the experience; they are threatened by it.* Far from motivating people, competition under these circumstances is quite likely to result in disillusionment and discouragement. People who do not see much chance of success cannot be inveigled into making an effort. They avoid competition whenever they are able. Any teacher knows that children who work for scholastic honors are those who feel a possibility of winning. The competitors

6. Adapted from A. W. Combs, "The Myth of Competition" (*Childhood Education* 33, 1957): 264–269.

work like crazy, while the noncompetitors go about more important business of their own.

Whether or not competition is challenging or threatening will depend upon how the situation seems to the competitor—not how it seems to an outsider. Left to themselves, people will compete only rarely, and then only when they feel a chance of success. Forcing people to compete can only result in discouragement or rebellion. When the cards are stacked against us, we give up playing or start a fight with the people responsible for the stacking. Forced to compete, people may simply go through the motions in a dispirited, listless manner, or revolt against the oppressors.

3. *When competition becomes too important, any means becomes justified to achieve the ends.* Winning is the aim of competition, and the temptation is to win at any cost. Although competition begins with the laudable aim of encouraging production, it quickly breaks down to a struggle to win at any price. When winning is not crucial, as in casual sports and games, competition can add excitement and fun so serve a useful and satisfying function. Competition as a way of life is quite a different matter. The means we use to achieve our ends are always bought at a price. When victory becomes too important, students cheat on exams, athletic teams begin to "play dirty," and businessmen lie to their customers. Price tags must be read not only in dollars and cents, but also in terms of human values—broken bodies, broken spirits, and disheartened and disillusioned people who do not appear in the winner's circle, on the sports pages, or as guests of honor at the testimonial banquet.

Competition encourages lone-wolf endeavors, and lone wolves can be dangerous to a cooperative society. We need to be able to count on other people to seek our best interests along with their own. In the headlong rush to win, competition too easily loses sight of this responsibility. It values aggression, hostility, and scorn. "Dog eat dog" becomes its philosophy. Too often the degree of glory involved for the victor is in direct proportion to the abasement and degradation of the loser.

Selected Readings

Starred entries indicate appearance in whole or in part in Donald L. Avila, Arthur W. Combs, and William W. Purkey, *The Helping Relationship Sourcebook,* Boston: Allyn and Bacon, 1977.

*Campbell, D. N. "On Being Number One: Competition in Education." *Phi Delta Kappan* 56, 1974, pp. 143–146.

Caplan, G. *Concepts of Mental Health and Consultation: The Application in Public Health Social Work.* Washington, D.C.: Children's Bureau, U.S. Department of Health, Education and Welfare, 1959.

Ginott, H. G. *Between Parent and Teenager.* New York: Macmillan Publishing Co., 1968.

Ginott, H. G. *Between Parent and Child: New Solutions to Old Problems.* New York: Macmillan Publishing Co., 1965.

Gordon, T. *Parent Effectiveness Training: The "No-Lose" Program for Raising Responsible Children.* New York: Peter H. Wyden, 1970.

Johnston, J. M., and Pennypacker, H. S. "A Behavioral Approach to College Training." *American Psychologist* 26, 1971, pp. 219–244.

Kirschenbaum, H.; Wapier, R.; and Simon, S. B. *Wad-Ja-Get: The Grading Game in American Education.* New York: Hart Publishing Co., 1971.

Koorland, M. A., and Mitchell, M. *Elementary Principles and Procedures of the Standard Behavior Chart.* Gainesville, Florida: Learning Environments, Inc., 1975.

MacMillan, D. L. *Behavior Modification in Education.* New York: Macmillan Publishing Co., 1973.

Marrow, A. J.; Bowers, D. G.; and Seashore, S. E. *Management by Participation.* New York: Harper & Row, Publishers, 1967.

Scott, W. W., and Spaulding, L. F. *What Do We Know about Leadership?* Washington, D.C.: U.S. Office of Health, Education and Welfare, 1972.

Simon, S. B., and Bellanca, J. A. *Degrading the Grading Myths: A Primer of Alternatives to Grades and Marks.* Washington, D.C.: Association for Supervision and Curriculum Development, 1976.

13

Being and Becoming Helpers

The helper's self is the primary tool with which helpers work. As we have seen, every human being has tremendous possibilities, and there is almost no limit to what a self may become. Understanding the self and learning to use it well is a lifelong process of personal discovery. Since every helper is unique, there cannot be universal rules, regulations, or procedures required for such explorations. Facilitating the growth of helpers is, itself, a helping process, however, and the principles we have been discussing throughout this book apply to aspiring helpers and professional training programs as well. Such concepts cannot be expressed as clear-cut do's and don't's. They can, however, serve as suggestions for personal growth and as hypotheses or guideposts for effective practice.

BECOMING HELPERS

Becoming Begins from Acceptance

Research demonstrates that self-acceptance is closely related to acceptance of others. People willing and able to confront who they are with clarity and honesty are much more likely to be able to do this with those they interact with. Acceptance is a major characteristic of adequate personalities and it is also a basic requirement for helping relationships. Becoming an effective professional worker is not a matter of trading one's old self in for a new one. Rather, it is a matter of learning how to use the self one has and of improving it slowly over a period of time. A very good place to start is with the principle of acceptance, to begin with the declaration, "It's all right to be me!"

In any group of beginners, the range of background, experience, attitudes, knowledge, maturity, and motivation will vary widely. Some people will be farther along at the beginning of a program than others will be at the end. Helpers will also vary greatly in the speed with which they can grow, and the needs students have for various kinds of experience will seldom be the same. The student-helper must learn to appreciate his own uniqueness and exhibit a readiness to confront whatever is needed for his own next steps in development, irrespective of where others in the process may be. Setting unreasonable goals and making invidious comparisons with others will only distort the focus of effort and result in anxiety.

Expert helpers do not develop overnight. *Techniques* of helping, like changes of costume, can sometimes be quickly put on. The development of an effective "self as instrument," however, is not achieved by the employment of gadgets or gimmicks. There are few substitutes for experience in the helping professions. The growth of helpers is a product of increasingly differentiated perceptions, of maturing beliefs, values, and understandings. This takes time, and many an otherwise likely candidate has destroyed effectiveness by impatience or lack of self-acceptance. Sudden changes rarely take place in students, clients, or patients. Nor do they occur in helper-learners.

Exploring Personal Meaning

Learning to use the self effectively is a highly personal matter, only slightly influenced by external manipulation. Growth of self can only occur with the cooperation of learners and a willingness to commit self in the processes of growth. It follows that the development of helpers must be predicated on high levels of self-direction and acceptance of primary responsibility by aspiring helpers for their own learning. Responsibility and self-direction are learned. They must be acquired from experience, from being given opportunities to be self-directing and responsible. You cannot learn to be self-directing if no one permits you to try. Human capacities are strengthened by use but atrophy with disuse. Autonomy, responsibility, and independence are the products of being willing to look and eager to try.

Changing the Self

Many people assume that to help a person change, the thing to do is to have him examine himself, decide what needs to be done, and then go do it. Some training programs also spend a great deal of time having young helpers indulge in self-examination, evaluating themselves and their behavior against long lists of the characteristics of "good" teachers, counselors, social workers, or whatever. Such approaches to changing self are rarely helpful. The self-concept is an organization of meanings, which cannot be changed by simply *deciding* to be different or concentrating attention on behavior. Persons discover who they are and what they are from the feedback they get in their interactions with the world and with other people or through the exploration of personal meanings. Intensive self-analysis often results in little more than maudlin self-indulgence. Having persons examine themselves with great intensity concentrates attention on behavior rather than the meanings producing behavior.

The authors' clients in psychotherapy do not get better when they examine themselves or their behavior. They get better when they look at their personal meanings, at how they feel about their wives, their kids, their jobs, the people they are working with. For example, let us suppose that Mary Johnson would like to make herself a more lovable person. To make herself more lovable, one thing she ought *not* do is sit around and think about her lovableness! She may, however, become more lovable by thinking about how she feels about other people—her friends, husband, parents, people she works with—or thinking about minority groups, social problems, and what she values and cares about. As a consequence of this exploration, she may come to feel better about these people and events. Feeling better toward them, her behavior will mirror her better feeling. Other people, reacting to her new behavior, will then respond by treating Mary as a nicer person. In turn, as Mary perceives this new reaction of others, she may discover she has become a more lovable person. Generally speaking, there are two ways in which one's self-concept may be changed: through new experience from events outside the person or through the discovery of new meanings achieved in the process of exploring existing ones.

The extensive, internally consistent organization of beliefs characteristic of effective helpers is only achieved after long and frequent confrontations with ideas. Helpers acquire personal understandings in the same ways their students, clients, and patients do—through a continuous, step-by-step process of exploration. Belief systems are the products of discussing, debating, trying, thinking, experimenting, making mistakes, and starting again in never-ending inquiry. All this takes time and a whole-hearted commitment to the process. It cannot be rushed. Nor is it simply a matter of acquiring new information. If it were true that people changed simply by knowledge about what ought to be done, then education professors would be by far the best teachers; psychologists and psychiatrists, the best adjusted; nurses and doctors, the healthiest; and ministers the most serene. But everyone knows that that is not so.

Earlier in our discussion of the principles of learning we observed that there is a vast difference between knowing and behaving. Effective learning comes about as a consequence of discovery of personal meaning. It is not enough simply to know; helpers must understand so deeply and personally that knowledge will affect behavior.

Practitioner-Scholar Dilemma

Most students entering programs for the helping professions begin with a quest for information. All their previous school experience has been primarily academic, emphasizing the acquisition of information. Their success has been evaluated by tests designed to measure the degree to which information was acquired, and success or failure was demonstrated by grades intended to reward or punish performance in the approved academic competition. As a consequence, aspiring helpers come to training programs, believing that they are not learning anything unless someone is telling them something new. This is a great pity, for failure to understand the scholar-practitioner distinction often delays progress in their new professional life.

The major goal for the scholar is to learn *about* something, to understand its relationship to other ideas, and perhaps, to teach it to someone else. To achieve this end, scholars seek out sources of information wherever they may be obtained, from lectures, reading, research, field trips, demonstrations, or discussions with experts. The problem of the practitioner is a different one. For professional workers it is not enough just to know—helpers have to *use* what they have learned. That goal requires a different educational experience. Practitioners must get involved. It may be enough for the educational psychologist to know about children as a group, for example; but teachers, counselors, or social workers will need to understand a particular child. Understanding persons as unique human beings is quite different from understanding about them academically.

This fundamental difference in objectives is the basis for the misunderstandings that often occur between students and teachers in liberal arts colleges and students and teachers in professional schools. One group is concerned primarily with the acquisition of knowledge; the other with professional performance. So the scholar observes the nurse, the teacher, the counselor, or clinical psychologist and exclaims, "Mickey Mouse stuff! How unscientific can you get?" Professional workers, on the other hand, look at the work of the scholar and exclaim, "What good is that? Imagine trying that with my patient!" (or student or client). Each observes the other through the glasses of his own values, beliefs, and decisions as to what is important, and each finds the other wanting. This breakdown of understanding between scholars and practitioners sometimes becomes very bitter.

Beginning students in the helping professions often complain that they aren't learning anything, because they spend many hours in observing,

202 **Helping Processes**

experimenting, and interminable talk. They do not understand that beliefs, values, and purposes are not acquired from information alone, but from the personal discovery of the meaning of information. For example, to make operational the basic principle of democracy, "when people are free, they can find their own best ways," does not require more information. For most of us, what is needed is a deeper understanding of the full meaning of that simple statement. Most persons can glibly state the principle, but comparatively few have so deeply comprehended its meaning that they consistently behave in truly democratic fashion.

Confronting Ultimate Questions

One of the ways in which helpers can test the depth of their grasp of purposes and dynamics is to come face to face with "ultimate" questions. For example, counselors who espouse belief in the confidentiality of counseling may ask themselves how far they are willing to stick by the principle. Would the counselor refuse information to a client's parent who demanded to know what her daughter said in the counseling hour? Would the counselor refuse information to another counselor? Would he or she defy a court order to reveal what a client confided?

How far would a social worker go in permitting a client to make her own decision? So far as to make a decision that seemed basically wrong to the social worker? To choose an antisocial act? To make a decision harmful to herself?

How far would a teacher go in maintaining the democratic belief? So far as to let students elect the "wrong" fellow student to office? To let children make their own rules? Or revolt against an autocratic school regulation?

Experienced helpers behave from instant to instant, apparently without ever thinking about what they ought to do next or how to go about it. Their behavior is a smoothly flowing, spontaneous response to students or clients determined, almost automatically, by well-established internally consistent belief systems. Beginners approach their tasks in a more tentative fashion, because they do not have such clear-cut guidelines. An internally consistent set of beliefs about themselves, other people, and appropriate purposes and processes makes smooth, effective practice possible.

Creating the Need to Know

One of the few principles of learning about which there is universal agreement is that people learn best when they have a need to know. Despite this understanding, a great deal of teaching is designed with almost total disregard for the principle. When people need to know they go to extraordinary lengths to find out. Without a need to know the most magnificent presentation may fall on deaf ears. Helper-learners can sometimes generate need from within their own experience, but real confrontation with problems is far more likely to provide effective motives for learning. Personal meaning is best achieved through problem solving: confronting dilemmas, questions, and events and seeking appropriate resolutions. Such problems can sometimes be manufactured and presented to student helpers as hypothetical situations in written form like case studies, in spoken directions as in role playing, or in some form of audiovisual presentation as in psychodrama, records, or television. Confrontation is far more effective, however, when problems faced are real and immediate.

The most vital source of problems for student-helpers is, of course, actual confrontation with students, clients, and patients. Once, practice teaching, counseling practicums, and social work internships were provided at the end of professional programs, as opportunities for the student-helper to practice what he had learned from his teacher-trainers. Many professional programs now regard such experience as far more valuable for aiding students to find out what the problems are. Consequently, practical experience is now often provided throughout the training program as a vehicle for creating needs to know.

While few student-helpers are ever able to choose precisely the nature of their experiences, they can welcome and take advantage of opportunities for new and positive experience. When this is done, the chances are that those experiences will lead to further possibilities. Successful experience contributes to positive feelings about self, and helpers can increase their chances for such experience by trying themselves to the limits of their capacities. The basic principle that good helping relationships are challenging without being threatening is also a useful guideline for the explorations of helpers themselves.

Methods and Becoming

Every helping profession has its special kinds of techniques and methods for carrying out its functions and the most immediate focus of the beginning helper's attention is usually concentrated on acquiring useful methods. It is a frightening thing to be placed in a helping role unequipped to carry out one's responsibilities. In the face of such threats, beginners beg for "tricks of the trade." The questions asked are likely to be, "What shall I do?" "How shall I do it?" "What do I do if . . . ?" Such questions are understandable. Survival is at stake, and of course, beginners need basic techniques with which to get started. Searching for "right" methods in the helping professions, however, is a blind alley.

Helping relationships are human interactions and the people involved in this process are unique human beings. The search for common methods to fit uniqueness is an exercise in futility. The task of the helper-learner is a matter of finding methods that fit, fit the client, fit the student or patient, fit the problems to be dealt with, fit the situations in which helper and helpee are involved, fit the purposes and dynamics of the particular helping profession, and of course, fit the nature and condition of the helper's self. The lack of right methods to be learned and practiced may be a disappointment to aspiring helpers. On the other hand, the uniqueness of methods means that no helper can be required to be like any other. Helpers can be who they are and what they are and the methods they use can be their very own.

A common fallacy in some training programs is the belief that the methods of experts can be taught directly to beginners. As a matter of fact, many methods of the experts work only because they are expert. For example, expert teachers handle most disciplinary problems by ignoring them, hardly a method to be recommended to the neophyte! Similarly, many techniques of expert counselors, social workers, or pastors are effective, because the background of experience, study, and assimilation of ideas have become so much a part of the effective worker as to make his interactions a smooth flowing expression of his personal meanings. Exhorting beginners to model themselves after the experts can prove to be more discouraging than motivating. Even when beginners find themselves in what is ostensibly the same practical problem as the expert, they do not have the understanding or belief system to make the method work. Beginning helpers need to find their own ways rather than adopting the ways of others. Helpers need experiences that make them stretch, but at which they have a fighting chance of success. Setting goals too high can be discouraging and self-defeating. Setting them too low can result in apathy and boredom.

Painters speak of searching for their "idiom," by which they mean the peculiar style of painting that fits the individual artist and best expresses his message. In similar fashion, effective helpers engage in a continual search for ways to create helping relationships that best fit their own and their clients' needs. Effective helpers know that when their methods are authentic, the relationships they establish are more likely to be successful. As most of us know from our own experience in dealing with other people, people who try to pretend to be what they are not only come across as phonies and put us on guard.

Special Experiences for Personal Growth

In addition to planned experiences provided by training programs and experiences sought out or contrived by helpers themselves helper-learners can take advantage of a wide variety of opportunities especially designed to further personal growth and actualization. Some of these are in the very professions and practices for which helper-learners are preparing. Others may be found outside professional or academic settings. In earlier chapters we mentioned some ways of increasing sensitivity and group experiences as aids to personal growth. Others may be found in modern techniques for expanding personal awareness and in various forms of counseling and psychotherapy.

Expanding Personal Awareness

A number of mind or consciousness expanding groups developed during the sixties, and many still continue. Some of these concentrate on aiding people to become more aware of their physical bodies. Others seek to free mental processes through various forms of meditation, through the use of hypnosis, or through the use of hallucinogenic drugs. Still others attempt to expand awareness in spiritual terms. Some of these attempts to expand awareness are very old, having deep roots in oriental cultures, while others are comparatively new.

Some consciousness expanding movements have evolved into religious cults, stoutly defended by adherents and accompanied by the trappings of religious ceremony. Others have been exploited for personal gain by self-anointed "masters" calling themselves psychologists, counselors, gurus, swamis, trainers or any of a hundred other titles. Some, however, continue to grow and bid fair to make important contributions to human health and fulfillment. Some have even been the subjects of empirical research and so have established themselves on more than testimonial grounds. Among these latter are several forms of meditation.

There seems little doubt that the practice of meditation is valuable for many people. Its techniques also seem to have considerable promise for the helping professions. To date, transcendental meditation has been subjected to the most research, and the resulting data indicate that meditation provides a kind of rest for the body apparently not achieved in other ways. It slows processes like heart rate, breathing, and galvanic skin response, to a rate below that of other forms of rest. It also seems to help reduce or eliminate various psychosomatic disorders and decreases drug and alcohol dependence. Psychological benefits, while not as well supported empirically, are rather convincing and directly related to the goals of the helping professions. The data suggest that transcendental meditation contributes to such things as increased sensitivity, awareness and tolerance of self and others, more positive feelings about self and others, and more self-actualizing-like characteristics.

If these early claims hold up, a significant new tool may have been discovered for use by helpers. Two factors make the possibilities of meditation especially valuable for the helping professions: the simplicity of acquisition and application. The technique can be learned very easily and can then be practiced by an individual without further involvement with other persons, further instruction, or cost. Such characteristics make meditation a valuable means for helping others, and they can also be used as important steps to growth for helpers themselves.

Doctor Heal Thyself

Beginning helpers sometimes hesitate to seek professional help for themselves, because they regard such actions as indications of personal weakness, which may be regarded as lack of fitness for the profession. Such attitudes are not only unfortunate, they are downright destructive to personal growth. The assumption that helpers must be extraordinary persons of vastly superior character is totally out of line with the basic nature of helping professions. Effective helpers are human beings like everyone else and suffer problems and frustrations like all other members of the human race. Being an effective helper does not require that one be totally without problems, only that they be sufficiently resolved to assure minimum interference in the work of helping others. Many successful helpers have personally experienced pain and suffering and periods of inadequacy. It may even be true that many people have been initially attracted to the helping professions precisely because they felt a need for personal help. After all, if one has problems it is an intelligent thing to seek help in solving them.

Helping relationships are only the application of the best we know about healthy human interaction, refined and concentrated for the needs of particular students, clients, or patients. As such, they have value for all persons. Growth is a continuous process and whatever helps it occur ought to be available to the largest possible number of persons. The authors of this book have frequently sought the help of colleagues in the helping professions to explore and discover more adequate ways of seeing themselves and the world. They have sometimes done this, because they confronted personal problems. They have also made frequent use of such services simply for their value in clarifying thinking and stimulating personal growth. So have most other professional helpers with whom the authors are acquainted.

Even if the above reasons for using the services of professional helpers were not enough, they have important value for helper-learners for two other reasons. One, persons entering the helping professions should demonstrate their faith in the processes they advocate for other people. Two, being in the helpee's role is, itself, an important learning experience for the aspiring helper. Sensitivity to others and the ability to perceive the world from another's frame of reference are vital skills for the helping professions. One important way in which helpers can sharpen these skills is through the experience of being a student-client, "on the other side" of the helping relationship.

THE HELPER'S OWN SELF-ACTUALIZATION

Helping relationships require that helpers either postpone their own immediate needs for fulfillment or find important satisfactions in being of service to their clients. To do this, helpers need to be well-disciplined. Self-discipline, however, is not an easy thing to maintain unless helpers themselves are achieving a significant degree of personal self-actualization. Deeply deprived persons find it difficult or impossible to be much concerned about fulfilling the needs of others. Their own needs are far too pressing.

Helpers need to have themselves well in hand. Otherwise, the question of who is helping whom is likely to become confused. A complete reversal of roles for helper and helpee is not uncommon in teaching and counseling. This can easily happen with a resistant student or client who has learned to keep outsiders from approaching his private feelings by asking them questions about their lives and experiences. The unwary helper can be seduced by this gambit. He responds to the questions, assuming that the client really wants to know, and because it eases the conversation and seems to contribute to rapport. Unless he is aware of what is going on, he may soon discover that he is doing all the talking and using the experience to ventilate his own feelings.

Self-discipline can sometimes cover up the effects of mild deprivation, but even with the most rigorous personal discipline it is probably not possible for highly inadequate persons to completely overcome that handicap to becoming an effective helper. All helping relationships require personal discipline. But self-discipline, no matter how strenuously applied, can rarely substitute sufficiently for positive feelings about self. Positive feelings about self make strenuous efforts at self-discipline less necessary.

Helpers do not have to be perfect. If they were, there would be very few in the profession. What *is* necessary is an accurate, realistic view of themselves, their assets, and their limitations. Persons engaged in the helping professions must be responsible. In accepting a request for help, the helper assumes the responsibility not to exceed his or her competence. To hold out a hope to someone that cannot be delivered is cruel and inhuman. Worse still, since clients can only judge the value of a helping relationship by their experience of it, a bad experience may prevent the client from ever getting the help he needs, because of loss of faith in the process. Good helpers do not exceed their competence. The greater the self-actualization of the helper, the greater the degree of freedom within which he can operate effectively. Whatever their level of personal fulfillment, however, professional helpers must have clear understandings of themselves, their talents, and their limitations.

The Personal Self and Professional Self

Beginners in the helping professions sometimes cause themselves and others much unhappiness by confusing their roles as persons and professional workers. A person's self and role are not the same. The self consists of a person's personal belief systems, his peculiar ways of seeing himself, and his relationship to the world. In contrast, the professional role defines a set of proper responsibilities and appropriate ways of behaving for helpers. These two concepts are related, but they are by no means identical. While the self must be expressed authentically in the professional role, the professional role does not have to pervade the private life of the helper. One can live the *philosophy* of helping and apply it to one's own life. Attempting to live the *practice* of the various forms of the helping professions, however, may only serve to complicate relationships in private life.

The relationships one has with wife, friends, or co-workers do not call for the person's professional role but for authentic behavior as husband, friend, or colleague. The helper who seeks to be teacher or counselor to wife, friends, or colleagues may only succeed in frustrating and antagonizing them. What they are likely to experience is a hidden agenda—a feeling of being tolerated, used, or manipulated. Beginning counselors, for example, often make themselves obnoxious by "treating" everyone they come in contact with. Treating a person who has not asked for it, or teaching a person who does not want such a relationship, can be a blatant lack of acceptance. It imposes a relationship, and so robs others of their right to choose for themselves.

Helpers are not immune to the effects of the self-concept on perception and may even be blinded by their professional roles. Pediatricians, concerned about a child's physical health, have been known to strap a child's arm to a board so that he could not bend his elbow and put his thumb in his mouth, without thinking about what this frustration does to the mental health of the child. Public health nurses and social workers often complain about people who live in shacks but nevertheless own television sets. They forget that if they lived in such squalid conditions, they, too, might wish to have what little joy and beauty a television set could bring them. Psychologists, deeply concerned about a client's behavior, have been known to overlook the evidence of brain damage in clients. Clergymen may be so deeply concerned with the problem of a parishioner's sins that instead of helping, they "cast the first stone."

Roles must be appropriate for the relationship in which they are used. It is important for helpers to keep perspectives clear.

The intense concentration of effort involved in many of the helping professions is most exhausting. In addition, the rigorous self-discipline required to carry out some of these relationships effectively requires setting one's self aside in the interests of other people. Even the healthiest self must still seek fufillment, and this search cannot long be denied. Successful performance in the helping professions may, in itself, be a form of self-fulfillment, but the self is more than "professional." It is also personal, man or woman, husband or wife, citizen, friend, or any of a thousand other definitions. These, too, require care and feeding. It is important, therefore, that persons engaged in the helping professions avail themselves of opportunities to engage in activities that are less demanding and more directly fulfilling of personal needs. The old adage that "all work and no play makes Jack a dull boy" has relevance for the helping professions. The most effective teachers, counselors, nurses, and psychologists known to the authors of this book are people who do not work at their professional roles full time.

THE HELPER AS PERSON AND CITIZEN

The Helper's Own Economy

Persons in the helping professions are likely to have many demands made upon them, especially if they are good at their jobs. The numbers of people needing help are very great, and the number of professional helpers is still very few. As a consequence, the demands for aid directed toward people in the helping professions will often be overwhelming. This raises difficult problems for the helper. Helpers usually enter the profession because they sincerely want to be of help to other people. When the number of requests so far outnumber their capacities to deliver, helpers may become discouraged, disillusioned, or embittered.

People in need of help can be terribly demanding of those who are in positions to assist them. This is especially true in those professions dealing with problems of mental health. Desperate people have little time to think of the problems of others. They are likely to be extraordinarily sensitive to slights and demand attention from helpers. To deal with such persons requires great patience, a capacity to absorb hostility, and a depth of concern sufficient to carry the helper through long periods of little or no apparent progress. Fundamental changes in people take place slowly, and helpers may often never see the effects of their work because they do not become manifest until long after helpees have left.

The effectiveness of helpers will be dependent upon how they choose to use themselves as instruments. Some of these decisions will be predetermined by the titles they bear or the accepted practices defined by their place of employment. But even in the most rigidly prescribed settings, there are still many decisions to be made about whom to work with, how to use time, and how to go about the helping task. A helper's success at coping with varied demands will be dependent upon his understanding of his clients, the nature of the helping task, the extent of his compassion, and the depth of his personal resources.

In making decisions about how to use themselves, helpers will inevitably make mistakes. Mistakes must be expected. They must also be forgiven. The compassion helpers advocate for others must be applied to themselves as well. The helper consumed by guilt or asking too much of himself may end by making himself ineffective.

Helpers are persons, too, and must be permitted the privileges of being human. There may even be times when helpers will have to say "no" to requests that are made of them. This may be an anguished decision for helpers, accompanied by the feeling that they have somehow betrayed their trust. Like everyone else, however, helpers have limitations, and because of those limitations or limits imposed by outside events, it will sometimes be necessary to reject requests for help. Indeed, not to do so may even result in compounding problems. Counselors, for example, who take on too many clients, may end up teaching their clients that the process has little to offer. Teachers who cannot bear to hurt a child by saying "no" when they should, may only lead their pupils to greater disillusionment and a sense of betrayal at a later date.

Because of their limitations or the circumstances in which they have to work, there may even be times when helpers decide to do less than their best. This is a decision that any human being has a right to make; but, having made it, it ought to be clearly perceived for what it is—a human decision and not an inevitable fact. A guidance counselor in high school may decide to see every member of the senior class for fifteen minutes instead of working more intensively with a few. That decision is the counselor's prerogative. It should not, however, be rationalized as being more effective.

A human being is a dynamic economy. Each has its assets and liabilities, its strengths and its weaknesses. This economy cannot long be violated. Instead, it must be accepted and worked with. Helpers need to accurately and realistically assess their limitations and accept them for what they are. They are not required to be all things to all people. Indeed, if they try, they are almost certainly doomed to failure. Being human, they, too, need times of respite to regain perspective and composure.

The Helper as Citizen

The professional role of helpers demands a special responsibility for assisting individuals to achieve greater fulfillment. This, in itself, is an important contribution to society, but the responsibility of helpers does not stop there. People in the helping professions live and work in society. They were citizens before they were teachers, counselors, social workers, or nurses, and the responsibilities of citizenship cannot be set aside by anyone. Persons in the helping professions, like everyone else, must come to some kind of terms with the world they live in. The helper's responsibility as a citizen requires more than repairing the casualties of the system as a counselor might, or preventing future failures as a teacher may. Responsibility as a citizen also requires contributing to the construction of a truly fulfilling society.

Professional helpers have several advantages in this, for their professions were established primarily to meet human needs. The successful completion of professional tasks leads directly to the enhancement of individuals and hence to the improvement of society. Both their professional training and job resposibilities provide helpers with opportunities to directly affect the social structure. Participation in the helping professions keeps one closely in touch with the basic emotions and perceptions of which human personality is composed. This insight and understanding of people and behavior can be of immense value for understanding the dynamics of society and contributing to its improvement.

A change in persons inevitably effects society as well. Helpers can make important contributions to social change by sharing their knowledge and by committing themselves to action wherever their special talents can be made useful. How they do this, of course, is an individual matter depending upon the helper's self, the situation, and the degree of involvement chosen.

The Helper as Agent of Change

Perhaps the most frequently heard excuse for personal inaction is the one that begins, "They won't let me." "They" may be bosses, parents, teachers, principals, supervisors, politicians, almost anybody. The implication is that one could do so much if only these nefarious influences were not in the way. The vast majority of reasons given by teachers, for example, for the failure of students to learn, lie almost anywhere except with the teacher—the children were unmotivated, were improperly prepared last year, were lazy, came from bad home situations. The tendency to place the blame for failure on others is by no means confined to teachers. It is a common excuse for inaction employed by helpers in all of the professions.

Sometimes supervisors, administrators, or other persons do impose restrictions upon freedom. Equally as often, these obstructions exist only in the minds of the complainants. When the accuracy of the "they won't let me" explanation for inaction is investigated, "they" are often amazed to hear of the roadblocks "they" are presumed to have placed in the way of progress. Obstructions to change do not have to be real. If someone thinks they exist, that is enough. Rosenthal and others have called this the "self-fulfilling prophecy" and demonstrated that when people believe a thing is so, they are likely to behave in ways that make it so. Counselors who believe their clients are resisting are likely to create resistance, and social workers convinced that nothing can be done do not make much of an effort to try and so increase the likelihood that nothing will be done.

Major changes often frighten people, especially if they are widely advertised in advance. This creates its own resistance. The very same changes can often be brought about without opposition if they are instituted as "normal" procedures minus trumpets and fanfare. In every life situation there is always room to maneuver, a degree of slack that permits a certain amount of movement. The helper who systematically takes up this slack soon finds still more room to maneuver because people get used to events. They assume it is normal, relax attention, and so provide a little more room to wriggle. Operating over a period of time by a continuous process of "taking up the slack," considerable change may be brought about. Later, because the matter never became an issue, no one is quite sure how it happened. Meanwhile, it has become well-established, and if successful, will probably be continued.

In the interest of maximum impact, behavior may sometimes have to be expressed less drastically than belief. At first glance, such a statement may sound like a denial of the authenticity we spoke of earlier. Not at all. People may *believe* whatever they wish. Behavior though, because it directly interacts with others, must be relevant and responsible. So, a man who believes he must be honest may speak out forcefully against racism knowing full well it will be threatening to his hearers, because he *intends* to force a distasteful confrontation. The same honest man may "pull punches" when his sister inquires how he likes her hat, because he is also kind and loves his sister—values that are more important at that moment than being impeccably honest.

Since individuals behave in terms of their perceptions, persons who hope to change behavior must be concerned with the relationship between the *meaning* of their action in the experience of those they influence. To be unconcerned with the consequences of one's behavior is to be little more than self-indulgent. Maximum change is likely to be produced when we successfully find ways to challenge people without threatening them. One reason for the ineffectiveness of many who take a radical position for social change is their insistence upon behaving in the full measure of belief without regard for its effects upon others. In the process they often make themselves so threatening to those they would like to change that they leave people no alternative but outright rejection.

Without compromising beliefs or abandoning eventual goals helpers may achieve more by adjusting demands to realistic appraisals of what is currently possible. There may be times and places when radical or revolutionary concepts are in order. Radicals can and have had stunning effects upon human affairs in the course of history. Persons who choose this way of forcing confrontation do so at the risk of destroying themselves in the process—but, on occasion, even that may be deemed a price well worth paying. There are social causes so important that personal considerations need to be sacrificed for larger goals.

As members of the social order, persons in the helping professions need to have a proper perspective of what can honestly be expected from society. People in the helping professions sometimes feel that they are not properly appreciated by the institutions they are involved in or the people they work with. Social workers bewail the fact that they are often misunderstood by the communities they are trying to help, teachers complain about the lack of public interest in the problems of the schools, counselors are shocked at the ingratitude of clients, and nurses are hurt that their patients so quickly forget them. Actually, this is a common fate of all workers in our society.

A democratic society *expects* each person to do his job. An interdependent society can only exist that way. This is especially true for the helping professions established expressly to serve other people. Society takes for granted they will do their jobs. It also reserves the right to protest, complain, and accuse if it does not believe the job is being done. This is the democratic way, and professional helpers who feel they are not appreciated by society need only to ask themselves, "When was the last time I dropped in at the police station to tell them what a good job they are doing?" "When did I last call up the sewage disposal works to express my appreciation for what they are doing?" For that matter, "When was the last time I wrote my congressman or senator with something other than a complaint?"

Conflicting Demands on Helpers

The professional role of helpers makes them responsible for aiding individuals to reach their maximum fulfillment. The personal role of helpers requires them to behave as citizens in ways that protect and enhance society. Fortunately, these goals are generally congruent, but at times they may come into conflict with one another. For example, a child caught in a disapproved act may beg his teacher not to inform his parents. A client tells his counselor that he has been shoplifting, or his social worker that he plans to commit suicide. The problems created by such confrontations must be met by helpers. Solutions are not simple. They are further complicated by the fact that helpers probably would not have the information in the first place had they not successfully created an atmosphere in which the student or client felt safe in talking about such matters.

Similar conflicts come about when some social agency attempts to impose upon helpers requirements contrary to the helper's conception of the professional role. This situation arose when teachers were told they could not teach evolution or were required to lead children in daily prayers (an act that has been declared unconstitutional). It might occur, too, when a counselor or nurse is requested by an authority to divulge what a client or patient said.

Matters like these raise difficult problems for the professional and citizenship roles of the helper. The resolution of such problems, for helpers confronted with them for the first time, is likely to involve a good deal of anguish. Pat answers seldom suffice. Each helper must think matters through for himself and arrive at his own decisions. After that, he must also be willing to take the consequences, whatever they may be. The process of making such decisions is painful. The pain is by no means worthless, however; it is precisely by wrestling with such problems that vision becomes clear, understandings are sharpened, philosophies are made more consistent, and further growth of the helper is achieved.

HELPING PROFESSIONS: A TWO-WAY STREET

Successful participation in helping relationships is, in itself, an experience in fulfillment. In earlier chapters we observed that whatever is experienced is experienced forever. We have also seen how the self may expand to include other persons. The helper's encounters with clients, students, and patients expand his own experience and influence. A friend once pointed out to the authors three sources of immortality available to everyone. One kind, he said, is the immortality we achieve through our blood lines. This, however, is a tenuous foothold. Hereditary links are easily broken by the failure of our children or descendants to reproduce. A second kind of immortality, he pointed out, is that promised us in the tenets of religion. Such concepts are comforting thoughts, but they could, conceivably, be wrong. The only kind of immortality we can all be sure of, he maintained, is that which we achieve as a consequence of our impact on the people in the world we live in. So the helper affects the client, and the client affects the helper, and each leaves the interaction changed in some way because of the experience. All future contacts will be affected because of this significant experience. "This," said our friend, "is a kind of immortality we can all be sure of. If in time we achieve the others also, that's like icing on the cake."

A helper is a warm-blooded, living, human being with his or her own needs, capacities, hopes, fears, loves, and aspirations. In addition to these characteristics, which they share in common with all other human beings, helpers have assumed, or have had thrust upon them, the responsibility for creating relationships that are helpful for other people. How effectively the helper carries out this task will depend upon how well he has learned to use his particular talents and personality for the realization of his own and society's purposes. We have called this the "self as instrument" concept.

When helpers perform effectively, it is not only clients, patients, or students who profit. The increased humanity and sensitivity to others that is a result of intimate interaction with others is also one of the fringe benefits for workers in the helping professions. Helping others is a two-way street. One cannot successfully enter deeply and meaningfully into the life of another person without having that experience affect one's self as well.

Counselors, for example, cannot walk hand in hand with clients through the intimate phases of their lives without adding something important to their own understanding. Similarly, successful experiences in teaching, nursing, supervision, administration, and social work must leave their inevitable mark upon the professional helper and enrich his own field of experience. With tongue in cheek, someone once described psychotherapy: "When two people get together to help each other!" The joke is probably true. Effective practice in the helping professions provides its practitioners with the rare privilege of engaging in work that results in a continuous process of personal growth.

Selected Readings

Starred entries indicate appearance in Donald L. Avila, Arthur W. Combs, and William W. Purkey, *The Helping Relationship Sourcebook,* Boston: Allyn and Bacon, 1977.

Bugental, J. F. T. *The Search for Authenticity: An Existential-Analytic Approach to Psychotherapy.* New York: Holt, Rinehart and Winston, 1965.

*Combs, A. W. "Fostering Self-Direction." *Educational Leadership* 23, 1966, pp. 373–387.

Combs, A. W.; Blume, R. A.; Newman, A. J.; and Wass, H. L. *The Professional Education of Teachers: A Humanistic Approach to Teacher Preparation.* Boston: Allyn and Bacon, 1974.

Lawton, G. "Neurotic Interaction between Counselor and Counselee." *Journal of Counseling Psychology* 5, 1958, pp. 28–33.

Rogers, C. R., and Stevens, B. *Person to Person: The Problem of Being Human.* New York: Pocket Books, 1967.

Simon, S.; Howe, L.; and Kirschenbaum, H. *Values Clarification: A Handbook of Practical Strategies for Teachers and Students.* New York: Hart, 1972.

Bibliography

Aaronson, D., and Markowitz, N. "The Temporal Course of Retrieval from Short Term Memory." Paper presented at meeting of the Eastern Psychological Association, Washington, D.C., April 1968.

Abramson, P., ed. "Discipline: Not the Worst Problem . . . but Bad." *Grade Teacher* 86, 1968, pp. 151–163.

Adams, H. B. "Mental Illness: Or Interpersonal Behavior Patterns?" *American Psychologist* 19, 1964, pp. 191–197.

Adams, J. S. "Reduction of Cognitive Dissonance by Seeking Consonant Information." *Journal of Abnormal and Social Psychology* 62, 1961, pp. 74–78.

Agee, J. *A Death in the Family.* New York: Grossett & Dunlap, 1967.

Allport, F. H. *Theories of Perception and the Concept of Structure.* New York: John Wiley & Sons, 1965.

Allport, G. W. "The Use of Personal Documents in Psychological Science. *Social Science Research Council Bulletin,* 1942.

Allport, G. W. *Becoming.* New Haven: Yale University Press, 1955.

Allport, G. W. *Pattern and Growth in Personality.* New York: Holt, Rinehart and Winston, 1961.

Ames, A. *An Interpretative Manual: The Nature of Our Perceptions, Prehensions and Behavior.* Princeton, New Jersey: Princeton University Press, 1955.

Amos, W. E., and Orem, R. C. *Managing Student Behavior.* St. Louis: Green Publishing Co., 1967.

Anastasi, A. "Psychology, Psychologists and Psychological Testing. *American Psychologist* 55, 1967, pp. 297–306.

Appelbaum, S. A. "The Problem Solving Aspect of Suicide." *Journal of Projective Techniques and Personality Assessment* 27, 1963, pp. 259–268.

Arbuckle, D. S. "Self-Ratings and Test Scores on Two Standardized Personality Inventories. *Personnel Guidance Journal* 37, 1958, pp. 292–293.

Arbuckle, D. S., and Boy, A. V. "Client-Centered Therapy in Counseling Students with Behavior Problems. *Journal of Counseling Psychology* 8, 1961, pp. 136–139.

Arkoff, A. "Some Workers in Improvement." In *Adjustment and Mental Health*, pp. 284–307. New York: McGraw-Hill Book Co., 1968.

Aronson E.; Carlsmith, J. M.; and Darley, J. M. "The Effects of Expectancy on Volunteering for an Unpleasant Experience. *Journal of Abnormal and Social Psychology* 66, 1963, pp. 220–224.

Association for Supervision and Curriculum Development. *Evaluation as Feedback and Guide*, 1967 Yearbook. Washington, D.C.: ASCD, 1967.

Association for Supervision and Curriculum Development. *Learning and Mental Health in the School*, 1966 Yearbook. Washington, D.C.: ASCD, 1966.

Association for Supervision and Curriculum Development. *Perceiving Behaving, Becoming: A New Focus for Education*, 1962 Yearbook. Washington, D.C.: ASCD, 1962.

Aspy, D. N. "Maslow and Teachers in Training." *Journal of Teacher Education* 20, 1969a, pp. 303–309.

Aspy, D. N. "How did he get there?" *Peabody Journal of Education* 47, 1969b, pp. 152–253.

Aspy, D. N. "The Effect of Teacher-Offered Conditions of Empathy, Positive Regard and Congruence upon Student Achievement." *Florida Journal of Educational Research* 11, 1969c, pp. 39–49.

Aspy, D. N. "Elephants in the Living Room." *Personnel and Guidance Journal* 48, 1969d, pp. 287–293.

Ausubel, D. P. "A New Look at Classroom Discipline." *Phi Delta Kappan* 43, 1961, pp. 25–30.

Ausubel, D. P. "A Teaching Strategy for Culturally Deprived Pupils: Cognitive and Motivational Considerations." *School Review* 71, 1963, pp. 454–463.

Averch, H. A.; Carroll, S. J.; Donaldson, T. S.; Kiesling, H. J.; and Pincus, J. *How Effective Is Schooling: A Critical Review of Research*. Englewood Cliffs, New Jersey: Educational Technology Publications, 1974.

Avila, D. L., and Purkey, W. W. "Intrinsic and Extrinsic Motivation: A Regrettable Distinction. *Psychology in the Schools* 3, 1966, pp. 206–208.

Avila, D. L.; Combs, A. W.; and Purkey, W. W. *The Helping Relationship Sourcebook*. Boston: Allyn and Bacon, 1971.

Avila, D. L., and Purkey, W. "Self-Theory and Behaviorism: A Rapprochement." *Psychology in the Schools*, 1972, pp. 124–126.

Axline, V. M. *Dibs: In Search of Self*. Boston: Houghton Mifflin Co., 1964.

Bach, G. R. "The Marathon Group: 1. Intensive Practice of Intimate Interaction." *Psychological Reports* 18, 1966, pp. 995–1002.

Baker, J. P., and Crist, J. L. "Teacher Expectancies: A Review of the Literature." In J. D. Elashoff and R. E. Snow, eds., *Pygmalion Reconsidered*, pp. 48–64. Worthington, Ohio: Charles A. Jones Publishing Co., 1971.

Ball, G. "Speaking without Words." *American Journal of Nursing* 60, 1960, pp. 692–693.

Barlow, J. A. *Stimulus and Response*. New York: Harper & Row, Publishers, 1968.

Bartlett, F. C., *Remembering*, rev. ed. Cambridge, England: Cambridge University Press, 1932.

Bartley, S. H. *Principles of Perception*. New York: Harpers, 1958.

Beard, R. M. *An Outline of Piaget's Developmental Psychology for Students and Teachers*. New York: Basic Books, 1969.

Beatty, W. H., and Clark, R. "A Self-Concept Theory of Learning: A Learning Theory for Teachers. In H. C. Lindgren, ed., *Readings in Educational Psychology*. New York: John Wiley & Sons, 1968.

Becker, A. H. "The Function of Relationship in Pastoral Counseling." Doctoral dissertation, Boston University. Boston: University Microfilms, 1958, no. 58–3087.

Beilin, H. "Teachers' and Clinicians: Attitudes toward the Behavior Problems of Children. *Child Development* 30, 1959, pp. 9–25.

Benson, H. *The Relaxation Response*. New York: William Morrow & Co., 1975.

Benton, J. A., Jr. "Perceptual Characteristics of Episcopal Pastors." Unpublished doctoral dissertation, University of Florida, 1964.

Beres, D. "Perception, Imagination and Reality." *International Journal of Psychoanalysis* 41, 1960, pp. 327–334.

Berger, E. M. "The Relation between Expressed Acceptance of Self and Expressed Acceptance of Others. *Journal of Abnormal and Social Psychology* 47, 1952, pp. 778–782.

Bergin, A. E. "Some Implications of Psychotherapy Research for Therapeutic Practice." *Journal of Abnormal Psychology* 71, 1966, pp. 235–246. See also, *International Journal of Psychiatry* 3, 1967, pp. 136–150.

Berkowitz, L., and Cottingham, D. R. "The Interest, Value and Relevance of Fear Arousing Communication." *Journal of Abnormal and Social Psychology* 60, 1960, pp. 37–43.

Berzon, B.; Pious, C.; and Farson, R. E. "The Therapeutic Event in Group Psychotherapy: A Study of Subjective Reports by Group Members." *Journal of Individual Psychology* 19, 1963, pp. 204–212.

Bettleheim, B. *Love Is Not Enough*. New York: Collier Books, 1965.

Bettelheim, B. *The Empty Fortress: Infantile Autism and the Birth of the Self*. New York: Free Press, 1967.

Bettelheim, B. "Where Self Begins." *Child and Family* 7, 1968, pp. 5–12.

Bieri, J., and Trieschman, A. "Learning as a Function of Perceived Similarity to Self." *Journal of Personality* 25, 1956, pp. 213–223.

Bigge, M. L. *Learning Theories for Teachers*. New York: Harper & Row, Publishers, 1964.

Bills, R. E. "Personality Changes during Student Centered Teaching." *Journal of Educational Research* 50, 1956, pp. 121–126.

Binet, A. *Les Idees Modernes sur les Enfants*. Paris: Ernest Flamarion, 1909.

Birdwhistell, R. L. *Kinesis and Context: Essays on Body Motion Communication*. Philadelphia: University of Pennsylvania Press, 1970.

Birney, R. C.; Burdick, H.; and Teevan, R. C. *Fear of Failure*. New York: Van Nostrand, 1969.

Bischof, L. *Interpreting Personality Theories*. New York: Harper & Row, Publishers, 1964.

Bloomfield, H. H.; Cain, P. M.; and Joffe, D. T. *TM: Discovering Inner Energy and Overcoming Stress*. New York: Delacorte Press, 1975.

Bogdan, R., and Taylor, S. "The Judged, Not the Judges: An Insider's View of Mental Retardation. *American Psychologists*, January 1976, pp. 47–52.

Bonner, H. *On Being Mindful of Man*. Boston: Houghton Mifflin, 1965.

Borislow, B. "Self-Evaluation and Academic Achievement." *Journal of Counseling Psychology* 9, 1962, pp. 246–254.

Botwinick, J. *Aging and Behavior: A Comprehensive Integration of Research Findings*. New York: Springer, 1973.

Boucher, J. D., and Ekman, P. "Facial Areas and Emotional Information. *Journal of Communication* 25, 1975, pp. 21–29.

Bowers, W. J. *Student Dishonesty and Its Control in College*. New York: Bureau of Applied Social Research, Columbia University, 1964.

Bowers, N. D., and Soar, R. S. *Evaluation of Laboratory Human Relations Training for Classroom Teachers. Studies of Human Relations in the Teaching-Learning Process: V. Final Report*. U.S. Office of Education Contract. No. 8143. Columbia, South Carolina: University of South Carolina, 1961.

Bradford, L.; Benne, K.; and Gibb, J. R. *T-Group Theory and Laboratory Method*. New York: John Wiley & Sons, 1964.

Bradway, K. P., and Robinson, N. M. "Significant I. Q. Changes in Twenty-Five Years." *Journal of Educational Psychology*, 52, 1961, pp. 74–79.

Brammer, L. *The Helping Relationship: Process and Skills*. Englewood Cliffs, New Jersey: Prentice-Hall, 1973.

Brandt, R. M. "The Accuracy of Self-Estimate: A Measure of Self-Concept Reality." *Genetic Psychology Monographs* 58, 1958, pp. 55–99.

Brennecke, J., and Amick, R. *The Struggle for Significance*. Beverly Hills, California: Glencoe Press, 1971.

Brill, N. "Communication with Low Income Families." *Journal of Home Economics* 58, 1966, pp. 631–635.

Brock, T. C., and Grant, L. D. "Dissonance, Awareness, and Motivation." *Journal of Abnormal and Social Psychology* 67, 1963, pp. 53–60.

Brookes, R. M., and Goldstein, A. G. "Recognition by Children of Inverted Photographs of Faces." *Child Development* 34, 1963, pp. 1033–1040.

Brookover, W. B. *"The Relationships of Self-Images to Achievement of Junior High School Subjects."* East Lansing, Michigan: United States Office of Education, no. 845, 1960.

Brookover, W. B.; Paterson, A.; and Thomas, S. "Self-Concept of Ability and School Achievement." *Sociology of Education* 37, 1964, pp. 271, 278.

Brophy, J. E., and Good, T. L. "Teachers' Communication of Differential Expectations for Children's Classroom Performance: Some Behavioral Data." *Journal of Educational Psychology* 61, 1970, pp. 364–374.

Brophy, J. E., and Good, T. L. *Teacher-Student Relationships: Causes and Consequences.* New York: Holt, Rinehart and Winston, 1974.

Brown, B. B. *An Investigation of Observer-Judge Ratings of Teacher Competence.* Final report no. D–182, Contract no. OF–6–10–288. Washington, D.C.: U.S. Department of Health, Education and Welfare, Office of Education, 1969.

Brown, I. C. *Understanding Other Cultures.* Englewood Cliffs, New Jersey: Prentice-Hall, 1963.

Brown, R. G. *A Study of the Perceptual Organization of Elementary and Secondary Outstanding Young Educators.* Unpublished doctoral dissertation, University of Florida, 1970.

Brownfain, J. J. "Stability of the Self-Concept as a Dimension of Personality." *Journal of Abnormal and Social Psychology* 47, 1952, pp. 597–606.

Bruner, J. S. *Toward a Theory of Instruction.* New York: W. W. Norton & Co., 1966.

Brunkan, R. J., and Sheni, F. "Personality Characteristics of Ineffective, Effective, and Efficient Readers. *Personnel and Guidance Journal* 44, 1966, pp. 837–344.

Bugental, J. F. T. *The Search for Authenticity 1965, An Existential-Analytic Approach to Psychotherapy.* New York: Holt, Rinehart and Winston, 1965.

Bugental, J. F. T., ed. *Challenges of Humanistic Psychology.* New York: McGraw-Hill Book Co., 1967.

Buhler, C. B. "Human Life Goals in the Humanistic Perspective." *Journal of Humanistic Psychology* 7, 1967, pp. 36–52.

Buhler, C. B., and Allen, M. *Introduction to Humanistic Psychology.* Belmont, California: Wadsworth, 1972.

Caliguri, J. "Self-Concept of the Poverty Child." *Journal of Negro Education* 35, 1966, pp. 280–282.

Calvin, A. D., and Holtzman, W. H. "Adjustment and Discrepancy between Self-Concept and Inferred Self. *Journal of Consulting Psychology* 17, 1953, pp. 39–44.

Campbell, David N. "On Being Number One: Competition in Education." *Phi Delta Kappan* 56, 1974, pp. 143–146.

Canfield, J., and Wells, H. C. *100 Ways to Enhance Self-Concept in the Classroom: A Handbook for Parents and Teachers.* Englewood Cliffs, New Jersey: Prentice-Hall, 1976.

Cantril, H. *Human Nature and Political Systems.* New Brunswick, New Jersey: Rutgers University Press, 1961.

Cantril, H. "The Human Design." *Journal of Individual Psychology* 20, 1964, pp. 129–136.

Cantril, H. "Sentio, Ergo Sum: 'Motivation' Reconsidered." *The Journal of Psychology* 65, 1967, pp. 91–107.

Caplan, G. *Concepts of Mental Health and Consultation: The Application in Public Health Social Work.* Washington, D.C.: U.S. Dept. of Health, Education and Welfare, 1959.

Caplan, M. D. "Self-Concept, Level of Aspiration, and Academic Achievement." *The Journal of Negro Education* 37, 1968, pp. 435–439.

Carkhuff, R. R., and Berenson, B. G. *Beyond Counseling and Therapy*. New York: Holt, Rinehart and Winston, 1967.

Carkhuff, R. R., and Truax, C. B. "Toward Explaining Success and Failure in Interpersonal Learning Experiences." *Personnel and Guidance Journal* 44, 1966, pp. 723–728.

Carkhuff, R. R., and Truax, C. B. *Toward Counseling and Psychotherapy: Training and Practice*. Chicago, Illinois: Aldine, 1967.

Carlson, R. "Stability and Change in the Adolescent's Self-Image." *Child Development* 36, 1965, pp. 659–666.

Carlton, L., and Moore, R. H. "Culturally Disadvantaged Children Can Be Helped." *NEA Journal* 9, 1966, pp. 13–14.

Carlton, L., and Moore, R. H. *Reading, Self-Directive Dramatization and Self Concept*. Columbus, Ohio: Charles E. Merrill Publishing Co., 1968.

Carr, D. E. *The Forgotten Senses*. Garden City, New York: Doubleday & Co., 1972.

Carter, T. P. "The Negative Self Concept of Mexican-American Students." *School and Society* 96, 1968, pp. 217–219.

Cartwright, R. D. "Self-Conception Patterns of College Life." *Journal of Counseling Psychology* 10, 1963, pp. 47–52.

Chansky, N. M., and Taylor, M. "Perceptual Training with Young Mental Retardates." *American Journal of Mental Deficiency* 68, 1964, pp. 460–468.

Child, I. L. *Humanistic Psychology and the Research Tradition: Their Several Virtues*. New York: John Wiley & Sons, 1973.

Chodorkoff, B. "Self-Perception, Perceptual Defense, and Adjustment." *Journal of Abnormal and Social Psychology* 49, 1954, pp. 508–512.

Choy, C. *The Relationship of College Teacher Effectiveness to Conceptual Systems Orientation and Perceptual Orientation*. Unpublished doctoral dissertation, University of Northern Colorado, 1969.

Clore, G.; Wiggins, H. H.; and Itkin, S. "Judging Attraction from Nonverbal Behavior: The Gain Phenomenon." *Journal of Consulting and Clinical Psychology* 43, 1975, pp. 491–497.

Cohen, J. "Psychological Time." *Scientific American* 211, 1964, pp. 116–124.

Cohen, L. D. "Level of Aspiration Behavior and Feelings of Adequacy and Self-Acceptance." *Journal of Abnormal and Social Psychology* 49, 1954, pp. 84–86.

Coller, A. R. *The Assessment of Self-Concept in Early Childhood Education*. Urbana Illinois: ERIC Clearinghouse on Early Childhood Education, University of Illinois, 1971.

Combs, A. W. "A Phenomenological Approach to Adjustment Theory." *Journal of Abnormal and Social Psychology* 44, 1949, pp. 29–35.

Combs, A. W. "Intelligence from a Perceptual Point of View." *Journal of Abnormal and Social Psychology* 47, 1952, pp. 662–673.

Combs, A. W. "Counseling as a Learning Process." *Journal of Counseling Psychology* 1, 1954, pp. 31–36.

Combs, A. W. "The Myth of Competition." *Childhood Education* 33, 1957, pp. 264–269.

Combs, A. W. "What Can Man Become?" *California Journal for Instructional Improvement* 4, 1961, pp. 15–23.

Combs, A. W. "The Personal Approach to Good Teaching." *Educational Leadership* 21, 1964, pp. 369–378.

Combs, A. W. "Fostering Self-Direction." *Educational Leadership* 23, 1966, pp. 373–387.

Combs, A. W. "The Perceptual Approach to the Helping Professions." *Journal of the Association for the Study of Perception* 5, 1970.

Combs, A. W. "Two Views of Motivation." In J. J. Frymier, ed., *Handbook of Research on Motivation*. Columbus, Ohio: Ohio State University, 1971a.

Combs, A. W. "Some Basic Guidelines for the Training of 'Helpers.'" *Proceedings, National Faculty Development Conference*. Atlanta Georgia: Southern Regional Education Board, 1971b.

Combs, A. W. *Educational Accountability: Beyond Behavioral Objectives*. Washington, D.C.: Association for Supervision and Curriculum Development, 1972.

Combs, A. W. "Why the Humanistic Movement Needs a Perceptual Psychology." *Journal of the Association for the Study of Perception* 9, 1974, pp. 1–13.

Combs, A. W. *Myths in Education: Beliefs that Hinder Progress and Their Alternatives*. Boston: Allyn and Bacon, in press.

Combs, A. W.; Blume, R. A.; Newman, A. J.; and Wass, H. L. *The Professional Education of Teachers: A Humanistic Approach to Teacher Preparation*. Boston: Allyn and Bacon, 1974.

Combs, A. W.; Courson, C. C.; and Soper, D. W. "The Measurement of Self-Concept and Self-Report. *Educational and Psychological Measurement* 23, 1963, pp. 439–500.

Combs, A. W.; Richards, A. C.; and Richards, F. *Perceptual Psychology: A Humanistic Approach to the Study of Persons*. New York: Harper & Row, 1976.

Combs, A. W., and Snygg, D. *Individual Behavior: A Perceptual Approach to Behavior*. New York: Harper & Brothers, Publishers, 1959.

Combs, A. W., and Soper, D. W. "The Self, Its Derivative Terms and Research." *Journal of Individual Psychology* 12, 1957, pp. 134–145.

Combs, A. W., and Soper, D. W. *The Relationship of Child Perceptions to Achievement and Behavior in the Early School Years*. Cooperative Research Project no. 814. Gainesville, Florida: University of Florida, 1963a.

Combs, A. W., and Soper, D. W. "Perceptual Organization of Effective Counselors. *Journal of Counseling Psychology* 10, 1963b, pp. 222–226.

Combs, A. W., and Soper, D. W. "The Helping Relationship as Described by Good and Poor Teachers." *Journal of Teacher Education* 14, 1963c, pp. 64–67.

Combs, A. W.; Soper, D. W.; Gooding, C. T.; Benton, J. A.; Dickman, J. F.; and Usher, R. H. *Florida Studies in the Helping Professions.* Social Science Monograph no. 37. Gainesville, Florida: University of Florida Press, 1969.

Combs, A. W., and Taylor, C. "The Effect of Perception of Mild Degrees of Threat on Performance." *Journal of Abnormal and Social Psychology* 47, 1952, pp. 420–424.

Combs, C. F. "Perception of Self and Scholastic Underachievement in the Academically Capable." *Personnel and Guidance Journal* 43, 1964a, pp. 47–51.

Combs, C. F. "A Study of the Relationship between Certain Perceptions of Self and Scholastic Underachievement in Academically Capable High School Boys. *Dissertation Abstracts* 24, 1964b, p. 620.

Connelly, C. J. "Threatening the Sense of Self-Worth." *Childhood Education* 4, 1964, p. 20.

Conwell, R. H. *Acres of Diamonds.* New York: Harper & Row, Publishers, 1943.

Coopersmith, S. *The Antecedents of Self-esteem.* San Francisco: W. H. Freeman and Co., 1967.

Coudert, J. *Advice from a Failure.* New York: Dell, 1965.

Courson, C. "The Relationship of Certain Perceptual Factors to Adequacy." Unpublished doctoral dissertation, University of Florida, 1963.

Courson, C. "The Use of Inference as a Research Tool. *Educational and Psychological Measurement* 25, 1965, pp. 1029–1038.

Courson, C. "Personal Adequacy and Self-Perception in High School Students: A Study of Behavior and Internal Perceptual Factors." *Journal of Humanistic Psychology* 8, 1968, pp. 29–38.

Craddick, R. A. "Height of Christmas Tree Drawings as a Function of Time." *Perceptual and Motor Skills* 17, 1963, pp. 335–339.

Craig, J. H., and Craig, M. *Synergic Power: Beyond Domination and Permissiveness.* Berkeley, California: ProActive Press, 1974.

Craig, M. "Patient—Heal Thyself." *Journal of Contemporary Psychotherapy* 6, 1974, pp. 157–164.

Crandall, V. J., and Sinkeldam, C. "Children's Dependent and Achievement Behaviors in Social Situations, and Their Perceptual Field Dependence." *Journal of Personality* 32, 1964, pp. 1–22.

Crovetto, L. L.; Fischer, A. M.; and Boudreaus, J. L. *The Pre-school Child and His Self-Image.* New Orleans: Division of Instruction and Division of Pupil Personnel, New Orleans Public Schools, 1967.

Culler, I. B. "Stability of Self-Concept in Schizophrenia." *Journal of Abnormal Psychology* 71, 1966, pp. 275–279.

Davids, A., and Lawton, M. H. "Self-Concept, Mother Aversions and Food Aversions in Emotionally Disturbed Children." *Journal of Abnormal and Social Psychology* 62, 1961, pp. 309–314.

Davidson, H., and Lang, G. "Children's Perceptions of Their Teacher's Feelings toward Them Related to Self-Perception, School Achievement and Behavior." *Journal of Experimental Education* 29, 1960, pp. 107–118.

Davitz, J. R. "Fear, Anxiety and the Perception of Others." *Journal of General Psychology* 61, 1959, pp. 169–173.

Davitz, J. R., and Davitz, L. J. "Nonverbal Vocal Communication of Feeling." *Journal of Communication* 2, 1961, pp. 81–86.

De Charms, R. *Personal Causation: The Internal Affective Determinants of Behavior.* New York: Academic, 1968.

Dedrick, C. V. L. "The Relationship between Perceptual Characteristics and Effective Teaching at the Junior College Level." Unpublished doctoral dissertation, University of Florida, 1972.

Dee, F. S.; Arndt, C.; and Meyer, B. "Self-Acceptance of Nurses and Acceptance of Patients: An Exploratory Investigation." *Nursing Research* 14, 1965, pp. 346–350.

Delaney, D. J., and Heiman, R. A. "Effectiveness of Sensitivity Training on the Perception of Non-Verbal Communication." *Journal of Counseling Psychology* 13, 1966, pp. 436–440.

Dellow, D. A. "A Study of the Perceptual Organization of Teachers and Conditions of Empathy, Congruence, and Positive Regard." Unpublished doctoral dissertation, University of Florida, March 1971.

Demos, G. D., and Zuwaylif, F. H. "Characteristics of Effective Counselors." *Counselor Education and Supervision* 5, 1966, pp. 163–165.

Deutsch, M. *The Resolution of Conflict: Constructive and Destructive Processes.* New Haven: Yale University Press, 1973.

Dexter, L. A. *The Tryanny of Schooling.* New York: Basic Books, 1964.

Dickman, J. F. "The Perceptual Organization of Person-Oriented versus Task-Oriented Student Nurses." Unpublished doctoral dissertation, University of Florida, 1967.

Diggory, J. *Self-Evaluation.* New York: John Wiley & Sons, 1966.

Dinitz, S.; Scarpitti, F. R.; and Reckless, W. C. "Delinquency Vulnerability: A Cross Group and Longitudinal Analysis." *The American Sociological Review* 27, 1962, pp. 515–517.

Dombrow, R. "A Study of the Relationship between Therapist's Empathy for Patients and Changes in Patients' Self-Concepts during Therapy." *Dissertation Abstracts* 27B, 1966, pp. 301–302.

Dove, A. "Soul Folk 'Chitling' Test (The Dove Counterbalance Intelligence Test)." In G. A. Davis and T. F. Warren, eds., *Psychology of Education: New Looks.* Lexington, Massachusetts: D. C. Heath and Co., 1974.

Doyle, E. J. "The Relationship between College Teacher Effectiveness and Inferred Characteristics of the Adequate Personality." Unpublished doctoral dissertation, University of North Carolina, 1969.

Doyle, W.; Hancock, G.; and Kifer, E. "Teachers' Perceptions: Do They Make a Difference?" *Journal of the Association for the Study of Perception* 7, 1972, pp. 21–30.

Drews, E. M., and Lipson, L. *Values and Humanity.* New York: St. Martins Press, 1971.

Durr, W. K., and Schmatz, R. R. "Personality Difference between High-Achieving and Low-Achieving Gifted Children." *Reading Teacher* 17, 1964, pp. 251–254.

Eisen, N. H. "Some Effects of Early Sensory Deprivation on Later Behavior: The Quandam Hard of Hearing Child." *Journal of Abnormal and Social Psychology* 65, 1962, pp. 338–342.

Eisner, W. W. *Think with Me about Creativity: Ten Essays on Creativity.* Dansville, New York: Owen Publishing Co., 1964.

Ellena, W. J.; Stevenson, M.; and Webb, H. V. *Who's a Good Teacher?* Washington, D.C.: American Association of School Administrators, National Education Association, 1961.

English, H. B. *Dynamics of Child Development.* New York: Holt, Rinehart and Winston, 1961.

Erikson, E. M. "The Concept of Identity in Race Relations." *Daedalus* 95, 1966, pp. 141–171.

Evans, J. T. *Characteristics of an Open Education: Results from a Classroom Observation Rating Scale and Questionnaire.* Newton, Massachusetts Educational Development Center, 1971.

Farquhar, W. W. *A Comprehensive Study of the Motivational Factors Underlying Achievement of Eleventh Grade High School Students.* United States Office of Education Cooperative Research Report No. 846. Michigan State University: United States Office of Education Office of Research and Publications, 1968.

Fausti, R. P., and Luker, A. H. "Phenomenological Approach to Discussion." *Speech Teacher* 14, 1965, pp. 19–23.

Festinger, L. *A Theory of Cognitive Dissonance.* Palo Alto, California: Stanford University Press, 1957.

Festinger, L. "Cognitive Dissonance." *Scientific American* 207, 1964, pp. 93–107.

Fiedler, F. E. "A Comparison of Therapeutic Relationships in Psychoanalytic, Non-Directive and Adlerian Therapy." *Journal of Consulting Psychology* 14, 1950a, pp. 436–445.

Fiedler, F. E. "The Concept of an Ideal Therapeutic Relationship." *Journal of Consulting Psychology* 14, 1950b, pp. 239–245.

Fiedler, F. E. *A Theory of Leadership Effectiveness.* New York: McGraw-Hill Series in Management, 1967.

Fink, M. B. "Self-Concept as It Relates to Academic Underachievement." *California Journal of Educational Research* 13, 1962, pp. 57–62.

Fisher, W. "Better Self-Images." *The Instructor* 78, 1968, p. 95.

Fleming, E., and Anttonen, R. "Teacher Expectancy, or My Fair Lady. *American Educational Research Journal* 8, 1971, pp. 241–252.

Ford, D. H., and Urhan, H. B. *Systems of Psychotherapy: A Comparative Study.* New York: John Wiley & Sons, 1963.

Frank, L. K. "The World as a Communication Network." In G. Kepes, ed., *Sign Image Symbol.* New York: Braziller, 1966.

Frankl, V. E. *Man's Search for Meaning: An Introduction to Logotherapy.* Boston: Beacon Press, 1963.

Frankl, Viktor E. "Self-transcendence as a Human Phenomenon." In J. Sutich and M. A. Vich, eds., *Readings in Humanistic Psychology.* New York: The Free Press, 1969.

Freud, A. *The Ego and the Mechanisms of Defense.* New York: International Universities Press, 1946.

Freud, S. *A General Introduction to Psychoanalysis.* Garden City, New York: Garden City Publishing Co., 1920.

Frick, W. B. *Humanistic Psychology: Interviews with Maslow, Murphy and Rogers.* Columbus, Ohio: Charles E. Merrill, 1971.

Friedman, M. *To Deny Our Nothingness.* New York: Dell, 1967.

Fromm, E. *Art of Loving: An Inquiry into the Nature of Love.* New York: Harper & Row, Publishers, 1956.

Fromm, E. *Man for Himself.* New York: Holt, Rinehart and Winston, 1957.

Frostig, M. "Visual Perception in Brain-Injured Children." *American Journal of Orthopsychiatry* 33, 1963, pp. 665–671.

Frymier, J. R. "The Relationship of Certain Behavioral Characteristics to Perception." Unpublished doctoral dissertation, University of Florida, 1957.

Frymier, J. R. "Professionalism in Context." *Ohio State Law Journal* 26, 1965a, pp. 53–65.

Frymier, J. R. *The Nature of Educational Method.* Columbus, Ohio: Charles E. Merrill, 1965b.

Frymier, J. R., and Thompson, J. H. "Motivation: The Learner's Mainspring." *Educational Leadership* 22, 1965, pp. 567–570.

Gage, N. L. "Exploration of Teacher's Perceptions of Pupils." *Journal of Teacher Education* 9, 1958, pp. 97–101.

Gage, N. L., ed. *Handbook of Research on Teaching.* Chicago: Rand McNally & Co., 1963.

Gergen, K. J., and Wishnov, B. "Others' Self-Evaluations and Interaction Anticipation as Determinants of Self-Presentation." *Journal of Personality and Social Psychology* 2, 1965, pp. 348–358.

Getzels, J. W., and Jackson, P. W. *Creativity and Intelligence: Explorations with Gifted Students.* New York: John Wiley & Sons, 1962.

Getzels, J. W., and Jackson, P. W. "The Teacher's Personality and Characteristics." In N. L. Gage, ed., *Handbook of Research on Teaching,* pp. 506–582. Chicago: Rand McNally & Co., 1963.

Gibb, J. R. "Defensive Communication." *The Journal of Communication* 11, 1961, pp. 141–148.

Gibb, J. R.; Platts, G. N.; and Miller, L. E. *Dynamics of Participative Groups.* New York: Jolin Swift, 1961.

Gibby, R. G., Sr., and Gibby, R. G., Jr. "The Effects of Stress Resulting from Academic Failure." *Journal of Clinical Psychology* 23, 1967, pp. 35–37.

Gibson, E. J. "Perceptual Learning." *Annual Review of Psychology* 14, 1963, pp. 29–56.

Ginott, H. G. *Group Psychotherapy with Children.* New York: McGraw-Hill Book Co., 1961.

Ginott, H. G. *Between Parent and Child: New Solutions to Old Problems.* New York: Macmillan Publishing Co., 1965.

Ginott, H. G. *Between Parent and Teenager.* New York: Macmillan Publishing Co., 1968.

Giorgi, A. *Psychology as a Human Science: A Phenomenologically-Based Approach.* New York: Harper & Row, Publishers, 1970.

Givner, A., and Graubord, P. S. *A Handbook of Behavior Modification for the Classroom.* New York: Holt, Rinehart and Winston, 1974.

Gladstone, R. *A Set of Principles of Teaching Derived from Experimental Psychology,* 2nd ed. Stillwater, Oklahoma: Oklahoma State University Press, 1967.

Glasser, W. *Reality Therapy: A New Approach to Psychiatry.* New York: Harper & Row, Publishers, 1965.

Glasser, W. *Schools without Failure.* New York: Harper & Row, Publishers, 1968.

Goble, F. G. *Third Force: The Psychology of Abraham Maslow.* New York: Grossman Publishers, 1970.

Goffman, E. *Frame Analysis: An Essay on the Organization of Experience.* Cambridge, Massachusetts: Harvard University, 1974.

Goldstein, A. P. *Therapist-Patient Expectancies in Psychotherapy.* Elmsford, New York: Pergamon, 1962.

Gollob, H. F., and Dittes, J. E. "Effects of Manipulated Self-Esteem on Persuasibility Depending on Threat and Complexity of Communication. *Journal of Personality and Social Psychology* 2, 1965, pp. 195–201.

Good, T. L.; Biddle, B. J.; and Brophy, J. E. *Teachers Make a Difference.* New York: Holt, Rinehart and Winston, 1975.

Gooding, C. T. "An Observational Analysis of the Perceptual Organization of Effective Teachers." Unpublished doctoral dissertation, University of Florida, 1964.

Goodman, M. "Expressed Self-Acceptance and Interspousal Needs: A Basis for Mate Selection." *Journal of Counseling Psychology* 11, 1965, pp. 129–135.

Gordon, C., and Gergen, K. J. *The Self in Social Interaction. Vol. I: Classic and Contemporary Perspectives.* New York: John Wiley & Sons, 1968.

Gordon, I. J. "Observing from a Perceptual Viewpoint." *Journal of Teacher Education* 10, 1959, pp. 280–284.

Gordon, I. J. *New Conceptions of Children's Learning and Development.* Washington, D.C.: Association for Supervision and Curriculum Development, National Education Association, 1966a.

Gordon, I. J. *Studying the Child in School.* New York: John Wiley & Sons, 1966b.

Gordon, I. J. *A Parent Education Approach to Provision of Early Stimulation for the Culturally Disadvantaged.* Gainesville, Florida: Institute for Development of Human Resources, 1967.

Gordon, I. J. *Human Development from Birth through Adolescence,* 2nd ed. New York: Harper & Row, Publishers, 1969.

Gordon, I. J., and Wood, P. C. "Relationship between Pupil Self-Evaluation, Teacher Evaluation of the Pupil and Scholastic Achievement." *Journal of Educational Research* 56, 1963, pp. 440–443.

Gordon, T. *Parent Effectiveness Training: The No-Lose Program for Raising Responsible Children.* New York: Peter H. Wyden, 1970.

Goslin, D. A. *The Search for Ability.* New York: Russell Sage Foundation, 1963.

Graff, R. W., and Bradshaw, H. E. "Relationship of a Measure of Self-Actualization to Dormitory Assistant Effectiveness. *Journal of Counseling Psychology* 17, 1970, pp. 502–506.

Greene, G. *Sex and the College Girl.* New York: Dial Press, 1964.

Grimes, J. W., and Allensmith, W. "Compulsivity, Anxiety, and School Achievement." *Merrill-Palmer Quarterly of Behavior and Development* 7, 1961, pp. 247–271.

Grossack, M. M. "Some Effects of Cooperation and Competition upon Small Group Behavior." *Journal of Abnormal and Social Psychology* 49, 1954a, pp. 341–348.

Grossack, M. M. "Perceived Negro Group Belongingness and Social Rejection." *The Journal of Psychology* 38, 1954b, pp. 127–130.

Grossack, M. M. "Some Personality Characteristics of Southern Negro Students." *The Journal of Social Psychology* 46, 1957, pp. 125–131.

Guilford, J. P. "Three Faces of Intellect." In R. E. Ripple, ed., *Readings in Learning and Human Abilities,* pp. 46–64. New York: Harpers, 1964.

Guller, I. B. "Stability of Self-Concept in Schizophrenia." *Journal of Abnormal Psychology* 71, 1966, pp. 275–279.

Haarer, D. L. "A Comparative Study of Self-Concept of Ability Institutionalized Delinquent Boys and Non-Delinquent Boys Enrolled in Public Schools. Unpublished doctoral dissertation, Michigan State University, 1964. See also *Dissertation Abstracts* 25, p. 6410.

Haas, H. I., and Maehr, M. L. "Two Experiments on the Concept of Self and the Reaction of Others." *Journal of Personality and Social Psychology* 1, 1965, pp. 100–105.

Haberman, M., and Raths, J. "High, Average, Low—and What Makes Teachers Think So." *Elementary School Journal* 68, 1968, pp. 241–245.

Haefner, D. "Some Effects of Situational Threat on Group Behavior." *Journal of Abnormal and Social Psychology* 49, 1954, pp. 445–453.

Hall, E. T. *The Silent Language.* New York: Fawcett World Library, 1959.

Halpin, A. W. "The Leader Behavior and Leadership Ideology of Educational Administrators and Aircraft Commanders." *Harvard Education Review* 25, 1955, pp. 18–32.

Hamachek, D. E. "A Study of the Relationships between Certain Measures of Growth and the Self-Images of Elementary School Children." *Dissertation Abstracts* 21, 1961, p. 2193.

Hamachek, D. E. "Dynamics of the Self." *Wisconsin Journal of Education* 101, 1969, pp. 7–9.

Hamachek, D. E. *Encounters with the Self*. New York: Holt, Rinehart and Winston, 1971.

Hamachek, D. E., and Mori, I. "Need Structure, Personal Adjustment and Academic Self-Concept of Beginning Education Students." *Journal of Educational Research* 58, 1964, pp. 158–162.

Hanna, Thomas. *Bodies in Revolt; a Primer in Somatic Thinking*. New York: Holt, Rinehart and Winston, 1970.

Harlow, H. "The Nature of Love." *The American Psychologist* 13, 1958, pp. 673–685.

Harlow, H., and Harlow, M. K. "Social Deprivation in Infant Monkeys." *Scientific American* 207, 1962, pp. 136–146.

Harman, W. W. "Two Contrasting Forecasts." In P. K. Piele and G. L. Eidell, eds., *Social and Technological Change: Implications for Education*. Eugene, Oregon: Center for Advanced Study of Educational Administration, 1970.

Harrington, M. *The Other America*. Baltimore, Maryland: Penguin Books, 1963.

Hastorf, A. H., and Myro, G. "The Effect of Meaning on Binocular Rivalry." *American Journal of Psychology* 72, 1959, pp. 393–400.

Hayakawa, S. I. "Suicide as a Communicative Act." *ETC: A Review of General Semantics* 15, 1957, pp. 46–51.

Hayakawa, S. I. *Language in Thought and Action*. New York: Harcourt, Brace & World, 1964.

Heine, R. W. "A Comparison of Patients' Reports on Psychotherapeutic Experience with Psychoanalytic, Non-Directive and Adlerian Therapists." *Journal of Psychotherapy* 7, 1953, pp. 16–23.

Henry, J. *Culture against Man*. New York: Random House, 1963.

Herman, M. "Self-Concept of the Negro Child." *Catholic School Journal* 66, 1966, pp. 62–63.

Hilgard, E., and Bowers, G. *Theories of Learning*. New York: Appleton-Century-Crofts, 1966.

Hinde, R. A., ed. *Non-Verbal Communication*. New York: Cambridge University Press, 1972.

Hitt, W. D. "Two Models of Man." *American Psychologist* 24, 1969, pp. 651–658.

Homme, F., and Tosti, D. *Behavior Technology: Motivation and Contingency Management*. San Rafael, California: Individual Learning Systems, 1971.

Honzik, M. P.; Macfarlane, J. W.; and Allen, J. "The Stability of Mental Test Performance between Two and Eighteen Years." In W. Dennis, ed., *Readings in Child Psychology* pp. 223–232. Englewood Cliffs, New Jersey: Prentice-Hall, 1963.

House, R. J. "T-group Education and Leadership Effectiveness: A Review of the Empiric Literature and a Critical Evaluation." *Personnel Psychology* 20, 1967, pp. 1–31.

Howe, M. J. *An Introduction to Human Memory*. New York: Harper & Row Publishers, 1970.

Howe, M. J. A. "Verbal Context as a Retrieval Cue in Long-Term Memory for Words." *Psychonomic Science* 9, 1967, pp. 453–545.

Hummel, R., and Sprinthall, N. "Underachievement Related to Interests, Attitudes, and Values." *The Personnel and Guidance Journal* 44, 1965, pp. 388–395.

Hunt, J. M. *Intelligence and Experience*. New York: Ronald Press, 1961.

Hunt, J. M. "The Implications of Changing Ideas on How Children Develop Intellectually. *Children* 11, 1964, pp. 83–91.

Hunt, J. M. "The Role of Experience in the Development of Competence." In J. McV. Hunt, ed., *Human Intelligence*. New Brunswick, New Jersey: Transaction, 1972.

Hunter, E. *Encounter in the Classroom*. New York: Holt, Rinehart and Winston, 1972.

Ittelson, W. H. "The Involuntary Bet." *Vogue*, March 15, 1952, pp. 76–77, 127.

Ittelson, W. H. *Visual Space Perception*. New York: Springer, 1960.

Ittelson, W. H., and Ames, A., Jr. *The Ames Demonstrations in Perception*. Darien, Connecticut: Hafner, 1968.

Ittelson, W. H. and Cantril, H. *Perception: A Transactional Approach*. Garden City, New York: Doubleday & Co., 1954.

Jackson, P. W. *Life in Classrooms*. New York: Holt, Rinehart and Winston, 1968.

Jennings, G. D. "The Relationship between Perceptual Characteristics and Effective Advising of University Housing Para-Professional Residence Assistants." Unpublished doctoral dissertation, University of Florida, 1973.

Jersild, A. T. "Voice of the self." *NEA Journal* 54, 1965, pp. 23–25.

Johnson, T. J.; Feigenbaum, R.; and Weiby, M. "Some Determinants and Consequences of the Teacher's Perception of Causation." *Journal of Educational Psychology* 55, 1964, pp. 237–246.

Johnston, J. M. and Pennypacker, H. S. "A Behavioral Approach to College Teaching." *American Psychologist* 26, 1971, pp. 219–244.

Jones, A.; Braden, I.; and Wilkinson, H. J. "Information Deprivation as a Motivational Variable." *Journal of Experimental Psychology* 62, 1961, pp. 126–137.

Jones, R. L., ed. *Black Psychology*. New York: Harper & Row, Publishers, 1972.

Jones, S. C., and Panitch, D. "The Self-Fulfilling Prophecy and Interpersonal Attraction." *Journal of Experimental Social Psychology* 7, 1971, 356–366.

Jourard, S. *Personal Adjustment*. New York: Macmillan Publishing Co., 1963.

Jourard, S. *The Transparent Self*. New York: Van Nostrand, 1964.

Jourard, S. *Disclosing Man to Himself*. New York: Van Nostrand, 1968.

Jourard, S. "Healthy Personality and Self-Disclosure." In H. G. Brown, R. A. Newell, and H. G. Vonk, eds., *Behavioral Implications for Curriculum and Teaching: Interdisciplinary Readings*. Dubuque, Iowa: William C. Brown, 1969.

Jourard, S. *Healthy Personality: An Approach from the Viewpoint of Humanistic Psychology*. New York: Macmillan Publishing Co., 1974.

Jourard, S., ed. *To Be or Not to Be . . . Existential-Psychological Perspectives on the Self*. Gainesville, Florida: University of Florida Press, 1967.

Katz, D., and Kahn, R. L. "Some Recent Findings in Human Relations Research in Industry." In G. E. Swanson, T. M. Newcomb, and E. L. Hartley, *Readings in Social Psychology*. New York: Holt, 1952.

Keen, E. *A Primer of Phenomenological Psychology*. New York: Holt, Rinehart and Winston, 1975.

Kelley, E. C. *Education for What Is Real*. New York: Harper, 1947.

Kelley, E. C. "Communication and the Open Self." *ETC: A Review of General Semantics* 10, 1954, p. 96.

Kelley, E. C. *In Defense of Youth*. Englewood Cliffs, New Jersey: Prentice-Hall, 1962a.

Kelley, E. C. *Another Look at Individualism*. Detroit, Michigan: Wayne State University, College of Education, 1962b.

Kelley, E. C. "The Meaning of Wholeness." *ETC: A Review of General Semantics* 26, 1969, pp. 7–15.

Kelley, E. C. "What May We Now Believe." In D. L. Avila, A. W. Combs, and W. W. Purkey, *Helping Relationship Sourcebook*. Boston: Allyn and Bacon, 1977.

Kelly, F. J., and Veldman, D. J. "Delinquency and School Dropout Behavior as a Function of Impulsivity and Non-Dominant Values." *Journal of Abnormal and Social Psychology* 64, 1969, pp. 190–194.

Kelly, G. A. *A Theory of Personality: The Psychology of Personal Constructs*. New York: Norton, 1963.

Kellog, R., and O'Dell, S. *The Psychology of Children's Art*. Camino, Del Mar, California: CRM, 1967.

Kemp, C. G. *Perspectives on the Group Process*. Boston: Houghton Mifflin, 1970.

Kemp, C. G. "Existential Counseling." *The Counseling Psychologist* 2, 1971, pp. 2–30.

Kester, S. "The Communication of Teacher Expectations and Their Effects on the Achievement and Attitude of Secondary School Students." *American Educational Research Journal* 66, 1972, pp. 51–58.

Kimbal, S. T. "Cultural Influence Shaping the Role of the Child." In G. D. Spindler, ed., *Education and Culture: Anthropological Approaches*. New York: Holt, Rinehart and Winston, 1963.

Kirk, S. A. *Early Education of the Mentally Retarded: An Experimental Study*. Urbana, Illinois: University of Illinois Press, 1958.

Kirschenbaum, H.; Wapier, R.; and Simon, S. B. *Wad-Ja-Get: The Grading Game in American Education*. New York: Hart Publishing Co., 1971.

Klein, G. S. *Perception, Motives, and Personality*. New York: Knopf, 1970.

Koffman, Roberta G. "A Comparison of the Perceptual Organizations of Outstanding and Randomly Selected Teachers in Open and Traditional Classrooms." Unpublished doctoral dissertation, University of Massachusetts, 1975.

Kohlberg, L. "Stage and Sequence: The Cognitive-Developmental Approach to Socialization." In D. A. Goslin, ed., *Handbook of Socialization Theory and Research*. Skokie, Illinois: Rand McNally & Co., 1969.

Kolers, P. A. "It Loses Something in the Translation." *Psychology Today* 2, 1969, pp. 32–35.

Kolesnik, W. B. *Humanism and/or Behaviorism in Education.* Boston: Allyn and Bacon, 1975.

Koorland, M. A. and Mitchell, M. *Elementary Principles and Procedures of the Standard Behavior Chart.* Gainesville, Florida: Learning Environments, 1975.

Korchin, S. J., and Basowitz, H. "Perceptual Adequacy in a Life Stress." *Journal of Psychology* 38, 1954, pp. 495–502.

Kounin, J. S. "Managing Emotionally Disturbed Children in Regular Classrooms: A Replication & Extension." *Journal of Special Education* 2, 1968, pp. 129–135.

Kounin, J. S., and Gump, P. V. "Ripple Effect in Discipline." *Elementary School Journal* 59, 1958, pp. 158–162.

Kowitz, G. T. "Test Anxiety and Self-Concept." *Childhood Education* 44, 1967, pp. 162–165.

Kratochvil, D.; Aspy, D.; and Carkhuff, R. R. "The Differential Effects of Absolute Level and Direction of Growth in Counselor Functioning upon Client Level of Functioning." *Journal of Clinical Psychology* 23, 1967, pp. 216–217.

Krech, D.; Crutchfield, R. S.; and Livson, N. *Elements of Psychology,* 2nd ed. New York: Alfred A. Knopf, 1969.

Kuenzli, A. E. *The Phenomenological Problem.* New York: Harper & Brothers, 1959.

Kvareceus, W. C. *Negro Self-Concept: Implications for School and Citizenship.* New York: McGraw-Hill Book Co., 1965.

Kvaraceus, W. C. "Poverty, Education and Race Relations." In W. C. Kvaraceus, J. S. Gibson, and T. J. Curtin, eds., *Poverty, Education and Race Relations: Studies and Proposals,* pp. 3–10. Boston: Allyn and Bacon, 1967.

La Benne, W. D., and Greene, B. J. *Educational Implications of Self-Concept Theory.* Pacific Palisades, California: Goodyear, 1969.

Lafferty, J. C. "Values that Defeat Learning." *National Association of Secondary School Principals Bulletin* 52, 1968, pp. 201–212.

Lakin, M. "Some Ethical Issues in Sensitivity Training." *American Psychologist* 24, 1969, pp. 923–928.

Lamy, M. E. "Relationship of Self-Perceptions of Early Primary Children to Achievement in Reading." In I. J. Gordon, ed., *Human Development: Readings in Research,* p. 251. Chicago: Scott, Foresman and Co., 1965.

Landsman, T. "Factors Influencing Individual Mental Health." *Review of Educational Research* 32, 1962, pp. 464–475.

Landsman, T. "Positive Experience and the Beautiful Person." Address given at meeting of the Southeastern Psychological Association, Roanoke, Virginia, April 1968.

Landry, R. G., and Edeburn, C. C. "Teacher Self-Concept and Student Self-

Concept." Paper presented at the American Educational Research Association Convention, Chicago, Illinois, April 1974.

Lantz, D. L. "Changes in Student Teachers' Concepts of Self and Others." *Journal of Teacher Education* 15, 1964, pp. 200–203.

Lantz, D. L. "Relationship between Classroom Emotional Climate and Concepts of Self, Others and Ideal among Elementary Student Teachers." *Journal of Educational Research* 59, 1965, pp. 80–83.

Lanzetta, J. T.; Axelrod, H.; Haefner, D.; and Langham, P. "Some Effects of Situational Threat on Group Behavior." *Journal of Abnormal and Social Psychology* 49, 1954, pp. 445–453.

Larson, C. V. *Communication: Everyday Encounters.* Belmont, California: Wadsworth Publishing Co., 1976.

Laszlo, E. *The Systems View of the World.* New York: Braziller, 1972.

Laury, G. V., and Murloo, A. M. "Subtle Types of Mental Cruelty to Children." *Child and Family* 6, 1967, pp. 28–34.

Lawton, G. "Neurotic Interaction between Counselor and Counselee." *Journal of Counseling Psychology* 5, 1958, pp. 28–33.

Lecky, P. *Self-Consistency: A Theory of Personality.* New York: Island Press, 1945.

Lee, L. C.; Kagan, J.; and Rabson, A. "Influence of Preference for Analytic Category upon Concept Acquisition." *Child Development* 34, 1963, pp. 433–442.

Lefcourt, H. M. "Risk Taking in Negro and White Adults." *Journal of Personality and Social Psychology* 2, 1965, pp. 765–770.

Leichty, M. M. "Family Attitudes and Self-Concept in Vietnamese and U.S. Children." *American Journal of Orthopsychiatry* 33, 1963, pp. 38–50.

Levanway, R. W. "The Effect of Stress on Expressed Attitude toward Self and Others." *Journal of Abnormal and Social Psychology* 50, 1955, pp. 225–226.

Lewin, K. *A Dynamic Theory of Personality: Selected Papers by Kurt Lewin.* New York: McGraw-Hill Book Co., 1935.

Liddle, G. P. "Psychological Factors Involved in Dropping Out of School." *High School Journal* 45, 1962, pp. 276–280.

Lifton, W. M. *Working with Groups.* New York: John Wiley & Sons, 1966.

Lilly, J., and Shurley, J. T. "Experiments in Solitude, in Maximum Achievable Physical Isolation with Water Suspension, of Intact Healthy Persons." In B. E. Flaherty, ed., *Psychophysiological Aspects of Space Flight,* pp. 238–247. New York: Columbia University Press, 1961.

Lippitt, R. *Feedback Process in the Community Context.* Washington, D.C.: National Training Laboratory, National Education Association, 1965.

Lippitt, R., and White, R. K. "An Experimental Study of Leadership and Group Life." In G. E. Swanson, T. M. Newcomb, and E. L. Hartley, eds., *Readings in Social Psychology,* rev. ed. New York: Henry Holt, 1952.

Livingston, R. B. "How Man Looks at His Own Brain: An Adventure Shared by Psychology and Neuro-Physiology." In S. Koch, ed., *Psychology: A Study of a Science,* pp. 51–99. New York: McGraw-Hill Book Co., 1962.

Lloyd, J. "The Self-Image of a Small Black Child." *Elementary School Journal* 67, 1967, pp. 406–411.

Logan, F. A., and Wagner, A. R. *Reward and Punishment*. Boston: Allyn and Bacon, 1965.

Long, B. H., and Henderson, E. H. "Certain Determinants of Academic Expectancies among Southern and Non-Southern Teachers." *American Educational Research Journal* 11, 1974, pp. 137–147.

Loss, S. P. "Nonverbal Behavior of Teachers and Students: Clues to Teaching Effectiveness." *American Vocational Journal* 48, 1973, pp. 23–24.

Luchins, A. S. "The Problem of Truth in the Study of Perception." *Psychological Record* 13, 1963, pp. 213–220.

Luckey, E. B. "Implications for Marriage Counseling of Self-Perceptions and Spouse Perceptions." *Journal of Counseling Psychology* 7, 1960, pp. 3–9.

Ludwig, D. L., and Maehr, M. L. "Changes in Self-Concept and Stated Behavior Preferences. *Child Development* 38, 1967, pp. 453–467.

Luft, J. "On Nonverbal Interaction." *Journal of Psychology* 63, 1966, pp. 261–268.

MacDonald, J. B. "Gamesmanship in the Classroom." *National Association of Secondary School Principals Bulletin* 50, 1966, pp. 51–68.

MacDonald, J. B., and Zaret, E. "A Study of Openness in Classroom Interactions." Unpublished manuscript, Marquette University, 1966.

MacKinnon, D. W. "The Nature and Nurture of Creative Talent." *American Psychologist* 17, 1962, pp. 484–495.

MacLeod, J. "Sensitivity Training, What's That? Is it for a Local Union?" *International Journal of Religious Education* 43, 1966, pp. 8–9.

MacMillan, Donald L. *Behavior Modification in Education*. New York: The Macmillan Co., 1973.

Maehr, M. L. "Some Limitations of the Application of Reinforcement Theory to Education." *School and Society* 96, 1968, pp. 108–110.

Maehr, M. L., Menking, J., and Nafeger, S. "Concept of Self and the Reaction of Others." *Sociometry* 25, 1962, pp. 353–357.

Mahler, C. A., and Caldwell, E. *Group Counseling in Secondary Schools*. Chicago: Science Research Associates, 1961.

Makarenko, A. S. *The Collective Family: A Handbook for Russian Parents*. Garden City, New York: Doubleday & Co., 1967.

Malcolm X. *The Autobiography of Malcolm X*. New York: Grove Press, 1964.

Marrow, A. J. *Behind the Executive Mask*. New York: American Management Association, 1964a.

Marrow, A. J. "Risks and Uncertainty in Action Research." *Journal of Social Issues* 20, 1964b, pp. 5–20.

Marrow, A. J.; Bowers, D. G.; and Seashore, S. E. *Management by Participation*. New York: Harper & Row, Publishers, 1967.

Marshall, H. H. "The Effect of Punishment of Children: A Review of the Literature and a Suggested Hypothesis." *Journal of Genetic Psychology* 106, 1965, pp. 23–33.

Marshall, J. "The Evidence." *Psychology Today* 2, 1969, pp. 48–52.

Maslow, A. H. *Toward a Psychology of Being.* New York: Van Nostrand, 1962.

Maslow, A. H. "The Creative Attitude." *The Structuralist* 3, 1963, pp. 4–10.

Maslow, A. H. "Synergy in the Society and in the Individual." *Journal of Individual Psychology,* November 1964, pp. 153–164.

Maslow, A. H. *Motivation and Personality,* 2nd ed. New York: Harper & Row, Publishers, 1970.

Maslow, A. H. *The Farther Reaches of Human Nature.* New York: Viking, 1971.

Matarayya, J. D. "Psychotherapeutic Processes." *Annual Review of Psychology* 16, 1965, pp. 181–224.

Matson, F. W., ed. *Being, Becoming, and Behavior.* New York: George Braziller, 1967.

May, R. *Love and Will.* New York: Norton, 1969.

May, R., ed. *Existence.* New York: Basic Books, 1958.

May, R., ed. *Existential Psychology.* New York: Random House, 1961.

Mayer, C. L. "The Relationship of Early Special Class Placement and the Self-Concepts of Mentally Handicapped Children." Exceptional Children 33, 1966, pp. 77–81.

McCallon, E. L. "Teacher Characteristics and Their Relationship to Change in the Congruency of Children's Perception of Self and Ideal-Self." *Journal of Experimental Education* 34, 1966, pp. 84–88.

McDaniel, S. W. "Counselor Selection: An Evaluation of Instruments." *Counselor Education and Supervision* 6, 1967, pp. 142–144.

McGrath, J. E., and McGrath, M. "Effects of Partisanship on Perceptions of Political Figures." *Public Opinion Quarterly,* Spring 1962.

McGreevy, P. "Factor Analysis of Measures Used in the Selection of Counselor Education Candidates." *Journal of Counseling Psychology* 14, 1967, pp. 51–56.

McIntyre, C. J. "Acceptance by Others and Its Relation to Acceptance of Self and Others." *Journal of Abnormal and Social Psychology* 47, 1952, pp. 624–625.

McNeil, E. B. *The Quiet Furies: Man and Disorder.* Englewood Cliffs, New Jersey: Prentice-Hall, 1967.

McNeil, E. B. *Being Human: The Psychological Experience.* New York: Harper & Row, Publishers, 1973.

Mead, G. H. *Mind and Society.* Chicago: University of Chicago Press, 1934.

Mead, M. "The Young Adult." In E. Ginzburg, ed., *Values and Ideals of American Youth,* pp. 37–51. New York: Columbia University Press, 1961.

Mehrabian, A. "Immediacy: An Indicator of Attitudes in Linguistic Communication." *Journal of Personality* 34, 1966, pp. 26–34.

Mehrabian, A. *Silent Messages.* Belmont, California: Wadsworth Publishing Co., 1971.

Mehrabian, A. *Nonverbal Communication.* Chicago: Aldine-Atherton, 1972.

Meinhart, N. T. "Love Is the Essence of Nursing." *RN,* August 1968, pp. 69–70.

Mendels, G. E., and Flanders, J. P. "Teachers' Expectations and Pupil Performance." *American Educational Research Journal* 10, 1973, pp. 203–212.

Menninger, K. A. *Man Against Himself*. New York: Harcourt, Brace & World, 1968.

Meyer, B. et al. "Self-Acceptance of Nurses and Acceptance of Patients: An Exploratory Investigation." *Nursing Research* 14, 1965, pp. 346–350.

Meyers, E. *Self Concept, Family Structure, and School Achievement: A Study of Disadvantaged Negro Boys*. Doctoral dissertation, Teachers College, Columbia University, 1966.

Milgram, S. *Obedience to Authority*. New York: Harper & Row, Publishers, 1974.

Mitchell, C. D.; Harlow, H. F.; Raymond, C. J., and Ruppenthal, G. C. "Long Term Effects of Total Social Isolation upon Behavior of Rhesus Monkeys." *Psychological Reports* 18, 1966, pp. 567–580.

Mon, G. R. "Nonverbal Teaching: Body Language." *Math Teacher* 67, 1974, pp. 172–174.

Morehouse, L. E., and Gross, L. *Total Fitness in 30 Minutes a Week*. New York: Simon and Schuster, 1975.

Morrison, K. *Management Counseling of Small Business in the United States*. University, Mississippi: Mississippi Industrial and Technological Research Commission, 1963.

Morse, W. C. "Self-Concept in the School Setting." *Childhood Education* 41, 1964, pp. 195–198.

Mouly, G. J. *Psychology for Effective Teaching*, 2nd ed. New York: Holt, Rinehart and Winston, 1968.

Moustakas, C. *The Self: Exploration in Personal Growth*. New York: Harper, 1956a.

Moustakas, C. *The Teacher and the Child*. New York: McGraw-Hill Book Co., 1956b.

Moustakas, C. E. *Loneliness*. Englewood Cliffs, New Jersey: Prentice-Hall, 1961.

Moustakas, C. E. *The Authentic Teacher: Sensitivity and Awareness in the Classroom*. Cambridge, Massachusetts: Howard A. Doyle Publishing Co., 1966.

Mudra, D. "A New Look at Leadership." *Journal of Health, Physical Education and Recreation* 35, 1964, pp. 30, 86.

Mullozzi, A., and Spees, E. R. "Factors in Selecting Residence Hall Fellows." *Journal of the National Association of Women Deans and Counselors* 34, 1971, pp. 185–190.

Murphy, G. *Personality: A Biosocial Approach to Origins and Structure*. New York: Harper, 1947.

Murphy, G., and Spohn, H. E. *Encounter with Reality*. Boston: Houghton Mifflin, 1968.

Mussen, P. H. *The Psychological Development of the Child*. Englewood Cliffs, New Jersey: Prentice-Hall, 1963.

Neil, A. S. *Summerhill*. New York: Hart Publishing, 1960.

Myrick, R. D., and Kelly, F. D. "A Scale for Evaluating Practicum Students in Counseling and Supervision." *Counselor Education and Supervision* 10, 1971, pp. 350–356.

O'Banion, T., and O'Connell, A. *The Shared Journey: An Introduction to Encounter.* Englewood Cliffs, New Jersey: Prentice-Hall, 1970.

Omwake, K. T. "The Relation between Acceptance of Self and Acceptance of Others Shown by Three Personality Inventories." *Journal of Consulting Psychology* 18, 1954, pp. 443–446.

Ornstein, R. E. *The Psychology of Consciousness.* San Francisco: Freeman, 1972.

O'Roark, A. "A Comparison of Perceptual Characteristics of Elected Legislators and Public School Counselors Identified as Most and Least Effective." Unpublished doctoral dissertation, University of Florida, 1974.

Ostler, R., and Kranz, P. L. "More Effective Communication through Understanding Young Children's Nonverbal Behavior." *Young Child* 31, 1976, pp. 113–120.

Otto, H. A. "The Minerva Experience: Initial Report." In J. F. Bugental, ed., *Challenges of Humanistic Psychology,* pp. 119–124. New York: McGraw-Hill Book Co., 1967.

Paris, N. M. "T-Grouping: A Helping Movement." *Phi Delta Kappan* 49, 1968, pp. 460–463.

Parker, J. "The Relationship of Self Report to Inferred Self Concept in Sixth Grade Children." Unpublished doctoral dissertation, University of Florida, 1964.

Parker, J. "The Relationship of Self-Report to Inferred Self-Concept." *Educational and Psychological Measurement* 26, 1966, pp. 691–700.

Paschal, B. J. "A Concerned Teacher Makes the Difference." *The Arithmetic Teacher* 13, 1966, pp. 203–205.

Patterson, C. H. "The Self in Recent Rogerian Theory." *Journal of Individual Psychology* 17, 1961, pp. 5–11.

Payne, D. A. "The Concurrent and Predictive Validity of an Objective Measure of Academic Self-Concept." *Educational and Psychological Measurement* 22, 1962, pp. 773–780.

Payne, D. A., and Farquhar, W. W. "The Dimension of an Objective Measure of Academic Self Concept." *Journal of Educational Psychology* 53, 1962, pp. 187–192.

Pendergrass, P. W. "The Relationship of Perceived Threat to Adolescent Students' Feelings of Adequacy in the Classroom." Unpublished doctoral dissertation, University of Florida, 1971.

Piaget, J. *Judgment and Reasoning in the Child.* Translated by M. Warden. Paterson, New Jersey: Littlefield, Adams, 1959.

Piaget, J. *The Mechanisms of Perception.* Translated by G. N. Seagrim. New York: Basic Books, 1969.

Piaget, J. *Science of Education and the Psychology of the Child.* Translated by D. Coltman. New York: Viking, 1971.

Piaget, J. *The Child and Reality: Problems of Genetic Psychology.* Translated by A. Rosin. New York: Grossman, 1973.

Pilisuk, M. "Cognitive Balance and Self-Relevant Attitudes." *Journal of Abnormal and Social Psychology* 65, 1962, pp. 95–103.

Pilisuk, M. "Anxiety, Self-Acceptance, and Open-Mindedness." *Journal of Clinical Psychology* 19, 1963, pp. 387–391.

Pinneau, S. R., and Milton, A. "The Ecological Veracity of the Self-Report." *Journal of Genetic Psychology* 93, 1958, pp. 249–276.

Pitts, Carl E., ed. *Operant Conditioning in the Classroom.* New York: Thomas Y. Crowell Co., 1971.

Postman, L., and Bruner, J. S. "Perception under Stress." *Psychological Review* 55, 1948, pp. 314–323.

Powers, W. T. *Behavior: The Control of Perception.* Chicago: Aldine, 1973.

Preston, M. G., and Heintz, R. K. "Effects of Participatory vs. Supervisory Leadership on Group Judgment." *Journal of Abnormal and Social Psychology* 44, 1949, pp. 345–355.

Privette, G. "Transcendent Functioning." *Teachers College Record* 66, 1965, pp. 733–739.

Pugh, R. W. *Psychology and the Black Experience.* Monterey, California: Brooks/Cole, 1972.

Purkey, W. W. "The Self and Academic Achievement." *Florida Educational Research and Development Council Research Bulletin* 3, 1967.

Purkey, W. W. "The Search for Self: Evaluating Student Self-Concepts." *Florida Educational Research and Development Council Research Bulletin* 4, 1968.

Purkey, W. W. *Self-Concept and School Achievement.* Englewood Cliffs, New Jersey: Prentice-Hall, 1970a.

Purkey, W. W. "The Task of the Teacher." In *Self-Concept and School Achievement.* Englewood Cliffs, New Jersey: Prentice-Hall, 1970b.

Putman, L. J. "A Communication on Communication." *Improving College and University Teaching* 14, 1966, pp. 148–150.

Rabinowitz, M. "The Relationship of Self-Regard to the Effectiveness of Life Experiences." *Journal of Counseling Psychology* 13, 1966, pp. 139–143.

Raimy, V. C. *The Self-Concept as a Factor in Counseling and Personality Organization.* Columbus, Ohio: Ohio State University Libraries, 1971.

Raimy, V. *Misunderstanding of the Self.* San Francisco: Jossey-Bass Publishers, 1975.

Reckless, W. C., and Dinitz, S. "Pioneering with Self-Concept as a Vulnerability Factor in Delinquency." *The Journal of Criminal Law, Criminology and Police Science* 58, 1967, pp. 515–523.

Reckless, W. C., Dinitz, S.; and Kay, B. "Self-Component in Potential Delinquency." *American Sociological Review* 22, 1957, pp. 566–570.

Reckless, W. C.; Dinitz, S.; and Murray, E. "Self-Concept as an Insulator Against Delinquency." *American Sociological Review* 21, 1956, pp. 744–756.

Redl, F., and Wineman, D. *Children Who Hate.* New York: Collier, 1962.

Reed, H. "Learning to Remember Dreams." *Journal of Humanistic Psychology* 13, 1973, pp. 33–48.

Reich, C. A. *The Greening of America*. New York: Random House, 1970.

Renzaglia, G. A.; Henry, D. R.; and Rybolt, G. A. "Estimation and Measurement of Personality Characteristics and Correlates of Their Congruence. *Journal of Counseling Psychology* 9, 1962, pp. 71–78.

Rezler, A. G. "Influence of Needs upon the Student's Perception of his Instructor." *Journal of Educational Research* 58, 1965, pp. 282–286.

Richards, A. C. "Humanistic Perspectives on Adequate and Artifactual Research." *Interpersonal Development* 1, 1970, pp. 77–86.

Richards, F. "Counselor Training: Educating for the Beautiful and Noble Person." Colorado *Journal of Educational Research* 12, 1972, pp. 11–16.

Richards, F., and Richards, A. C. *Homonovus: The New Man*. Boulder, Colorado: Shields, 1973.

Richmond, B. O.; Mason, R. L., Jr.; and Padgett, H. G. "Self-Concept and Perception of Others." *Journal of Humanistic Psychology* 12, 1972, pp. 103–111.

Riessman, F. *The Culturally Deprived Child*. New York: Harper, 1962.

Risley, T. R. "Learning and Lollipops." *Psychology Today* 7, 1968, pp. 28–31.

Roberts, W. "Believing Is Seeing." *Saturday Review,* October 19, 1968, p. 62.

Roethlisberger, F. J. "Barriers to Communication between Men." In S. I. Hayakawa, ed., *The Use and Misuse of Language,* pp. 41–46. Greenwich, Connecticut: Fawcett Publications, 1962.

Rogers, C. R. *Client-Centered Therapy*. Boston: Houghton Mifflin, 1951.

Rogers, C. R. "A Note on 'the Nature of Man.'" *Journal of Counseling Psychology* 4, 1957, pp. 199–203.

Rogers, C. R. "The Characteristics of a Helping Relationship." *Personnel and Guidance Journal* 37, 1958, pp. 6–16.

Rogers, C. R. "A Theory of Therapy, Personality, and Interpersonal Relationships, as Developed in the Client-Centered Framework." In S. Koch, ed., *Psychology: A Study of a Science,* pp. 184–256. New York: McGraw-Hill Book Co., 1959.

Rogers, C. R. *On Becoming a Person: A Therapist's View of Psychotherapy*. Boston: Houghton Mifflin, 1961.

Rogers, C. R. "The Therapeutic Relationship: Recent Theory and Research." *Australian Journal of Psychology* 17, 1965, pp. 95–108.

Rogers, C. R. "The Interpersonal Relationship in the Facilitation of Learning." In R. R. Leeper, ed., *Humanizing Education: The Person in the Process,* pp. 1–18. Washington, D.C.: Association for Supervision and Curriculum Development, National Education Association, 1967a.

Rogers, C. R. *Coming into Existence*. Cleveland: World Publishing Co., 1967b.

Rogers, C. R., *Freedom to Learn*. Columbus, Ohio: Charles E. Merrill Publishing Co., 1969.

Rogers, C. R. *Carl Rogers on Encounter Groups*. New York: Harper & Row, Publishers, 1970.

Rogers, C. R., and Skinner, B. F. "Some Issues Concerning the Control of Behavior." *Science* 124, 1956, pp. 1057–1066.

Rogers, C. R., and Stevens, B. *Person to Person: The Problem of Being Human.* New York: Pocket Books, 1967.

Rokeach, M. *Beliefs, Attitudes and Values. A Theory of Organization and Change.* San Francisco: Jossey-Bass, Publishers, 1968.

Rokeach, M. *The Nature of Human Values.* New York: Free Press, 1973.

Rosenfeld, H., and Zander, A. "The Influence of Teachers on Aspirations of Students." *Journal of Educational Psychology* 52, 1961, pp. 1–11.

Rosenthal, R., and Jacobson, L. F. "Teacher Expectations for the Disadvantaged." *Scientific American* 218, 1968a.

Rosenthal, R., and Jacobson, L. F. *Pygmalion in the Classroom.* New York: Holt, Rinehart and Winston, 1968b.

Rotman, C. B., and Golburgh, S. J. "Group Counseling of Mentally Retarded Adolescents." *Mental Retardation* 5, 1967, pp. 13–16.

Rotter, J. C. "The Perceptual Characteristics of Elementary, Secondary and Community College Counselors." Unpublished doctoral dissertation, Wayne State University, 1971.

Ruesch, J., and Kees, W. *Nonverbal Communication.* Berkeley, California: University of California Press, 1956.

Ruff, G. E. "Isolation and Sensory Deprivation." In S. Arieti, ed., *American Handbook of Psychiatry,* pp. 385–405. New York: Basic Books, 1966.

Ryans, D. *Characteristics of Teachers: Their Description and Appraisal.* Washington, D.C.: American Council on Education, 1960.

Ryans, D. G. "Some Relationships between Pupil Behavior and Certain Teacher Characteristics." *Journal of Educational Psychology* 52, 1961, pp. 82–90.

Sampson, E. E. "Achievement in Conflict." *Journal of Personality* 31, 1963, pp. 510–516.

Sarason, I. G. "The Effects of Anxiety and Threat on the Solution of a Difficult Task." *Journal of Abnormal Social Psychology* 62, 1961, pp. 165–168.

Sarason, I. G. *Personality: An Objective Approach.* New York: John Wiley & Sons, 1966.

Sarason, I. G. "Verbal Learning, Modeling and Juvenile Delinquency." *American Psychologist* 23, 1968, pp. 254–266.

Sargent, S. S. "Humanistic Methodology in Personality and Social Psychology." In J. F. T. Bugental, ed., *Challenges of Humanistic Psychology,* pp. 127–132. New York: McGraw-Hill Book Co., 1967.

Scarpitti, F. R.; Murray, E.; Dinitz, S.; and Reckless, W. C. "The Good Boy in a High Delinquency Area: Four Years Later." *American Sociological Review* 25, 1960, pp. 555–558.

Scheerer, M. "Problem Solving." *Scientific American* 208, 1963, pp. 118–128.

Scheidell, T. M., and Crowell, L. "Feedback in Small Group Communication." *Quarterly Journal of Speech* 2, 1966, pp. 273–278.

Schmuck, R. A., and Schmuck, P. A. *Group Processes in the Classroom.* Dubuque, Iowa: William C. Brown, 1971.

Schrank, W. R. "The Labeling Effect of Ability Grouping." *The Journal of Educational Research* 62, 1968, pp. 51–52.

Schrank, W. R. "Further Study of the Labeling Effects of Ability Grouping." *The Journal of Educational Research* 63, 1970, pp. 358–360.

Schroeder, P., and Dowse, E. "Selection, Function and Assessment of Residence Hall Counselors." *Personnel and Guidance Journal* 47, 1968, pp. 151–156.

Schultz, D. P. *Sensory Restrictions: Effects on Behavior.* New York: Academic Press, 1965.

Schultz, J. L. "A Cross-Sectional Study of the Development, Dimensionality, and Correlates of the Self-Concept in School-Age Boys." *Dissertation Abstracts* 26, 1966, p. 5883.

Schutz, W. C. *Joy: Expanding Human Awareness.* New York: Grove Press, 1967.

Scott, W. W., and Spaulding, L. F. "What Do We Know about Leadership?" Washington, D.C.: U.S. Office of Health, Education and Welfare, 1972.

Sears, P. S., and Sherman, V. S. *In Pursuit of Self-Esteem: Case Studies of Eight Elementary School Children.* Belmont, California: Wadsworth Publishing Co., 1964.

Selye, H. "The Two-Edged Sword of Stress." In R. G. Brown, R. A. Newell, and H. G. Vonk, eds., *Behavioral Implications for Curriculum and Teaching: Interdisciplinary Readings.* Dubuque, Iowa: William Brown Book Co., 1969.

Sennett, R. *The Uses of Disorder.* New York: Random House, 1970.

Severin, F. T. *Humanistic Viewpoints in Psychology.* New York: McGraw-Hill Book Co., 1965.

Shainberg, D. "Personality Restriction in Adolescents." *Psychiatric Quarterly* 40, 1966, pp. 258–270.

Shapiro, J. G. "Agreement between Channels of Communication in Interviews." *Journal of Consulting Psychology* 30, 1966, pp. 535–538.

Shapiro, J. G.; Foster, C. P.; and Powell, T. "Facial and Bodily Cues of Genuineness, Empathy, and Warmth." *Journal of Clinical Psychology* 24, 1968, pp. 233–236.

Shaw, M. C., and Alves, G. J. "The Self-Concept of Bright Academic Underachievers." *Personnel and Guidance Journal* 42, 1963, pp. 401–403.

Shaw, M. E. "A Comparison of Two Types of Leadership Style in Various Communication Nets." *Journal of Abnormal and Social Psychology* 50, 1955, pp. 127–134.

Shaw, M. E., and Blum, J. M. "Effects of Leadership Style upon Group Performance as a Function of Task Structure." *Journal of Perspective in Social Psychology* 3, 1966, pp. 238–242.

Sheerer, E. T. "An Analysis of the Relationship between Acceptance of and Respect for Self and Acceptance of and Respect for Others in Ten Counseling Cases." *Journal of Consulting Psychology* 13, 1949, pp. 169–175.

Short, J. F., and Strodtbeck, F. L. *Group Process and Gang Delinquency.* Chicago, Illinois: The University of Chicago Press, 1974.

Silverman, I. "Self-Esteem and Differential Responsiveness to Success and Failure." *Journal of Abnormal and Social Psychology* 69, 1964, pp. 115–119.

Bibliography

Simon, S. B., and Bellanca, J. A. *Degrading the Grading Myths: A Primer of Alternatives to Grades and Marks.* Washington, D.C.: Association for Supervision and Curriculum Development, National Education Association, 1976.

Simon, S.; Howe, L.; and Kirschenbaum, H. *Values Clarification: A Handbook of Practical Strategies for Teachers and Students.* New York: Hart Publishing Co., 1972.

Simon, S. B., and Napier, R. W. *Wad Ja Get? The Grading Game in American Education.* New York: Hart Publishing Company, 1971.

Skinner, B. F. *Science and Human Behavior.* New York: Macmillan Publishing Co., 1953.

Skinner, B. F. *The Technology of Teaching.* New York: Appleton-Century-Crofts, 1968.

Skinner, B. F. *Beyond Freedom and Dignity.* New York: Alfred A. Knopf, 1971.

Smith, H. C. *Sensitivity to People.* New York: McGraw-Hill Book Co., 1966.

Snyder, W. U. *Casebook of Non-Directive Psychotherapy.* Boston: Houghton Mifflin, 1947.

Snygg, D. "The Psychological Basis of Human Values." In D. Ward, ed., *Goals of Economic Life,* pp. 335–364. New York: Harper & Brothers, 1953.

Snygg, D. "A Cognitive Field Theory of Learning." In W. B. Waetjen, and R. R. Leeper, eds., *Learning and Mental Health in the School.* Washington, D.C.: Association for Supervision and Curriculum Development, National Education Association, 1966.

Snygg, D., and Combs, A. W. "The Phenomenological Approach and the Problems of 'Unconscious' Behavior." *Journal of Abnormal and Social Psychology* 45, 1950, pp. 523–528.

Soar, R. S. "Teacher-pupil Interaction." In *A New Look at Progressive Education,* 1972 Yearbook, pp. 166–204. Washington, D.C.: Association for Supervision and Curriculum Development, National Education Association, 1972.

Solley, C. M., and Murphy, G. *Development of the Perceptual World.* New York: Basic Books, 1960.

Sontag, L. W.; Baker, C. T.; and Nelson, V. L. "Mental Growth and Personality Development: A Longitudinal Study." In W. R. Goller, ed., *Readings in the Psychology of Human Growth and Development,* pp. 418–429. New York: Holt, Rinehart and Winston, 1962.

Soper, D. W., and Combs, A. W. "The Helping Relationship as Seen by Teachers and Therapists." *Journal of Consulting Psychology* 26, 1962, p. 288.

Spielberger, C. D. "The Effects of Manifest Anxiety on the Academic Achievement of College Students." *Mental Hygiene* 46, 1962, pp. 420–426.

Staines, J. W. "The Self-Picture as a Factor in the Classroom." *British Journal of Education Psychology* 28, 1958, pp. 97–111.

Stevens, J. O. *Awareness: Exploring, Experimenting, Experiencing.* Lafayette, California: Real People Press, 1971.

Stinnett, T. M., and Huggett, A. J. "The Profession of Teaching." In *Professional Problems of Teachers.* New York: Macmillan Publishing Co., 1966.

Stoller, H. "The Long Weekend." *Psychology Today* 1, 1967, pp. 28–33.

Stotland, E. "Effects of Public and Private Failure on Self-Evaluation." *Journal of Abnormal and Social Psychology* 56, 1958, pp. 223–229.

Stotland, E. "Self-Esteem Group Interaction, and Group Influence on Performance. *Journal of Personality* 29, 1961, pp. 273–284.

Strong, D. J., and Feder, D. "Measurement of the Self-Concept: A Critique of the Literature. *Journal of Counseling Psychology* 8, 1961, pp. 170–180.

Strunk, O. *Religion: A Psychological Interpretation.* New York: Abingdon Press, 1962.

Sullivan, H. S. *Conceptions of Modern Psychiatry,* 2nd ed. New York: W. W. Norton & Co., 1955.

Sulzer, B., and Mayer, G. R. *Behavior Modification Procedures for School Personnel.* Hinsdale, Illinois: Dryden Press, 1972.

Swanson, J. L. "The Relationship between Perceptual Characteristics and Counselor Effectiveness Ratings of Counselor Trainees." Unpublished doctoral dissertations, University of Florida, 1975.

Swinn, R. M.; Osborne, D.; and Winfree, P. "The Self-Concept and Accuracy of Recall of Inconsistent Self-Related Information." *Journal of Clinical Psychology* 18, 1963, pp. 473–474.

Swinn, R. M., and Hill, M. "Influence of Anxiety on the Relationship between Self-Acceptance and Acceptance of Others." *Journal of Consulting Psychology* 28, 1964, pp. 116–119.

Tate, G. A. "Re-Mythologization: Toward a Black Psychology of the Healthy Personality." In F. Richards, and I. D. Welch, eds., *Sightings: Essays in Humanistic Psychology.* San Francisco: Shields, 1973.

Taylor, C., and Combs, A. W. "Self-Acceptance and Adjustment." *Journal of Consulting Psychology* 16, 1952, pp. 89–91.

Taylor, D. M. "Consistency of the Self-Concept." Unpublished doctoral dissertation, Vanderbilt University, 1953.

Tessar, A., Rosen, S., and Waranch, E. "Communicator Mood and the Reluctance to Transmit Undesirable Messages: The MUM Effect." *Journal of Communication* 23, 1973, pp. 266–283.

Thomas, S. "An Experiment to Enhance Self-Concept of Ability and Raise School Achievement among Low-Achievement Ninth Grade Students." *Dissertation Abstracts* 26, 1966, p. 4870.

Thoresen, C. E., and Mahoney, M. J. *Behavioral Self-Control.* New York: Holt, Rinehart and Winston, 1974.

Tillich, P. *The Courage to Be.* New Haven: Yale University Press, 1959.

Toffler, A. *Future Shock.* New York: Random House, 1970.

Torrance, E. P. "Creative and Critical Evaluative Attitudes of Teachers." In *Rewarding Creative Behavior,* pp. 75–84. Englewood Cliffs, New Jersey: Prentice-Hall, 1965.

Tournier, P. *The Meaning of Persons.* New York: Harper, 1957.

Trent, R. D. "The Relationship between Expressed Self-Acceptance and Expressed Attitudes toward Negro and White in Negro Children." *Journal of Genetic Psychology* 91, 1957, pp. 25–31.

Truax, C. B. "An Approach toward Training for the Aide-Therapist: Research and Implications." Symposium presented at meeting of the American Psychological Association, Chicago, September 1965.

Truax, C. B. "Empathy, Warmth, Genuineness." *Rehabilitation Record* 7, 1966, pp. 10–11.

Truax, C. B., and Carkhuff, R. R. *Toward Effective Counseling and Psychotherapy: Training and Practice.* Chicago: Aldine, 1967.

Truax, C. B.; Carkhuff, R. R.; and Kodman, F. "Relationships between Therapist-Offered Conditions and Patient Change in Group Psychotherapy." *Journal of Clinical Psychology* 21, 1965, pp. 327–329.

Truax, C. B., and Wargo, D. G. "Psychotherapeutic Encounters that Change Behavior: For Better or for Worse." *American Journal of Psychotherapy* 22, 1966, pp. 499–520.

Truax, C. B.; Wargo, D. G.; Carkhuff, R. R.; Kodman, F.; and Moles, E. A. "Changes in Self-Concepts during Group Psychotherapy as a Function of Alternate Sessions and Vicarious Therapy Pretraining in Institutionalized Mental Patients and Juvenile Delinquents." *Journal of Consulting Psychology* 30, 1966a, pp. 309–314.

Truax, C. B.; Wargo, D. G.; Frank, J. D.; Imber, S. D.; Battle, C. C.; Hoehn-Sauc, R.; Nash, E. H.; and Stone, A. R. "Therapist Empathy, Geunineness, and Warmth and Patient Therapeutic Outcome." *Journal of Consulting Psychology* 3, 1966b, pp. 395–401.

Tryon, W. W., and Radzin, A. B. "Purpose-in-Life as a Function of Ego Resiliency, Dogmatism, and Biographical Variables." *Journal of Clinical Psychology* 28, 1972, pp. 544–545.

Turkel, S. *Working.* New York: Pantheon Books, 1972.

Usher, R. H. "The Relationship of Perceptions of Self, Others and the Helping Task to Certain Measures of College Faculty Effectiveness." Unpublished doctoral dissertation, University of Florida, 1966.

Van Buskirk, C. "Performance on Complex Reasoning Tasks as a Function of Anxiety." *Journal of Abnormal and Social Psychology* 62, 1961, pp. 201–249.

Van Kaam, A. *Existential Foundations of Psychology.* Pittsburgh: Duquesne University Press, 1966.

Verba, S. *Small Groups and Political Behavior: A Study of Leadership.* Princeton, New Jersey: Princeton University Press, 1961.

Vonk, H. G. "The Relationship of Teacher Effectiveness to Perceptions of Self and Teaching Purposes." Unpublished doctoral dissertation, University of Florida, 1970.

Vontress, C. E. "Cultural Barriers in the Counseling Relationship." *Personnel and Guidance Journal* 48, 1969, pp. 11–17.

Walker, J. E., and Shea, T. M. *Behavior Modification: A Practical Approach for Educators.* St. Louis: The C. V. Mosby Company, 1976.

Walsh, A. M. *Self-Concepts of Bright Boys with Learning Difficulties.* New York: Bureau of Publications, Teachers College, Columbia University, 1956.

Walton, F. X., and Sweeny, T. J. "Useful Predictions of Counseling Effectiveness." *Personnel and Guidance Journal* 45, 1967, pp. 579–584.

Wann, T. W., ed. *Behaviorism and Phenomenology: Contrasting Bases for Modern Psychology.* Chicago: University of Chicago Press, 1964.

Wapner, S., Werner, H., eds. *The Body Percept.* New York: Random House, 1965.

Ward, P., and Bailey, J. A. "Community Participation and Attitudinal Changes among Teacher Education Students." *The Personnel and Guidance Journal* 44, 1966, pp. 628–630.

Wass, H.; Blume, R. A.; Combs, A. W.; and Hedges, W. D. *Humanistic Teacher Education: An Experiment in Systematic Curriculum Innovation.* Ft. Collins, Colorado: Shields Publishing Co., 1974.

Wass, H., and Combs, A. W. "Humanizing the Education of Teachers." *Theory into Practice* 13, 1974, pp. 123–129.

Wattenberg, W. W., and Clifford, C. "Relation of Self-Concepts to Beginning Achievement in Reading." *Child Development* 35, 1964, pp. 461–467.

Weaver, T. T. "Effects of Positive and Negative Personality Evaluations on the Self-Concepts of High School Seniors." *Dissertation Abstracts* 26, 1965, pp. 1785–1786.

Webster, S. W. *Discipline in the Classroom.* San Francisco: Chandler, 1968.

Webster, S. W., and Kroger, M. N. "A Comparative Study of Selected Perceptions and Feelings of Negro Adolescents with and without White Friends in Integrated Urban High Schools." *Journal of Negro Education* 35, 1966, pp. 55–60.

Welch, I. D., and Richards, F. "Recreating the Experiences of Early Childhood." *The Group Leader's Workshop* 16, 1973, pp. 11–16.

Werkman, S. L., and Greenberg, E. S. "Personality and Interest Patterns in Obese Adolescent Girls." *Psychosomatic Medicine* 29, 1967, pp. 72–80.

Wessels, H. M. "Four Teachers I Have Known." *Saturday Review of Literature,* June 7, 1961.

White, W., and Porter, T. "Self-Concept Reports among Hospitalized Alcoholics during Early Periods of Sobriety." *Journal of Counseling Psychology* 13, 1966, pp. 352–355.

Wilhelms, F. T., and Siemans, R. E. "A Curriculum for Personal and Professional Development." In *Changes in Teaching Education: An Appraisal.* Washington, D.C.: National Commission of Teacher Education and Professional Standards, National Education Association, 1963.

Williams, W. C. "The Use of Force." In *The Farmer's Daughter and Other Stories.* Philadelphia: New Directions, 1961.

Winick, C., and Holt, H. "Seating Position as Nonverbal Communication in Group Analysis." *Psychiatry* 24, 1961, pp. 171–182.

Wittmer, J., and Lister, J. L. "The Graduate Record Examination, 16PF Questionnaire and Counselor Effectiveness." *Counselor Education and Supervision* 10, 1971, p. 293.

Wohlwill, J. F. "Perceptual Learning." *American Review of Psychology* 17, 1966, pp. 201–232.

Wolman, B. B. *The Unconscious Mind: The Meaning of Freudian Psychology.* Englewood Cliffs, New Jersey: Prentice-Hall, 1968.

Wolpe, Joseph. *Psychotherapy by Reciprocal Inhibition.* Palo Alto, California: Stanford University Press, 1958.

Wolpe, Joseph. *The Practice of Behavior Therapy.* New York: Pergamon Press, 1969.

Wolpe, J.; Salter, A.; and Reyna, L. J., eds. *The Conditioning Therapies: The Challenge in Psychotherapy.* New York: Holt, Rinehart and Winston, 1964.

Woolfolk, A. E. "Student Self-Disclosure in Response to Teacher Nonverbal Behavior." *Journal of Experimental Education* 44, 1975, pp. 36–40.

Worth Commission on Educational Planning. *A Future of Choices: A Choice of Futures.* Edmonton, Alberta, Canada: Hurtig, 1972.

Wrightsman, L. S., Jr. "Effects of Anxiety, Achievement, Motivation, and Task Importance upon Performance on an Intelligence Test." *Journal of Educational Psychology* 53, 1962, pp. 150–156.

Wylie, R. C. *The Self-Concept: A Critical Survey of Pertinent Research Literature.* Lincoln, Nebraska: University of Nebraska Press, 1961.

Zimmerman, I. L., and Allebrand, G. N. "Personality Characteristics and Attitudes toward Achievement of Good and Poor Readers." *The Journal of Educational Research* 59, 1965, pp. 28–30.

Zoolalion, C. "Factors Related to Differential Achievement among Boys in Ninth Grade Algebra." *Journal of Education Research* 58, 1965, pp. 205–207.

Zunich, M. "Perceptions of Indian, Mexican, Negro, and White Children Concerning the Development of Responsibility." *Perceptual and Motor Skills* 32, 1971, pp. 796–798.

REFERENCE GUIDE
TO RELEVANT RESEARCH
AND WRITING

The work of several thousand authors has contributed in one way or another to our current understanding of helping relationships. Detailed inclusion of the work of so many in the text of this book would seriously interfere with readability. The authors have, therefore, chosen to cite in the text only those directly quoted or those whose work is specifically referred to. To assist readers who wish to explore the literature on helping relationships at greater depth the Reference Guide To Relevant Research and Writing will prove useful. Page and paragraph references indicate points throughout the text where the work of other writers is especially relevant. Complete standard citations of works referred to will be found in the Bibliography, pages 217 to 247.

CHAPTER 1/ WHAT IS A PROFESSIONAL HELPER?

Page Para.

4	5	Arkoff 68; Carkhuff 67; Frymier 65
5	5	Brown 69; Ellena 61; Fiedler 50; Gage 63
6	1	Getzels 63
6	3	Combs 64; Combs & Blume 74; Combs & Soper 63a
8	5	Aspy 69b
9	2	Combs 64; Combs & Soper 63a
9	4	Benton 64; Combs 64, 69; Combs & Soper 63a; Dickman 67; Gooding 64; Soper 62; Stinnett 66

Page Para.

10	3	Johnson 64; Kelley 47; Klein 70
10	4	Brown 70; Choy 69; Combs 69; Combs & Blume 74; Dedrick 72; Dellow 71; Doyle 69; Jennings 73; Koffman 75; O'Roark 74; Pendergrass 71; Swanson 75; Usher 66; Vonk 70
11	3	Allport, G. 61
14	3	Arkoff 68; Brammer 73; Carkhuff 67; Combs 69; Combs & Blume 74; Purkey 70b; Rogers 58; Wass 74

CHAPTER 2/ PERCEPTIONS AND THE SELF

Page Para.

15 2 Bartley 58; Combs 74; Combs
& Richards 76; Frank 66;
Ittelson 52; Murphy 68
15 4 Combs & Richards 76
16 2 Allport, F. 65; Ames 55;
Buhler 67; Keen 75; Sargent
67; Strunk 62
16 5 Freud 20; Ittelson 54; Ornstein
72; Richards 70; Snygg 50;
Wolman 68
17 2 Frymier 57; Matson 67
17 3 Combs & Richards 76; Combs
& Soper 57
17 4 Wylie 61
18 2 Chodorkoff 54; Kelley 46, 62a;
Sullivan 55
18 3 Combs & Courson 63; Kelly 63
18 6 Mussen 63
19 2 Jersild 65
19 3 Allport, G. 55; Wapner 65
19 5 Carter 68
20 2 Brennecke 71; Caplin 68;
Cartwright 63; Combs &
Soper 63a; Crovetto 67;
Purkey 67; Swinn 63;
Zimmerman 65
20 3 Brock 63; Brookover 60, 64;
Brunkan 66; Combs, C. 64,
64a; Courson 63; Durr 64;
Haarer 64; Purkey 70a;
Tate 73
20 4 Haas 65
20 5 Allport, G. 61; Aronson 63;
Borislow 62; Carlton 68;
Coudert 65; Courson 68;
Farquhar 68; Hamachek 61;
Jones 71; Jourard 64
21 2 Baker 71; Connelly 64;
Coopersmith 67; Lamy 65;
Walsh 56
21 3 Brooks 63; Dinitz 62; Reckless
57; Scarpitti 60; Shaw 63
22 3 Cantril 64; Caplin 68;
Carlton 66; Carter 68; Fink
62; Gordon 68; Grossack 54;
Herman 66; Kvaraceus 65,
67; Pugh 72; Trent 57

Page Para.

23 2 Bettelheim 68; Caliguri 66;
Chansky 64; Combs & Soper
63a; Maehr 62; Mead 34;
Rosenthal 68a; Schronk 68,
70; Welch 73; Werkman 67
23 3 Beatty 68; Hamachek 69;
Kester 66; Pilisuk 62
23 4 Bettelheim 67; Brophy 74;
Davidson 60; Doyle 72;
Friedman 67; Gordon 66a;
Leichty 63; McCallon 66;
Zunick 71
24 1 Bogdan 76; Davids 61; Landry
74; Mayer 66; Meyers 66;
Purkey 68; Rosenthal 68b;
Schultz 66
24 2 Boucher 75; Brophy 70; Clore
75; Davitz 61; Hall 59;
Kimball 63; Loss 73;
Mehrabian 71, 72; Ruesch 56
25 2 Freud 20; Wattenberg 64
25 4 Carlson 65; Guller 66; Payne
62; Payne & Farquhar 62;
Taylor 53
26 2 Brownfain 52
26 5 Arbuckle 58; Coller 71; Combs
& Courson 63; Combs &
Soper 57; Gordon & Wood
73; Pineau 58
27 2 Parker 64, 66; Strong 61
27 3 Pineau 58
27 3 Brandt 58; Courson 65;
Diggory 66
28 2 ASCD 62
28 3 Staines 58
29 2 Canfield 76; Combs & Richards
76; LaBenne 69; Moustakas
56, 56a; Patterson 61; Sears 64
29 3 Crandall 64; Jourard 68;
Raimy 71, 75; Thomas 66
29 4 Ludwig 67
29 5 Combs 66
30 2 Kelley 77; Stotland 61
32 3 Bettelheim 68; Canfield 76;
Combs & Richards 76; Giorgi
70; Hamachek 71; Kelley 77;
LaBenne 69; Patterson 61;
Piaget 69; Purkey 70a

CHAPTER 3/ A HUMANISTIC VIEW OF MOTIVE

34 2 Combs 71
34 3 Klein 70

35 2 Cantril 67; Johnson 64
35 4 Freud 20

Page Para.

36	2	Menninger 68
37	3	Combs & Richards 76; Frymier 65; Giorgi 70
38	2	Bettelheim 65; Bugental 67; Combs 49; Kelley 47; Sears 64; Tournier 57
38	4	Buhler 67; Cantril 64; Hayakawa 57; Severin 65
38	5	Appelbaum 63; Brock 63; Courson 63; Jourard 64
39	2	Allport, G. 55; Brennecke 71; Combs & Snygg 59; Festinger 64, 71; Frankl 63; Goble 70; Lecky 45; Murphy 47; Rogers 57, 61
39	3	Maslow 70
39	5	Cantril 67
39	6	Maslow 64
40	3	Combs 66
40	5	Craddick 63; DeCharms 68; Farquhar 68; Goffman 74; McGrath 62
41	2	Hamachek 64; Rezler 65; Snygg 53
41	3	Greene 64
42	1	Combs & Richards 76; Kelley 62a
42	2	Neill 60
43	1	Caliguri 66; Guller 66

Page Para.

43	2	Combs 49; Davids 61; Frankl 63; Riessman 62; Short 74
43	3	Adams 64; Calvin 53; Davitz 59; Eisen 62; Guller 66; Harrington 63; Redl 62
43	4	Birney 69; Caplin 68; Herman 66; Lloyd 67
44	1	Jourard 63; Kelley 62; Korchin 54; McNeil 67
44	2	Bogdan 76; Kelly 64
44	4	Liddle 62
44	5	Cantril 61; Kohlberg 69; Webster 68
45	3	Maslow 62
45	4	Maslow 64; May 58, 61; Richards 73
45	6	Frymier & Thompson 65; Richards 73
46	2	Sullivan 55
46	4	Avila 66
47	3	Frymier & Thompson 65
47	4	Johnson 64
48	2	Bonner 65; Torrance 65
48	3	Combs 74; Rogers 65
49	2	Piaget 59
49	3	ASCD 66; Brennecke 71; Buhler 67; Cantril 67; Combs & Richards 76; Frankl 63; Fromm 56; Kelley 69; Redl 62; Snygg 53

CHAPTER 4/ LEARNING AND HELPING AS CHANGE IN PERSONAL MEANING

51	2	Combs & Richards 76; Ittelson 60, 68; Keen 75; Kemp 71; Luchins 63; Murphy 68
52	2	Ames 55; Beres 60; Brown 63; Fromm 57; Ittelson 54
52	4	Brock 63; Gibson 63; Solley 60
53	3	Lilly 61; Rugg 66; Schultz 65
53	5	Beard 69; Brookes 63; Festinger 62; Gladstone 67; Goffman 74; Harrington 63
54	1	Allport, F. 65; Piaget 59, 71, 73
54	2	Frymier 65; Hastorf 59; Kelley 47; McGrath 62; Smith 66
55	2	Baker 71; Brownfain 52; Scheidell 66; Schrank 68, 70
55	3	Tillich 59
55	4	Gibson 63; Howe 67, 70; Kelley 69; Roberts 62; Sarason 68
55	5	Ausubel 63; Wohlwill 66
56	2	Bruner 66; Crandall 64; Long 74; Sheerer 63; Shapiro 66; Welch 73

56	3	Beatty 68; Combs 59; Kelley 78
57	4	Bieri 56
57	5	Averch 74; Brophy 74; Combs C. 64, 64a
58	2	Jersild 65
58	3	ASCD 66; Bigge 64
58	4	Averch 74; Cohen 54; Dexter 64; Ornstein 72; Simon 72
59	2	Combs & Richards 76; Davitz 59; Sampson 63
59	3	Freud 46; Gibby 67; Grimes 61; Pilisuk 63; Sennett 70; Van Buskirk 61
59	4	Berkowitz 60; Connelly 64; Craig 74; Haefner 54; Postman 48; Sarason 61
60	2	Combs & Taylor 52; Lanzetta 54; Powers 75; Wrightsman 62
60	3	Levanway 55
60	4	Chodorkoff 54; Gollob 65; Spielberger 62

Page Para.   *Page Para.*

60	5	Combs 64; Selye 69; Swinn 64	65	4	Axline 64; Snygg 66
61	5	Aaronson 68; Bartlett 32; Krech 69; Reed 73	66	2	Aspy 69c; Smith 66
62	3	Marshall 69	66	3	Delaney 66; Gordon 70; Kemp 70
62	4	Fromm 56	66	4	Axline 64; Ward 66
62	5	Craddick 63	67	3	Combs 54; Ryans 61
64	3	ASCD 62; Ittelson 68	68	2	Beard 69; Combs 78; DeCharms 68; Jones 72; Kelley 47;
65	2	Courson 65; Dombrow 66; Gibson 63; Lee 63			Kohlberg 69; Rogers 67, 69;
65	3	Combs 69			Rosenthal 68a

CHAPTER 5/ THE RANGE OF HUMAN POTENTIAL

69	1	Combs 61	77	2	Brookover 60, 64; Coopersmith 67; Zoolalion 65
69	2	Combs & Richards 76			
71	3	Botwinick 73	77	3	Selye 69
71	4	Combs 52, 61; Hunt 64, 72; Piaget 69	77	4	Frostig 63
			77	5	Combs & Richards 76
73	3	Frankl 69	78	2	Cohen 64
73	4	Jones 72; Liddle 62; Otto 67	78	4	Caliguri 66; Grossack 57
74	1	Combs & Richards 76	79	2	Gordon 67, 69; Kirk 58
74	2	Binet 09; Getzels 62	79	3	Hummel 65; Lafferty 68; Rokeach 68, 73
74	4	Guilford 64; Hunt 61			
75	3	Goslin 63; Honzik 63			
75	4	Anastasi 67; Combs 61; Dove 74; Kvaraceus 65, 67; Lamy 65	81	3	Bradway 61
			81	4	Bogdan 76; Carlton 66
75	5	Bogdan 76; Bradway 61; Kowitz 67; Wrightsman 62	81	5	Chansky 64
			82	3	Eisner 64
75	6	Hunt 61	83	1	Combs 52; Henry 63; Hunt 61, 72; Jourard 68; Maslow 63;
77	1	Combs & Richards 76; Frank 66; Mussen 63			Piaget 73

CHAPTER 6/ DIMENSIONS OF SELF-FULFILLMENT

84	2	Allport, G. 61; ASCD 62; Friedman 67; Fromm 57; Jourard 74; Maslow 70; Rogers 67	89	4	Davidson 60
			89	6	ASCD 62; Aspy 69d; Hamachek 64; Rabinowitz 66; Raimy 71
85	1	ASCD 62; Bettelheim 65; Combs & Richards 76; Goble 70; Kelley 62a; Klein 70	90	2	ASCD 62; Ausubel 63; Fisher 68; Morse 64; Patterson 61; Purkey 70a; Reckless 56, 67; Renzaglia 62; Truax 66
85	2	Calvin 53; Cohen 54; Courson 63; Haarer 64; Jersild 65; Raimy 75; Reckless 56	90	3	Allport, G. 61; Hanna 70; Maslow 63; Reich 70; Richmond 72; Rogers 67; Toffler 70
85	3	Hamachek 69; Landsman 68			
86	1	Bonner 65; Rogers 61; Stotland 61	90	4	Brandt 58; Dee 65; Gollob 65; Jourard 67
86	3	English 61	90	5	Jones 72; Kelley 54; Taylor 52
86	4	Borislow 62; Mudra 64	91	2	Goodman 65; Tate 73; Tryon 72
87	3	Courson 68			
87	4	Carter 68; Gibby 67; Kelley 62; Silverman 64	91	3	Drews 71; Sontag 62
			92	5	Adams 61; McIntyre 52; Mead 61; Omwake 54; Reed 73; Sheerer 49; Swinn 64
88	1	Herman 66; Kelly 64; Reckless 67; Sarason 61; Stotland 58			

Page Para.

92	6	Dee 65; Jourard 64; Kelley 54; MacKinnon 62; Stevens 71; Woolfolk 75
93	3	Arbuckle 61; Davitz 59; Eisner 64
93	4	Combs 70; Kounin 68; Pilisuk 63; Truax & Carkhuff 65
93	5	MacDonald & Zaret 66
94	2	Fromm 56; Harlow 58, 62; Kimball 63; Mitchell 66
94	3	Aronson 63
95	3	Berger 52; Bettelheim 68; Eriksen 66; Grossack 54; Kohlberg 69
96	2	Bieri 56; Harlow 58; Maslow 70; Webster 66
96	4	Allport, G. 61; Bettelheim 67; Friedmann 67; Turkel 72; White 66
97	2	Coudert 65
97	3	Makarenko 67; Meinhart 68; Shainberg 66

Page Para.

97	4	Kemp 71; Redl 62
98	1	Aspy 69b; Axline 64; Carkhuff & Truax 66, 67; Fromm 56; Paschal 66; Rogers 58, 59; Truax 66; Truax et al. 66a, 66b
98	2	Moustakas 61
99	1	ASCD 66; Bugental 65; Getzels 62; Landsman 68; Maslow 71; Richards 73; Rogers 67
99	2	Maslow 70; McNeil 67
99	3	Combs 66; Frankl 69; Frick 71; Landsman 62; Lefcourt 65; Maslow 62, 70; Privette 65; Toffler 70
99	4	LaBenne 69
100	4	Combs 61, 62; Eisner 64; Goble 70; Harlow 58; Jourard 74; Maslow 71; May 69; Toffler 70; Richards 73

CHAPTER 7/ TWO FRAMES OF REFERENCE FOR WORKING WITH PEOPLE

101	2	Harmon 70; Homme 71; Kelly 63; Laszlo 72; Worth 72
101	3	Combs 74, Hitt 69, Laszlo 72
102	2	Cantril 61
102	3	Lee 63; Mudra 64
102	4	Hitt 69; Koffman 75; Lewin 35; Sargent 67; Scott 72
103	2	Lippitt 52; Marrow 64a
103	4	Laszlo 72
103	5	Ford 63; Hitt 67; Morrison 63
104	3	Johnson 64
104	5	Fiedler 67
105	2	Amos 67; Ausubel 61
106	4	Lewin 35
106	6	Anastasi 67; Avila 72; Barlow 68; Child 73; Freud 20, 46; Hilgard 66; Hitt 69; Kuenzli 59; Livingston 62; Sarason 66; Skinner 53, 71; Wann 64
107	2	Freud 20, 46

108	3	Combs 74; DeCharms 68; Giorgi 70
108	4	Bischof 64; Bugental 67; Child 73; Goble 70; Maslow 62; Severin 65; Van Kaam 66
108	5	Allport, G. 61; Buhler 72; Cantril 61; Frick 71; Jourard 74; May 58, 61
109	2	Grossack 54; Hitt 69; Rogers & Skinner 56
109	3	Avila 72; Combs 74; Hitt 69
110	4	Skinner 53, 68, 71; Wolpe 58, 64, 69
111	2	Combs & Richards 76
111	4	Krech 69
111	5	Avila 72; Jourard 63
112	3	Avila 72; Bonner 65; Bugental 67; Child 73; Combs 74; Frick 71; Hitt 69; Keen 75; Laszlo 72; Severin 65; Shaw 70; Skinner 71; Wann 64

CHAPTER 8/ GOALS AND RESPONSIBILITIES OF HELPING

115	1	Arkoff 68; Calvin 65
116	1	Combs 69; Dedrick 72; Dellow 71; Jennings 73; Koffman 75; O'Roark 74; Vonk 70
116	2	Bergin 66; Soper 62

117	2	Buhler 67
119	1	Kelley 62
119	2	Raimy 75
120	2	Luckey 60
121	6	Ford 63

Page Para.

121	7	Bergin 66; Fiedler 50, 50a
122	2	Heine 53
122	3	Bills 56; Combs 54; Kemp 71; Matarayya 65
122	4	ASCD 62; Dexter 64
123	3	Lawton 58
124	3	Lakin 69

Page Para.

125	2	Combs 72; Stinnett 66
125	6	Combs 72
126	4	Brophy 74; Carkhuff 67
127	2	Frymier 65
127	6	Truax & Wargo 66
129	1	Combs 72; Fiedler 67; Lakin 69; Raimy 75; Rokeach 73; Soar 72; Truax & Carkhuff 67

CHAPTER 9/ EMPATHY: ESSENTIAL SKILL OF HELPING

130	2	Combs 69; Combs & Soper 63a, Brown 70; Dedrick 72; Jennings 73; Koffman 75; O'Roark 74; Swanson 75
130	3	Combs 54, 69, 70, 74; Combs & Soper 63b; Fiedler 50; Long 74; Rogers 58, 59
131	1	Aspy 69a, 69c, 69d; Aspy & Roebuck 74; Gage 58; Rogers 51
131	2	Dombrow 66; Gordon 70; Jourard 68; Moustakas 66; Raimy 71, 75
131	3	Smith 66
131	4	Ausubel 61; Ginott 65, 68; Vontress 69
132	3	Combs & Richards 76; Truax 66; Truax et al. 66a
133	2	Courson 65
133	4	Allport, G. 42
134	2	Aspy 69a

134	3	Axline 64; Rogers 58
134	5	Jackson 68
135	7	Jackson 68
136	2	Kounin 68
136	3	Ginott 65, 68; Gordon 70
136	5	Ginott 65, 68
137	3	Carlton 68
137	4	Agee 67; Malcolm X 64
138	2	Gordon 59, 66
138	3	Gordon 59
139	5	Bugental 65; Carkhuff 67; Combs 64, 69; McIntyre 52; Omwake 54; Richards 72; Sheerer 49; Swinn 64
141	3	Freud 20; Benton 64
142	2	Aspy 69a; Glasser 68; Jackson 68; Moustakas 66; McNeil 73; O'Banion & O'Connell 70; Richards 72; Rogers 70; Stevens 71

CHAPTER 10/ THE HELPING-LEARNING ATMOSPHERE

143	2	Truax & Carkhuff 65; Ryans 61
144	2	MacDonald & Zaret 66; Lippitt 52
144	4	Lippitt 52; Mudra 64; Roethlisberger 62
144	5	Kratochvil 67
145	2	Beilin 59; Carkhuff 67; Mudra 64; Shapiro 68
145	3	Combs 72
145	4	Webster 58
146	2	Getzels 63; Gordon 63
146	4	Beilin 59; Hall 59; Jones 71; MacDonald 66; McCallon 66; Rezler 65; Rosenthal 68a
146	5	Baker 71; Fleming 71; Goldstein 62; Kester 66; Loss 73; Mendels 73; Rosenthal 68a
147	2	Brophy 70; Rosenfeld 61

147	3	Aronson 63; Aspy 69b; Bugental 65; Carkhuff & Truax 66, 67; Jourard 64, 68; Mudra 64; Rogers 58, 69; Truax 66; Truax et al. 66a
147	4	Jourard 67, 69; Mon 74; Moustakas 66; Redl 62
148	3	Aspy 69c, 69d; Benton 64; Berger 52; Omwake 54
148	4	Becker 58; Goldstein 62; McIntyre 52; Meyer 65; Omwake 54; Rogers 67; Sheerer 49; Swinn 64
149	3	Axline 64; Webster 68
150	2	Campbell 74; Davitz 59; Gollob 65; Haefner 54; Van Buskirk 61
150	3	Connelly 64

Page Para.

151   3   Combs & Taylor 52

151   4   Craig 74a; Vontress 69

153   2   ASCD 62; Combs 66; Courson 68; Kelley 77; Richards 73

153   5   Combs 78

154   2   Averch 74; Birney 69; Jones 71; Jourard 69; Kirschenbaum 71; Lippitt 65; Simon 76

154   3   ASCD 67; Bowers 61; Combs 72; Gergen 65; Rosenthal 68a; Weaver 65

Page Para.

154   4   Kirschenbaum 71; Simon 76

155   2   Haberman 68; Lefcourt 65; Spielberger 62; White 66

156   1   Bruner 66

156   2   Jackson 68

157   2   Fromm 56

158   3   Brophy 74; Combs 64; Glasser 65; Makarenko 67; Rogers 61; Schmuck 71; Schutz 67; Webster 68

CHAPTER 11/ PROVIDING EXPERIENCE AND INFORMATION

159   2   Fausti 65; Hayakawa 64; Hinde 72

159   3   Brown 63; Davitz 61; Kohlers 69

160   5   Carr 72; Hayakawa 64; Ruesch 56

161   2   Larson 76

161   3   Ball 60; Clore 75; Lafferty 68

162   7   Aspy 69b; Boucher 75; Clore 75; Hall 59; Hinde 72; Larson 76; Loss 73; Luft 66; Mehrabian 71, 72; Ostler 76

163   2   Ball 60; Carr 72; Davitz 61; Rogers 61; Winick 61

163   3   Combs & Snygg 59

163   4   Adams 61; Birdwhistell 70; Brill 66; Brock 63; Hall 59; Putnam 66

163   5   Hinde 72; Larson 76; Tessar 73

164   3   ASCD 66; Farquhar 68

164   4   Adams 61; Brill 66; Bieri 56; Mehrabian 66; Roberts 68

164   5   Snygg 66

167   2   Sarason 68

168   3   Adams 61; Beard 69; Festinger 62, 64; Lecky 45; Piaget 59, 71, 73

170   8   Bruner 66; Conwell 43; Howe 70

171   3   Boucher 75; Eisner 64; Kelley 54; Sarason 61

172   2   Craig 74; Gibb 61; Postman 48; Reed 73

173   2   Gollob 65

173   4   Deutsch 73

173   5   Pendergrass 71

175   4   Marrow 64, 67; Milgram 74

176   3   Wessels 61

176   5   Carr 72; Hall 59; Hayakawa 64; Hinde 72; Larson 76; MacDonald 66; Mehrabian 72

CHAPTER 12/ MODES OF HELPING

177   1   Arkoff 68

178   4   Good 75

180   2   Arbuckle 61; Rogers 65; Truax & Wargo 66; Wolpe 64

180   3   Gladstone 67; Goldstein 62

180   4   Aspy 69c; Becker 58; Good 75; Hamachek 71; Kelley 77; Kratochvil 67; Mendels 73; Truax & Carkhuff 65

180   5   Gibb 61; House 67; Hunter 72; Lanzetta 54; McLeod 66; Marrow 64a, 67; Rogers 70; Rotman 67; Scheidell 66; Short 74; Truax 66; Verba 61; Welch 73

181   3   Bowers 61; Schmuck 71

182   2   MacDonald 66

182   3   Bach 66; Lifton 66; O'Banion 70; Paris 68; Simon 72

182   4   Bradford 64; Gibb 61; House 67; Stevens 71

183   2   Berzon 63

183   3   Bowers 61; Hunter 72

183   4   Bach 66; Kemp 70; Lakin 69; Lifton 66; MacLeod 66; O'Banion 70

183   6   Rogers 70; Delaney 66

184   2   Kemp 70; Mahler 61; Morrison 63; Stoller 67

184   3   Caplan 59; Marrow 67

184   5   Rogers 70

185   2   Caplan 59

186   2   Amos 67; Ausubel 61; Barlow 68; MacMillan 73

Page Para.

187	1	Homme 71; Maehr 68
187	2	Avila 72
187	3	Howe 67, 70; Lippitt 65
188	2	Bigge 64
188	5	Snyder 47
190	4	Snyder 47
190	17	Combs 47; Ginott 65
191	7	Risley 68
192	2	Johnston 71; Koorland 75; Morehouse 75; Pitts 71; Walker 76
192	3	Kounin 68; Laury 67; Marshall 65; Milgram 74; Mouly 68; Skinner 53
192	4	Koorland 75

Page Para.

193	2	Avila 66; Kounin 58; Logan 65
193	3	Williams 61
193	4	Berkowitz 60
193	7	Skinner 53
194	5	Abramson 68
196	2	Campbell 74; Combs 57; Grossack 54
196	4	Birney 69
196	7	Combs 57
197	3	Bowers 64
197	5	Campbell 74; Caplan 59; Ginott 65, 68; Gordon 70; Johnston & Pennypacker 71; Kirschenbaum 71; Koorland 75; MacMillan 73; Marrow 67; Scott 72; Simon 76

CHAPTER 13/ BEING AND BECOMING HELPERS

199	1	Combs 69, 71, 71a; Combs & Blume 74; Richards 72; Rogers 67a; Wass 74; Wilhelms 63
199	2	Bugental 65
199	3	Hamachek 64; Wass 74
200	2	Gage 63; Hunter 72; Keen 75
200	3	Combs 66; Jourard 74
200	4	Aspy 69a; Combs 64, 69; Lantz 65; McIntyre 52; Sheerer 49; Swinn 64; Truax 65
201	3	Combs & Soper 63b; Fiedler 50
202	2	Combs 69; Combs & Blume 74
202	3	Aspy & Roebuck 74
202	4	Bills 56; Bischof 64; Gooding 64; Kemp 71
202	5	Aspy 69a; Combs & Blume 74; Wass & Blume 74
203	6	Snygg 66; Wilhelms 63
204	3	Ward 66
204	4	Wass & Blume 74; Wass & Combs 74
205	1	Aspy & Roebuck 74
205	4	Murphy 68

206	2	Bradford 64; Kemp 70; McNeil 73; Schutz 67
206	4	Benson 75; Bloomfield 75; Stevens 71
207	2	Craig 74a
208	2	Berger 52; Landsman 62; Richmond 72
208	3	Lantz 65
208	4	Gooding 64
209	2	Omwake 54
209	4	Combs, in press; Gergen 65
210	2	Combs 71a; McNeil 73; Rogers 67b
210	3	Richards 72
210	4	Jourard 68, 69
210	5	Gordon 68; Lippitt 65
211	3	Craig 74
211	5	Lecky 45; Maslow 64
211	6	Maslow 71
212	5	ASCD 62
214	4	Sampson 63
216	4	Bugental 65; Combs 66; Combs & Blume 74; Lawton 58; Rogers & Stevens 67; Simon 72

INDEX

Acceptance, 148
  and learning, 199
  and openness, 90
  of self and others, 91
Accountability, 125
Adequacy and fulfillment, 54
Agee, J., 138
Alienation and identification, 97
Allport, G., 19, 39
Amick, R., 49
Anchorages, 52
Arkoff, A., 14
Aspy, D., 142
Atmosphere, helping-learning, 143
Attack-appease dilemma, 174
Authenticity, 146
Authority and communication, 175
Authority figures, 178
Avila, D., 14, 32, 49, 68, 82, 112
Awareness, expanding, 206

Barriers
  in communication, 172
  to involvement, 151
  removing, 119
Beard, R., 68
Becoming, 39, 199
Becoming a helper, 12
Behavioral principles in helping, 186
Behaviorist-humanist argument, 109
Behaving and knowing, 201
Being and becoming, 199
Beliefs
  crucial effects of, 8
  helper, 128
  as reality, 51

Bellanca, J., 154, 198
Benedict, R., 45
Benton, J., 14
Berenson, B., 14
Bettelheim, B., 32
Binet, A., 74
Blume, R., 14, 216
Bonner, H., 113
Bowers, D., 198
Brammer, L., 14
Brennecke, J., 49
Brophy, J., 158
Brown, R., 10, 122
Bugental, J., 113, 216
Buhler, C., 49
Building personal resources, 119

Campbell, D., 197
Canfield, J., 32
Cantril, H., 49
Capacity, 71
Caplan, G., 198
Carkhuff, R., 14
Carr, D., 176
Censorship, 165
Challenge, 61
  and self-actualization, 87
  and threat, 61, 150
Change agent, 212
Charting behavior, 192
Child, I., 113
Choy, C., 10, 122
Client, who is the?, 185
Closed system psychologies, 107
Closed systems, 101
Cognitive dissonance, 54

Combs, A., 9, 14, 15, 26, 32, 39, 49, 56, 60, 68, 77, 82, 83, 85, 100, 113, 125, 129, 153, 158, 190, 216
Competition, 196
Communication, 159
  and need, 164
  non-verbal, 161
  and openness, 171
  principles and details in, 170
  responsibility for, 163
Concept of self, 39
Conflicts, 214
Confrontation, 166
  of ultimate questions, 203
Consultant, 178, 184
Control in open and closed systems, 104
Conwell, R., 171
Costanzo, P., 113
Counseling, reinforcement in, 188
Creating intelligence, helper's role in, 80
Cultism, 124

Decision groups, 182
Dedrick, C., 10, 122
Defense of self, 61
Delinquency, 26
  and need, 41
Dellow, D., 10, 122
Demands on helpers, 214
Democracy and open systems, 106
Democratic ideal, 4
Dependence, 125
Dependence barrier, 153
Dickman, J., 14
Discovery and differentiation, 67
Disease and deprivation, 88
Doyle, E., 10, 122

Eclecticism, 8
Effective helper, 5
Eisner, W., 100
Emotion, 61
  defined, 63
  and meaning, 62
Empathy, 130
  use of self in, 139
Environment, changing, 178
Ethical considerations, 123
Evaluation in helping, 154
Existentialists, 108
Expectancy, 147
Experience and information, 159
Extinction, 191

Facts as beliefs, 51
Failure
  effects of, 86
  fallacy of, 87
  value of, 89

Feeling, 61
  and knowing, 65
  and meaning, 63
Festinger, L., 39
Fiedler, F., 121, 129
Field experience, 204
Fit, importance of, 168
Frames of reference, 101
Frankl, V., 39, 50
Freedom
  and identification, 94
  and license, 156
  and self-actualization, 99
Freud, S., 107
Frick, W., 113
Fromm, E., 50
Frymier, J., 45, 47
Fulfillment, 37
  and conflict, 42
  and psychological health, 43
Functional capacity, 71

Ginott, H., 136, 190, 198
Giorgi, A., 33
Glasser, W., 142, 158
Goals, 101
Goals
  changing, 120
  of helping, 115, 150
  of open and closed systems, 102
Goble, F., 100
Good, T., 158
Gooding, C., 14
Gordon, I., 79
Gordon, T., 136, 198
Grades in helping, 154
Groups
  conversation, 181
  decision, 182
  discovery, 182
  encounter, 183
  instruction, 181
  learning, 183
  sensitivity, 182
Group therapy, 183
Growth principle, 38
  and behavior, 40

Hall, E., 176
Hamachek, D., 33
Harlow, H., 100
Hayakawa, S., 160, 176
Heine, R., 122
Helper
  authenticity, 12, 146
  becoming a, 13
  beliefs about people, 11, 47

Helper (continued)
  as change agent, 212
  choices, 145
  as citizen, 178, 211
  as client, 207
  as consultant, 184
  demands on, 214
  frame of reference, 10
  fulfillment, 215
  goals of, 48
  as model, 146
  perceptual organization of, 10
  as person and citizen, 210
  personal control, 141
  purposes, 12, 146
  responsibility, 115, 124, 127, 208
  roles, 126, 146
  and society, 212
  similarities, 121
  teaching role of, 122
  visibility, 147
Helper's
  own economy, 210
  own need, 141
  own self-actualization, 208
  task, 118
Helping
  atmosphere, 143
    challenge and threat in, 150
  beliefs in, 7
  closed and open systems in, 101
  and control, 36
  dynamics of, 117
  and eclecticism, 8
  by environment change, 178
  and the factor of time, 66
  as learning and teaching, 122
  and methods, 5
  modes of, 177
  one-to-one relationships, 180
  and positive self, 89
Helping-learning atmosphere, 143
Helping professions, 48
  changing goals, 116
  defined, 3
  and knowledge, 5
  likeness, 121
Helping relationship, 134
  acceptance in, 148
  changing goals, 120
  choices in, 145
  communication in, 159
  and competition, 196
  empathy in, 130
  extinction in, 191
  focus of, 117
  goals of, 115, 150
  information in, 159

Helping relationship (continued)
  limits in, 156, 210
  and management, 186
  methods in, 204
  modes of working, 177
  objectives, 145
  and openness to experience, 90
  and positive self, 89
  preoccupation with past, 153
  punishment in, 192
  purposes in, 146
  techniques, 111, 147
Helping through groups, 180
Henry, J., 83
Hierarchy of needs, 39
Hinde, R., 163, 176
Hitt, W., 113
Howe, L., 216
Humanist-behaviorist argument, 109
Humanistic psychology, 108
Human nature, 40
Human potential, 69
  behavioral, 72
  and heredity, 69
  physical, 72
  and psychotic behavior, 71
  range of, 69
Hunt, J., 74, 75, 83

Identification
  and compassion, 96
  and freedom, 94
  implications for practice, 97
  and needs, 40
  and self-actualization, 95
  with ideas, 94
Inference in helping, 133
Information
  and censorship, 165
  and experience, 159
  and fit, 168
  and need, 167
  and simplicity, 169
  speed and pacing, 168
Intelligence, 70
  and age, 78
  creating, 80
  and environment, 78
  and experience, 74, 79
  as functional capacity, 71
  helping and, 80
  and opportunity, 78
  and physical condition, 77
  tests, 75
  tests and labeling, 76
  values and goals, effects of, 79

Jackson, P., 134, 142

Jacobson, L., 68
Jennings, G., 10, 122
Johnston, J., 198
Jones, R., 68
Jourard, S., 83, 100

Keen, E., 113
Kelley, E., 18, 33, 50, 68, 83, 85
Kirk, S., 79
Kirschenbaum, H., 154, 198, 216
Knowing, 56, 65
  and behaving, 56
  and feeling, 65
Knowledge and helping, 5
Koffman, R., 10, 122
Kohlberg, L., 68
Koorland, M., 192, 198

La Benne, W., 33
Lakin, M., 129
Larson, C., 163, 176
Laszlo, E., 113
Lawton, G., 216
Leadership, 144
Learning, 51
  basic principle of, 56
  challenge and threat in, 150
  as discovery of meaning, 51, 55
  and feeling, 65
  and forgetting, 58
  groups, 183
  incidental, 161
  and need, 203
  and self, 56, 200
  and time, 65
Lecky, P., 39
Lewin, K., 102, 144
Limits
  on environmental helping, 178
  in helping relationships, 156
  stability of, 157
Listening, 134
Listening game, 135
Loneliness and identification, 97

Malcolm X, 138
Management and manipulation, 186
Management techniques, 192
Marrow, A., 198
Maslow, A., 39, 44, 83, 84, 99, 100
May, R., 100
McNeill, E., 142
Meaning, 52
  circular effect of, 55
  discovery of, 55, 65
  and emotion, 61
  and feeling, 61
  listening to, 136

Meaning (continued)
  and memory, 61
  selective effect of, 53
  stability of, 52
Medical model, 118
Meditation, 206
Mehrabian, A., 176
Memory, 61
  and meaning, 61
Mentors, 178
Methods
  and becoming, 204
  of experts, 205
  and helping, 5
Mistakes
  fear of, 155
  and growth, 211
Mitchell, M., 192, 198
Motivation, 34
  competition in, 196
  constancy of, 47
  external approach to, 34
  and fulfillment, 37
  humanistic view of, 34
  and need, 39, 41
  older concepts of, 35
  two views of, 34, 37
Moustakas, C., 142
Mudra, D., 86

Napier, R., 154
Need
  and behavior, 40
  and belongingness and love, 39
  and communication, 164
  hierarchy of, 39
  physiological, 39
  safety, 39
  self-actualization, 39
  and self-esteem, 39
  to know, 203
Newman, A., 14, 216

O'Banion, T., 142
Objectives, 101
Objectives of relationship, 145
Objectivity, 64
  fetish of, 64
  and the scientific method, 65
Observation, 138
O'Connell, A., 142
One-to-one relationship, 180
Openness
  and communication, 171
  implications for practice, 92
  to experience, 90
  and values, 92

Open system, 101
  psychologies of, 108
Organism, predictable and trustworthy, 43
O'Roark, A., 10, 122

Parent-child relationship, 190
Parker, J., 10, 122
Patterson, C., 33
Peak experience, 140
Pendergrass, R., 10, 122
Pennypacker, H., 198
Perception
  and empathy, 130
  and selective effect of need, 41
Perceptual field, 17
  and intelligence, 77
  and learning, 51
Perceptual psychology, 15
  and learning, 51
  and maladjustment, 43
  and perception, 15
Permissiveness, 156
Person
  at war with self, 36
  as basically evil, 35
  fully functioning, 85
  in open and closed systems, 103
  self-actualizing, 85
Personal growth experiences, 205
Personalists, 108
Perspective and social change, 214
Phenomenologists, 108
Philosophy
  in closed and open systems, 106
  and practice, 209
Physical model and capacity, 69
Positive view of self, 85
Profession, defined, 4
Professional accountability, 125
Professional roles, 126
Professional self and personal self, 209
Professional workers, beliefs of, 9
Piaget, J., 33, 54, 83
Practitioner-scholar dilemma, 202
Precision teaching, 192
Psychoanalysis, 107
Psychology
  of closed and open systems, 106
  humanistic, 109
  open system, 108
Punishment, 192
Purkey, W., 14, 32, 33, 49, 68, 82, 113
Purposes, 127
  in helping, 115

Raimy, V., 129
Reading behavior backwards, 27, 132
Reading programs and sensitivity, 136

Reality, 51, 132
Reckless, W., 21
Redl, F., 26, 50
Reinforcement
  in counseling, 188
  and feedback, 188
  in helping, 187
  in parent-child relations, 190
  schedules, 188
Responsibility, 124
  as citizen, 211
  helper, 115, 208
  in closed and open systems, 105
Richards, A., 15, 33, 45, 49, 77, 85, 100
Richards, F., 15, 33, 45, 49, 77, 85, 100, 142
Rogers, C., 7, 14, 39, 68, 84, 86, 130, 142,
  147, 158, 184, 216
Rokeach, M., 129
Role
  definitions, 126
  of expert, 105
  professional, 209
Rosenthal, R., 68, 213

Scholar-practitioner dilemma, 202
Schmuck, R., 158
Schutz, W., 158
Scientific method, 65
Scott, W., 198
Seashore, S., 198
Self
  beliefs about, 27
  center of personal universe, 19
  changing, 200
  personal and professional, 209
  positive and helping practice, 89
  relationship of learning to, 56
  use in empathy, 139
Self-actualization, 38, 86
  and freedom, 99
  helper's own, 208
  and identification, 95
  and maladjustment, 43
  and openness, 91
  and positive self, 85
  and threat, 86
Self as instrument, 6, 139, 199
  and empathy, 131
  and knowledge, 7
Self-concept
  acquisition of, 23
  changing of, 29
  circular effect of, 20
  defense of, 60
  defined, 17
  and delinquency, 21
  as determiner of behavior, 20
  expanded, 40

Self-concept (continued)
  extension of, 18
  helper's, 11
  and helping professions, 28
  and identification, 18
  and incidental learning, 24
  and learning, 56
  and maladjustment, 43
  and openness, 91
  and physical self, 18, 38
  and self-actualization, 38
  and self-corroboration, 87
  and self-report, 27
  and significant others, 23
  and social problems, 23
  stability of, 25
Self-consistency, 39
Self-enhancement, 39
  and challenge, 61
  and self-actualization, 39
  and threat, 61
Self-esteem, 61, 86
  and self-actualization, 85
  and threat, 61
Self-examination, 200
Self-fulfilling prophecy, 213
Self-fulfillment
  of helper, 215
  and identification, 95
Self-ideal, 167
Sensitivity, 130
  groups, 182
  and literature, 136
Severin, F., 113
Shaw, M., 113
Significant others, 128
Simon, S., 154, 198, 216
Skinner, B., 110, 113, 193
Social change, 212
Snyder, W., 8, 190
Snygg, D., 39, 50, 165
Soar, R., 129
Soper, D., 14
Spaulding, L., 198
S-R psychology, 106
Staines, J., 28, 29
Stevens, B., 216

Stevens, J., 142
Subjective observation, 139
Swanson, J., 10
Synergy, 45

Teaching, as helping, 122
Techniques
  in closed and open systems, 102
  of helping, 200
  and positive self, 89
  selecting, 111
Tessar, A., 163
Theory of closed and open systems, 106
Therapy
  listening in, 136
  and teaching, 122
Thompson, J., 45, 47
Threat, 59
  and acceptance, 148
  and challenge, 61, 150
  in communication, 172
  and defense of self, 60
  and learning, 59
  and perception, 59
  and self-actualization, 87
  and tunnel vision, 59
Threat-counterthreat cycle, 173
Tillich, P., 55
Toffler A., 100
Token economies, 191
Transactionalist, 108
Trauma, 25
Truax, C., 129
Tunnel vision, 59

Ultimate questions, 203
Unconscious stimuli, 107
Usher, R., 10, 14, 122

Wann, T., 113
Wapier, R., 198
Wass, H., 14, 216
Webster, S., 158
Wells, H., 33
Wessels, H., 176
Wineman, D., 50
Wolpe, J., 110